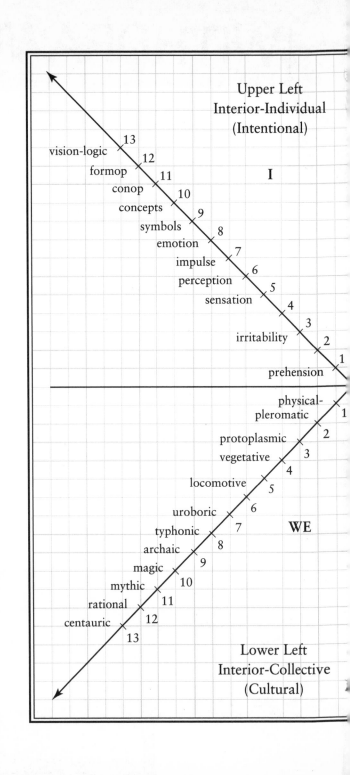

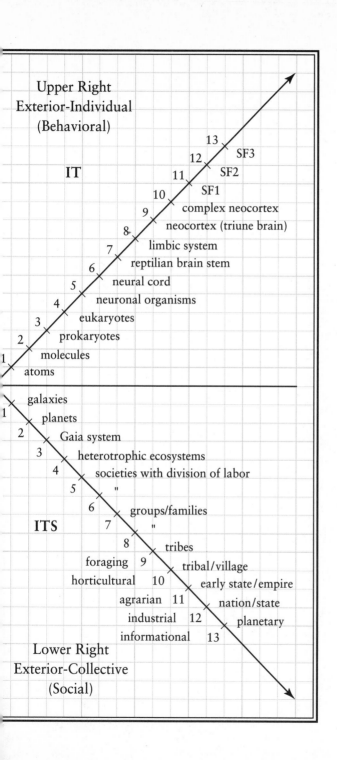

A BRIEF
HISTORY OF
EVERYTHING

SECOND EDITION

Ken Wilber

Gateway

Gateway
an imprint of
Gill & Macmillan
Hume Avenue
Park West
Dublin 12

Published by arrangement with Shambala Publications, Inc.,
PO Box 308, Boston, MA 02117, USA

Second edition first published by Gateway 2001
© Ken Wilber 1996, 2000

0 7171 3233 1

Printed by ColourBooks Ltd, Dublin

Group IX Series SUW The Swan Nr 12 by Hilma af Klint is reproduced on the
cover with the permission of The Hilma af Klint Foundation

*The paper used in this book is made from the wood pulp of
managed forests. For every tree felled, at least one tree is
planted, thereby renewing natural resources.*

A catalogue record is available for this book
from the British available.

3 5 7 6 4

Contents

Foreword

SIX YEARS AGO, IN 1989, I set out across the country on my own search for wisdom. In the course of my travels, I interviewed and worked with more than two hundred psychologists, philosophers, physicians, scientists, and mystics who claimed to have the answers I was after. By the time I wrote *What Really Matters: Searching for Wisdom in America*, it was clear to me that Ken Wilber was in a category by himself. He is, I believe, far and away the most cogent and penetrating voice in the recent emergence of a uniquely American wisdom.

It has been nearly twenty years since Ken Wilber published *The Spectrum of Consciousness*. Written when he was twenty-three, it established him, almost overnight, as perhaps the most comprehensive philosophical thinker of our times. *Spectrum*, which Wilber wrote in three months after dropping out of graduate school in biochemistry, made the case that human development unfolds in waves or stages that extend beyond those ordinarily recognized by Western psychology. Only by successfully navigating each developmental wave, Wilber argued, is it possible first to develop a healthy sense of individuality, and then ultimately to experience a broader identity that transcends—and includes—the personal self. In effect, Wilber married Freud and the Buddha—until then divided by seemingly irreconcilable differences. And this was just the first of his many original contributions.

The title of this book is deceptively breezy. *A Brief History of Everything* delivers just what it promises. It covers vast historical ground, from the Big Bang right up to the desiccated postmodern present. Along the way, it seeks to make sense of the often contradictory ways that human beings have evolved—physically, emotionally, intellectually, morally, spiritually. And for all its breadth, the book is remarkably lean and compact.

Indeed, what sets *A Brief History of Everything* apart both from *Spectrum* and from Wilber's eleven subsequent books is that it not only extends the ideas advanced in those earlier works, but presents them now in a simple, accessible, conversational format. Most of Wilber's books require at least some knowledge of the major Eastern contemplative traditions and of Western developmental psychology. *A Brief History* is addressed to a much broader audience—those of us grappling to find wisdom in our everyday lives, but bewildered by the array of potential paths to truth that so often seem to contradict one another—and to fall short in fundamental ways. For those readers who want still more when they finish this book, I recommend Wilber's recent opus, *Sex, Ecology, Spirituality,* which explores many of the ideas here in more rigorous detail.

No one I've met has described the path of human development—the evolution of consciousness—more systematically or comprehensively than Wilber. In the course of my journey, I ran into countless people who made grand claims for a particular version of the truth they were promoting. Almost invariably, I discovered, they'd come to their conclusions by choosing up sides, celebrating one set of capacities and values while excluding others.

Wilber has taken a more embracing and comprehensive approach, as you will soon discover. In the pages that follow, he lays out a coherent vision that honors and incorporates the truths from a vast and disparate array of fields—physics and biology; the social and the systems sciences; art and aesthetics; developmental psychology and contemplative mysticism—as well as from opposing philosophical movements ranging from Neoplatonism to modernism, idealism to postmodernism.

What Wilber recognizes is that a given truth-claim may be valid without being complete, true but only so far as it goes, and this must be seen as part of other and equally important truths. Perhaps the most powerful new tool he brings to bear in *A Brief History* is his notion that there are four "quadrants" of development. By looking at hundreds of developmental maps that have been created by various thinkers over the years— maps of biological, psychological, cognitive, and spiritual development, to name just a few—it dawned on Wilber that they were often describing very different versions of "truth." Exterior forms of development, for example, are those that can be measured objectively and empirically. But what Wilber makes clear is that this form of truth will only take you so far. Any comprehensive development, he points out, also includes an interior dimension—one that is subjective and interpretive, and depends on consciousness and introspection. Beyond that, Wilber saw, both interior and exterior development take place not just individually, but in a social or cultural context. Hence the four quadrants.

None of these forms of truth, he argues in a series of vivid examples, can be reduced to another. A behaviorist, to take just a single case, cannot understand a person's interior experience solely by looking at his external behavior—or at its physiological correlates. The truth will indeed set you free, but only if you recognize that there are many kinds of truth.

A Brief History of Everything operates on several levels. It's the richest map I've yet found of the world we live in, and of men and women's place in it. In the dialectic of progress, Wilber suggests, each stage of evolution transcends the limits of its predecessor, but simultaneously introduces new ones. This is a view that both dignifies and celebrates the ongoing struggle of any authentic search for a more conscious and complete life. "No epoch is finally privileged," Wilber writes. "We are all tomorrow's food. The process continues, and Spirit is found in the process itself, not in any particular epoch or time or place."

At another level, Wilber serves in *A Brief History* as a demystifier and a debunker—a discerning critic of the teachers, techniques, ideas, and systems that promise routes to encompassing truth, but are more commonly incomplete, misleading, misguided, or distorted. Too often we ourselves are complicit. Fearful of any change and infinitely capable of self-deception, we are too quick to latch on to simple answers and quick fixes, which finally just narrow our perspective and abort our development.

Wilber's is a rare voice. He brings to the task both a sincere heart and a commitment to truth. He widens his lens to take in the biggest possible picture, but he refuses to see all the elements as equal. He makes qualitative distinctions. He values depth. He's unafraid to make enemies, even as he is respectful of many voices. The result is that *A Brief History of Everything* sheds a very original light, not just on the cosmic questions in our lives, but on dozens of confusing and unsettling issues of our times—the changing roles of men and women; the continuing destruction of the environment; diversity and multiculturalism; repressed memory and childhood sexual abuse; and the role of the Internet in the information age—among many others.

I cannot imagine a better way to be introduced to Ken Wilber than this book. It brings the debate about evolution, consciousness, and our capacity for transformation to an entirely new level. More practically, it will save you many missteps and wrong turns on whatever wisdom path you choose to take.

TONY SCHWARTZ

Preface to the Second Edition

A *Brief History of Everything* is one of the most popular books I have written, which is heartening in that it contains a good deal of the integrative vision that I have tried to develop. "Integrative" simply means that this approach attempts to include as many important truths from as many disciplines as possible—from the East as well as the West, from premodern and modern and postmodern, from the hard sciences of physics to the tender sciences of spirituality. As one critic put it, this integrative approach "honors and incorporates more truth than any approach in history." I would obviously like to believe that is true, but you can best be the judge of that as you read the following pages.

And even if it were true, so what? What does an "integrative approach" even mean? And what does it have to do with me in today's world? Well, let's have a quick look at what it might mean in business, science, and spirituality.

Scholars of the many and various human cultures—premodern, modern, and postmodern—have increasingly been struck by their rich *diversity*: the beautiful, multicultural, many-hued rainbow of humanity, with multiple differences in religion, ethics, values, and beliefs. But many scholars have also been struck by some of the *similarities* of these cultures as well. Certain patterns in language, cognition, and human physiology, for example, are quite similar wherever they appear. Humans everywhere have the capacity to form images, symbols, and concepts, and although the contents of those concepts often vary, the capacity is universal. These universal and cross-cultural patterns tell us some very important things about the human condition, because if you have found something shared by most or even all humans, you have probably found something of profound significance.

What if we took all of these common patterns and put them together? What kind of picture would we get?

This would be very much like the human Genome Project (the complete mapping of the genes of human DNA), except that this would be a type of human Consciousness and Culture Project: the mapping of all those cultural capacities that humans everywhere have access to. This would give us a rather extraordinary map of human potentials, a great map of human possibilities. And it would further help us to recognize any of those potentials that we—that you and I—might not yet be fulfilling. It would be a map of our own higher stages of growth and a map of our own greater opportunities.

You might be surprised to know that a good deal of this Consciousness and Culture Project has in fact been completed. The result of the research of thousands of workers from around the world, the Consciousness and Culture Project has already disclosed a profound range of higher states of consciousness, stages of growth, patterns of spirituality, and forms of science that often dwarf the more restricted versions sanctioned in our present culture of scientific materialism, on the one hand, and, on the other, the postmodern celebration of surfaces.

As you will see, these greater potentials and possibilities are a crucial ingredient in the bigger picture that is presented in the following pages—a bigger picture that is a kind of "theory of everything." A "theory of everything" is just that: if we assume that all the world's cultures have important but partial truths, then how would all of those truths fit together into a richly woven tapestry, a unity-in-diversity, a multicolored yet single rainbow?

And once that rainbow is clear, how does it apply to me? Perhaps very simply: a more accurate, comprehensive map of human potentials will directly translate into a more effective business, politics, medicine, education, and spirituality. On the other hand, if you have a partial, truncated, fragmented map of the human being, you will have a partial, truncated, fragmented approach to business, medicine, spirituality, and so on. In garbage, out garbage.

Thus, no matter what your field of endeavor, a "theory of everything" will likely make it much more effective. So it is not surprising that this more comprehensive map of human possibilities has seen an explosion of interest in virtually all fields, including politics, business, education, health care, law, ecology, science and religion. For those interested in some of these recent applications, see *A Theory of Everything—An Integral Vision for Business, Politics, Science, and Spirituality.*

But the basics are all here, in this volume, which will give you all that you need of this comprehensive map to see if it is useful for you. And although this comprehensive map might sound complex, once you get the hang of it—as I will try to show in the following pages—it is surprisingly simple and easy to use, and by the time you finish reading, you will have all the tools you need to begin applying it if you wish.

One last point: the whole idea of a more comprehensive map is to enrich, not deny, your own present understanding. Some people are threatened by a more integral approach, because they imagine that it somehow means that what they are doing now is wrong. But this would be like a great French chef being threatened by Mexican cooking. We are simply adding new styles, not condemning those that already exist. I love French cooking, but I also like Mexican. They are not going to cease being what they are if both are fully appreciated. Most of the resistance to an integral approach comes from French chefs who despise Mexican cooking—an attitude that is perhaps less than helpful.

And so, in the following pages, you will find an international style of "cooking"—a universal smorgasbord of human possibilities, all arrayed as a shimmering rainbow, an extraordinary spectrum of your own deeper and higher potentials. This map is simply an invitation to explore the vast terrain of your own consciousness, the almost unlimited potentials of your own being and becoming, the nearly infinite expanse of your own primordial awareness, and thus arrive at that place which you have never left: your own deepest nature and your own original face.

A Note to the Reader

IN DOUGLAS ADAMS'S *Hitchhiker's Guide to the Galaxy,* a massive supercomputer is designed to give the ultimate answer, the absolute answer, the answer that would completely explain "God, life, the universe, and everything." But the computer takes seven and a half million years to do this, and by the time the computer delivers the answer, everybody has forgotten the question. Nobody remembers the ultimate question, but the ultimate answer the computer comes up with is: 42.

This is amazing! Finally, the ultimate answer. So wonderful is the answer that a contest is held to see if anybody can come up with the question. Many profound questions are offered, but the final winner is: How many roads must a man walk down?

"God, life, the universe, and everything" is pretty much what this book is about, although, of course, the answer is not quite as snappy as "42." It deals with matter, life, mind, and spirit, and the evolutionary currents that seem to unite them all in a pattern that connects.

I have written this book in a dialogue format—questions and answers. Many of these dialogues actually occurred, but most have been written specifically for this book. The questions are real enough—they are the questions I have most often been asked about my books in general and my most recent book in particular (*Sex, Ecology, Spirituality*). But there is no need whatsoever to have read that or any of my books: the following topics are interesting in themselves, I believe, and the dialogues demand no previous or specialized knowledge in these areas. (Scholars interested in references, bibliography, notes, and detailed arguments can consult *Sex, Ecology, Spirituality*.)

The first chapters deal with the material cosmos and the emergence of life. What drove chaos into order? How did matter give rise to life? What currents are afoot in this extraordinary game of evolution? Is there a "spirit" of ecology? Does it really matter?

The middle chapters explore the emergence of mind or consciousness, and we will follow the evolution of this consciousness through five or six major stages in human development, from foraging to horticultural to agrarian to industrial to informational. What was the status of men and women in each of those stages? Why did some of those stages emphasize the male, and some the female, gender? Does this shed any light on today's gender wars? Are the same currents at work in human evolution as in the cosmic game at large? How does past human development relate to today's human problems? If we do not remember the past, are we condemned to repeat it?

We will then look to the Divine Domain and how it might indeed be related to the creative currents in matter and life and mind. How and why did religion historically give way to psychology? Used to be, if you were inwardly disturbed and agitated and seeking answers, you talked to a priest. Now you talk to a psychiatrist—and they rarely agree with each other. Why? What happened? Do they both perhaps have something important to tell us? Should they perhaps be not feuding but kissing cousins?

In our own lives, to whom do we turn for answers? Do we look to Adams's supercomputer for ultimate answers? Do we look to religion? politics? science? psychologists? gurus? your psychic friend? *Where* do we finally place our ultimate trust for the really important questions? Does this tell us something? Is there a way to tie these various sources together? to have them each speak their own truths in ways that balance and harmonize? Is this even possible in today's splintered world?

The last chapters deal with flatland—with the collapse of the richly textured Kosmos into a flat and faded one-dimensional world, the bleak and monochrome world of modernity and postmodernity. But we will do so not simply with an eye to condemning the modern world, but rather in an attempt to discover the radiant Spirit at work, even in our own apparently God-forsaken times. Where is God, and where the Goddess, in these shallow waters?

How many roads must we each walk down? There might be an answer to this after all, for wonder continues to bubble up, and joy rushes to the surface, with release in the recognition and liberation in the awakening. And we all know how to wonder, which speaks in the tongues of that God within, and inexplicably points home.

K.W.
Boulder, Colorado
Spring 1995

A BRIEF HISTORY
OF EVERYTHING

Introduction

Q: Is there any sex in *Sex, Ecology, Spirituality?*

KW: With diagrams, actually.

Q: You're kidding.

KW: I'm kidding. But yes, sexuality is one of the main themes, and especially its relation to gender.

Q: Sex and gender are different?

KW: It's common to use "sex" or sexuality to refer to the *biological* aspects of human reproduction, and "gender" to refer to the *cultural* differences between men and women that grow up around the sexual or biological differences. The sexual differences are usually referred to as *male* and *female*, and the cultural differences as *masculine* and *feminine*. And while male and female might indeed be given biologically, masculine and feminine are in large part the creation of culture.

Q: So the trick is to decide which characteristics are sex and which are gender.

KW: In a sense, yes. The sexual differences between male and female, because they are primarily biological, are universal and cross-cultural— males everywhere produce sperm, females produce ova, females give birth and lactate, and so on. But the differences between *masculine* and *feminine* are created and molded primarily by the different cultures in which the male and female are raised.

And yes, part of the turmoil between the sexes nowadays is that, while male/female differences are biological and universal—and therefore can't really be changed very much—nonetheless masculine and feminine are in many ways the product of culture, and these roles can indeed be changed in at least some significant ways. And we, as a culture, are in the difficult and tricky process of trying to change some of these gender roles.

Q: For example?

KW: Well, while it's true that, on average, the male body is more muscular and physically stronger than the female, it does not follow that masculine therefore must mean strong and assertive and feminine must mean weak and demure. And we are in a transition period where masculine and feminine roles are being redefined and re-created, which has thrown both men and women into a type of rancorous sniping at each other in various types of gender wars.

Part of the problem is that, whereas masculine and feminine roles can indeed be redefined and refashioned—a long-overdue and much-needed refurbishing—nonetheless male and female characteristics cannot be changed much, and in our attempt to level the differences between masculine and feminine, we are dangerously close to trying to erase the differences between male and female. And while the former is a fine idea, the latter is impossible. And the trick is to know the difference, I suppose.

Q: So some of the differences between men and women are here to stay, and some need to be changed?

KW: It seems so. As we continue to investigate the differences between men and women, related to both sex and gender, there are indeed certain differences, even in the cultural domain, that crop up again and again across cultures. In other words, not only certain sex differences, but certain gender differences tend to repeat themselves cross-culturally.

It's as if the biological sex differences between men and women are such a strong basic platform that these biological differences tend to invade culture as well, and thus tend to show up in gender differences also. So, even though gender is culturally molded and not biologically given, nonetheless certain constants in masculine and feminine gender tend to appear across cultures as well.

Q: Even a decade ago, that was a rather controversial stance. Now it seems more commonly accepted.

KW: Yes, even the radical feminists now champion the notion that there are, generally speaking, very strong differences between the male and female value spheres—that is, in both sex and gender. Men tend toward hyperindividuality, stressing autonomy, rights, justice, and agency, and women tend toward a more relational awareness, with emphasis on communion, care, responsibility, and relationship. Men tend to stress autonomy and fear relationship, women tend to stress relationship and fear autonomy.

Carol Gilligan's and Deborah Tannen's work has been central here, of course, but it's amazing that, in the span of just a decade or so, as you say, most orthodox researchers and most feminist researchers are now in general agreement about certain fundamental differences in the male and female value spheres. This is also central to the new field of study known as "evolutionary psychology"—the effects of biological evolution on psychological traits.

And the tricky part now is: how to acknowledge these differences without using them, once again, to disenfranchise women. Because as soon as any sort of *differences* between people are announced, the privileged will use those differences to further their advantage. You see the problem?

Q: Yes, but it seems the opposite is now occurring. It seems that these differences are being used to demonstrate that men are rather inherently insensitive slobs and testosterone mutants who "just don't get it." The message is, men should be more sensitive, more caring, more loving, more relational. What you call the male value sphere is everywhere under attack. The message is, why can't a man be more like a woman?

KW: Yes, it's a certain amount of "turnabout is fair play." Used to be that women were defined as "deficient men"—"penis envy" being the classic example. Now men are being defined as "deficient women"—defined by the feminine characteristics that they lack, not by any positive attributes that they possess. Both approaches are unfortunate, I think, not to mention demeaning to both genders.

The tricky part, as I started to suggest, is how to do two very difficult things: one, to reasonably decide just what are the major differences between the male and female value spheres (à la Gilligan), and then, two, to learn ways to value them more or less equally. Not to make them the same, but to value them equally.

Nature did not split the human race into two sexes for no reason; simply trying to make them the same seems silly. But even the most conservative theorists would acknowledge that our culture has been predominantly weighted to the male value sphere for quite some time now. And so we are in the delicate, dicey, very difficult, and often rancorous process of trying to balance the scales a bit more. Not erase the differences, but balance them.

Q: And these differences have their roots in the biological differences between male and female?

KW: In part, it seems so. Hormonal differences, in particular. Studies on testosterone—in the laboratory, cross-culturally, embryonically, and even on what happens when women are given testosterone injections for medical reasons—all point to a simple conclusion. I don't mean to be crude, but it appears that testosterone basically has two, and only two, major drives: fuck it or kill it.

And males are saddled with this biological nightmare almost from day one, a nightmare women can barely imagine (except when they are given testosterone injections for medical purposes, which drives them nuts. As one woman put it, "I can't stop thinking about sex. Please, can't you make this stop?") Worse, men sometimes fuse and confuse these two drives, with fuck it and kill it dangerously merging, which rarely has happy consequences, as women are more than willing to point out.

Q: And the female equivalent?

KW: We might point to oxytocin, a hormone that tends to flood the female even if her skin is simply stroked. Oxytocin has been described as the "relationship drug"; it induces incredibly strong feelings of attachment, relationship, nurturing, holding, touching.

And it's not hard to see that both of these, testosterone and oxytocin, might have their roots in biological evolution, the former for reproduction and survival, the latter for mothering. Most sexual intercourse in the animal kingdom occurs in a matter of seconds. During intercourse, both parties are open to being preyed upon or devoured. Brings new meaning to "dinner and sex," because you *are* the dinner. So it's slam-bam-thank-you-ma'am. None of this sharing feelings, and emoting, and cuddling—and that about sums up men. Mr. Sensitive—the man, the myth, the weenie—is a very, very recent invention, and it takes men a bit of getting used to, we might say.

But the sexual requirements of mothering are quite different. The mother has to be constantly in tune with the infant, twenty-four hours a day, especially alert to signs of hunger and pain. Oxytocin keeps her right in there, focused on the relationship, and very, very attached. The emotions are not fuck it or kill it, but continuously *relate to it*, carefully, diffusely, concernfully, tactilely.

Q: So Mr. Sensitive is a gender role that is at odds with the sex role?

KW: In some ways, yes. That doesn't mean men can't or shouldn't become more sensitive. Today, it's an imperative. But it simply means men usually have to be *educated* to do so. It's a role they have to *learn*. And there are many reasons why this role should be learned, but we have to cut men some slack as they grope toward this strange new landscape.

But likewise for women. Part of the new demands of being a woman in today's world is that she has to fight for her autonomy, and not simply and primarily define herself in terms of her relationships. This, of course, is the great call of feminism, that women begin to define themselves in terms of their own autonomy and their own intrinsic worth, and not merely in terms of relationship to an Other. Not that relationships should be devalued, but that women find ways to honor their own mature self and not merely resort to self-abnegation in the face of the Other.

Q: So both men and women are working against their biological givens?

KW: In some ways, yes. But that is the whole point of evolution: it always goes beyond what went before. It is always struggling to establish new limits, and then struggling just as hard to break them, to transcend them, to move beyond them into more encompassing and integrative and holistic modes. And where the traditional sex roles of male and female were once perfectly necessary and appropriate, they are today becoming increasingly outmoded, narrow, and cramped. And so both men and women are struggling for ways to transcend their old roles, without—and this is the tricky part—without simply erasing them. Evolution always *transcends* and *includes*, incorporates and goes beyond.

And so, males will always have a base of testosterone drivenness—fuck it or kill it—but those drives can be taken up and worked into more appropriate modes of behavior. Men will always, to some degree, be incredibly driven to break limits, push the envelope, go all out, wildly, insanely, and in the process bring new discoveries, new inventions, new modes into being.

And women, as the radical feminists insist, will always have a base of relational being, oxytocin to the core, but upon that base of relational being can be built a sturdier sense of self-esteem and autonomy, valuing the mature self even as it continues to value relationships.

So for both men and women, it's transcend and include, transcend and include. And we are at a point in evolution where the primary sex roles—hyperautonomy for men and hyperrelationship for women—are both being transcended to some degree, with men learning to embrace relational being and women learning to embrace autonomy. And in this difficult process, both sexes appear to be monsters in the eyes of the other, which is why a certain kindness on both sides is so important, I think.

Q: Now you said that our society has been male-oriented for some time, and that a certain balancing of the books seems to be in order.

KW: This is what is generally meant by the "patriarchy," a word which is always pronounced with scorn. The obvious and perhaps naive solution is to simply say that men *imposed* the patriarchy on women—a nasty and brutal state of affairs that easily could have been different— and therefore all that is now required is for men to simply say, "Oops, excuse me, didn't mean to crush and oppress you for five thousand years. What *was* I thinking? Can we just start over?"

But, alas, it is not that simple, I don't believe. It appears there were certain inescapable circumstances that made the "patriarchy" an un-avoidable arrangement for an important part of human development, and we are just now reaching the point where that arrangement is no longer necessary, so that we can begin, in certain fundamental ways, to "deconstruct" the patriarchy, or more charitably balance the books between the male and female value spheres. But this is not the undoing of a brutal state of affairs that could easily have been otherwise; it is rather the outgrowing of a state of affairs no longer necessary.

Q: Which is a very different way of looking at it.

KW: Well, if we take the standard response—that the patriarchy was imposed on women by a bunch of sadistic and power-hungry men—then we are locked into two inescapable definitions of men and women. Namely, men are pigs and women are sheep. That men would intention-ally want to oppress half of the human race paints a dismal picture of men altogether. Testosterone or not, men are simply not that malicious in the totality of their being.

But actually, what's so altogether unbelievable about this explanation of the patriarchy is that it paints an incredibly *flattering* picture of men. It says that men managed to collectively get together and agree to op-press half of the human race, and more amazingly, they *succeeded totally* in every known culture. Mind you, men have never been able to create a domineering government that lasted more than a few hundred years; but according to the feminists, men managed to implement this other and massive domination for five thousand—some say one hundred thou-sand—years. Those wacky guys, gotta love 'em.

But the real problem with the "imposition theory"—men oppressed women from day one—is that it paints a horrifyingly dismal picture of women. You simply cannot be as strong and as intelligent *and op-pressed*. This picture necessarily paints women basically as sheep, as weaker and/or stupider than men. Instead of seeing that, at every stage of human evolution, men and women *co-created* the social forms of their interaction, this picture defines women primarily as molded by an Other. These feminists, in other words, are assuming and enforcing precisely the picture of women that they say they want to erase. But men are simply not that piggy, and women not that sheepy.

So one of the things I have tried to do, based on more recent feminist scholarship, is to trace out the hidden power that women have had and that influenced, co-created, the various cultural structures throughout our history, including the so-called patriarchy. Among other things, this releases men from being defined as schmucks, and releases women from being defined as duped, brainwashed, and herded.

Q: In various writings, you have traced five or six major epochs of human evolution, and you examine the status of men and women in each of those stages.

KW: Yes, one of the things we want to do, when looking at the various stages of human consciousness evolution, is also to look at the *status* of men and women *at each of those stages*. And that allows certain important conclusions to stand out, I believe.

Q: So this approach involves what, exactly? In general terms.

KW: What we want to do is *first*, isolate the biological constants that do not change much from culture to culture. These biological constants appear very simple and even trivial, such as: men on average have an advantage in physical strength and mobility, and women give birth and lactate. But those simple biological differences turn out to have an enormous influence on the types of cultural or gender differences that spring up around them.

Q: For example?

KW: For example, what if the means of subsistence in your particular culture is horse and herding? As Janet Chafetz points out, women who participate in these activities have a very high rate of miscarriage. It is to their Darwinian *advantage* not to participate in the productive sphere, which is therefore occupied almost solely by men. And indeed, over 90 percent of herding societies are "patriarchal." But *oppression* is not required to explain this patriarchal orientation. The evidence suggests, on the contrary, that women freely participated in this arrangement.

If, on the other hand, we fall into the naive and reflex action, and assume that if women in these societies weren't doing exactly what the modern feminist thinks they should have been doing, then those women *must* have been oppressed, then off we go on the men-are-pigs, women-are-sheep chase, which is horribly degrading to both sexes, don't you think?

Nobody is denying that some of these arrangements were very difficult, gruesome even. But what we find is that when the sexes are polarized or rigidly separated, then both sexes suffer horribly. The evidence suggests, in fact, that the patriarchal societies were much harder on the average male than on the average female, for reasons we can discuss if you like. But ideology and victim politics don't help very much in this particular regard. Trading female power for female victimhood is a self-defeating venture. It presupposes and reinforces that which it wishes to overcome.

Q: So you said we want to do two things, and the first was look at the universal biological differences between the sexes.

KW: Yes, and second, to look at how these constant *biological* differences played themselves out over the five or six stages of human *cultural* evolution. The general point is that, with this approach, we can isolate those factors that historically led to more "equalitarian" societies—that is, societies that gave roughly equal status to the male and female value spheres. They never *equated* male and female; they balanced them. And thus, in our present-day attempts to reach a more harmonious stance, we will have a better idea about just what needs to be changed, and what does not need to be changed.

So perhaps we can learn to value the differences between the male and female value spheres. Those differences, even according to the radical feminists, appear to be here for good—but we can learn to value them with more equal emphasis. *How* to do so is one of the things we might want to talk about.

The Scope of These Discussions

Q: The human stages of development are part of a larger project of looking at *evolution in general*. And in all sorts of domains—physical, mental, cultural, spiritual—ranging from subconscious to self-conscious to superconscious. You have done this in a dozen books, from *The Spectrum of Consciousness* to *The Atman Project* to *Up from Eden* to *Sex, Ecology, Spirituality*. What we want to do is go over these ideas—about the evolution of consciousness, spiritual development, the role of men and women, ecology and our place in the Kosmos—and see if we can discuss them in a simple and brief fashion. See if we can make them more accessible.

KW: We could start with the rather amazing fact that there seems to be a common evolutionary thread running from matter to life to mind. Certain *common patterns*, or laws, or habits keep repeating themselves in all those domains, and we could begin by looking at those extraordinary patterns, since they seem to hold the secrets of evolution.

Q: You have also looked at the higher stages of consciousness evolution itself, stages that might best be called spiritual.

KW: Yes. This takes up various themes suggested by Schelling, Hegel, Aurobindo, and other evolutionary theorists East and West. The point is that, according to these luminaries, evolution is best thought of as *Spirit-in-action*, God-in-the-making, where Spirit unfolds itself at every stage of development, thus manifesting more of itself, and realizing more of itself, at every unfolding. Spirit is not some particular stage, or some favorite ideology, or some specific god or goddess, but rather the entire process of unfolding itself, an infinite process that is completely present at every finite stage, but becomes more available to itself with every evolutionary opening.

And so yes, we can look at the higher stages of this evolutionary unfolding, according to the world's great wisdom traditions—the higher or deeper stages where Spirit becomes conscious of itself, awakens to itself, begins to recognize its own true nature.

These higher stages are often pictured as mystical or "far out," but for the most part they are very concrete, very palpable, very real stages of higher development—stages available to you and to me, stages that are our own deep potentials.

Q: You found that the world's great spiritual traditions fall into two large and very different camps.

KW: Yes, if we look at the various types of human attempts to comprehend the Divine—both East and West, North and South—what we find are two very different types of spirituality, which I call *Ascending* and *Descending*.

The Ascending path is purely transcendental and otherworldly. It is usually puritanical, ascetic, yogic, and it tends to devalue or even deny the body, the senses, sexuality, the Earth, the flesh. It seeks its salvation in a kingdom not of this world; it sees manifestation or samsara as evil or illusory; it seeks to get off the wheel entirely. And, in fact, for the Ascenders, any sort of Descent tends to be viewed as illusory or even evil. The Ascending path glorifies the One, not the Many; Emptiness, not Form; Heaven, not Earth.

The Descending path counsels just the opposite. It is this-worldly to the core, and it glorifies the Many, not the One. It celebrates the Earth, and the body, and the senses, and often sexuality. It even identifies Spirit with the sensory world, with Gaia, with manifestation, and sees in every sunrise, every moonrise, all the Spirit a person could ever want. It is purely immanent and is often suspicious of anything transcendental. In fact, for the Descenders, any form of Ascent is usually viewed as evil.

Q: One of the things we want to discuss is the history of the "war" between the Ascenders and the Descenders. They are each the devil in the other's eyes.

KW: Yes, it's at least a two-thousand-year-old war, often brutal and always rancorous. In the West, from the time roughly of Augustine to Copernicus, we have a purely Ascending ideal, otherworldly to the core. Final salvation and liberation could not be found in this body, on this Earth, in this lifetime. I mean, your present life could be okay, but things got really interesting once you died. Once you went otherworldly.

But then, with the rise of modernity and postmodernity, we see a complete and profound reversal—the Ascenders were out, the Descenders were in.

Q: You call this "the dominance of the Descenders," which is another major topic we will cover. You point out that the modern and postmodern world is governed almost entirely by a purely Descended conception, a purely Descended worldview.

KW: Yes, the idea that the sensory and empirical and material world is the only world there is. There are no higher or deeper potentials available to us—no higher transcendental stages of consciousness evolution, for example. There is merely what we can see with our senses or grasp with our hands. It is a world completely bereft of any sort of Ascending energy at all, hollow of any transcendence. And, in fact, as is usually the case with Descenders, any sort of Ascent or transcendence is looked upon as being misguided at best, evil at worst.

Q: But the point, I take it, is to integrate and include the best of both the Ascending and the Descending paths, yes?

KW: Yes. They both have some very important things to teach us, I believe.

Q: On the other hand, when they are divorced from each other, or when they try to deny each other, certain limited, partial, and oppressive schemes tend to result.

KW: I believe that is true. We all know the downsides of the merely Ascending path: it can be very puritanical and oppressive. It tends to deny and devalue and even repress the body, the senses, life, Earth, sexuality, and so forth.

The Descending path, on the other hand, reminds us that Spirit can be joyously found in body, sex, Earth, life, vitality, and diversity. But the

Descending path, in and by itself, has its own limitations. If there is no transcendence at all, then there is no way to rise above the merely sensory; no way to find a deeper, wider, higher connection between us and all sentient beings. We are merely confined to the sensory surfaces, the superficial facades, which separate us much more than join and unite us. Without some sort of transcendence or Ascent, we have *only* the Descended world, which can be shallow, alienated, and fragmented.

Q: You call the merely Descended world "flatland."

KW: Flatland, yes. We moderns and postmoderns live almost entirely within this purely Descended grid, this flat and faded world of endless sensory forms, this superficial world of drab and dreary surfaces. Whether with capitalism or Marxism, industrialism or ecopsychology, patriarchal science or ecofeminism—in most cases, our God, our Goddess, is one we can register with our senses, see with our eyes, wrap with feelings, worship with sensations, a God we can sink our teeth into, and that exhausts its form.

Whether or not we consider ourselves spiritual, we flatlanders worship at the altar of the merely Descended God, the sensory Goddess, the sensational world, the monochrome world of simple location, the world you can put your finger on. Nothing higher or deeper for us than the God that is clunking around in our visual field.

Q: You have pointed out that the great Nondual traditions, East and West, attempt instead to integrate both the Ascending and the Descending paths.

KW: Yes, to balance both transcendence and immanence, the One and the Many, Emptiness and Form, nirvana and samsara, Heaven and Earth.

Q: "Nonduality" refers to the integration of Ascending and Descending?

KW: That's right.

Q: So that is another point we want to discuss—the currents of Ascending and Descending spirituality, and how those currents can be integrated in our own daily lives.

KW: I think that is important, because, again, both paths have incredibly important things to teach us. It is in the union of the Ascending and the Descending currents that harmony is found, and not in any war between the two. It seems that only when Ascending and Descending are united can both be saved. And if we—if you and I—do not contribute to this union, then it is very possible that not only will we destroy the only Earth we have, we will forfeit the only Heaven we might otherwise embrace.

PART ONE

SPIRIT-IN-ACTION

1

The Pattern That Connects

Q: So we'll start the story with the Big Bang itself, and then trace out the course of evolution from matter to life to mind. And then, with the emergence of mind, or human consciousness, we'll look at the five or six major epochs of human evolution itself. And all of this is set in the context of spirituality—of what spirituality means, of the various forms that it has historically taken, and the forms that it might take tomorrow. Sound right?

KW: Yes, it's sort of a brief history of everything. This sounds altogether grandiose, but it's based on what I call "orienting generalizations," which simplifies the whole thing enormously.

Q: An orienting generalization is what, exactly?

KW: If we look at the various fields of human knowledge—from physics to biology to psychology, sociology, theology, and religion—certain broad, general themes emerge, about which there is actually very little disagreement.

For example, in the sphere of moral development, not everybody agrees with the details of Lawrence Kohlberg's moral stages, nor with the details of Carol Gilligan's reworking of Kohlberg's scheme. But there is general and ample agreement that human moral development goes through at least *three broad stages*.

The human at birth is not yet socialized into any sort of moral system—it is "preconventional." The human then learns a general moral scheme that represents the basic values of the society it is raised in—it becomes "conventional." And with even further growth, the individual may come to reflect on his or her society and thus gain some modest distance from it, gain a capacity to criticize it or reform it—the individual is to some degree "postconventional."

Thus, although the actual details and the precise meanings of that developmental sequence are still hotly debated, everybody pretty much agrees that something like those three broad stages do indeed occur, and occur universally. These are *orienting generalizations*: they show us, with a great deal of agreement, where the important forests are located, even if we can't agree on how many trees they contain.

My point is that if we take these types of largely-agreed-upon orienting generalizations from the various branches of knowledge—from physics to biology to psychology to theology—and if we string these orienting generalizations together, we will arrive at some astonishing and often profound conclusions, conclusions that, as extraordinary as they might be, nonetheless embody nothing more than our already-agreed-upon knowledge. The beads of knowledge are already accepted: it is only necessary to string them together into a necklace.

Q: And so in these discussions we will build toward some sort of necklace.

KW: Yes, in a sense. In working with broad orienting generalizations, we can suggest a broad orienting map of the place of men and women in relation to Universe, Life, and Spirit. The details of this map we can all fill in as we like, but its broad outlines really have an awful lot of supporting evidence, culled from the orienting generalizations, simple but sturdy, from the various branches of human knowledge.

The Kosmos

Q: We'll follow the course of evolution as it unfolds through the various domains, from matter to life to mind. You call these three major domains matter or cosmos, life or the biosphere, and mind or the noosphere. And all of these domains together you call the "Kosmos."

KW: Yes, the Pythagoreans introduced the term "Kosmos," which we usually translate as cosmos. But the original meaning of Kosmos was the patterned nature or process of all domains of existence, from matter to mind to God, and not merely the *physical* universe, which is usually what both "cosmos" and "universe" mean today.

So I would like to reintroduce this term, Kosmos. And, as you point out, the Kosmos contains the cosmos (or the physiosphere), the bios (or biosphere), psyche or nous (the noosphere), and theos (the theosphere or divine domain).

So, for example, we might haggle about where exactly it is that matter becomes life—or cosmos becomes bios—but as Francisco Varela points out, autopoiesis (or self-replication) occurs only in living systems. It is found nowhere in the cosmos, but only in the bios. It's a major and profound *emergent*—something astonishingly novel—and I trace several of these types of profound transformations or emergents in the course of evolution in the Kosmos.

Q: So in these discussions we're not interested in just the cosmos, but the Kosmos.

KW: Yes. Many cosmologies have a materialistic bias and prejudice: the physical cosmos is somehow supposed to be the most real dimension, and everything else is explained with ultimate reference to this material plane. But what a brutal approach that is! It smashes the entire Kosmos against the wall of reductionism, and all the domains except the physical slowly bleed to death right in front of your eyes. Is this any way to treat a Kosmos?

No, I think what we want to do is Kosmology, not cosmology.

Twenty Tenets: The Patterns That Connect

Q: We can begin this Kosmology by reviewing the characteristics of evolution in the various realms. You have isolated *twenty patterns* that seem to be true for evolution wherever it occurs, from matter to life to mind.

KW: Based on the work of numerous researchers, yes.

Q: Let's give a few examples of these twenty tenets to show what's involved. Tenet number 1 is that reality is composed of whole/parts, or "holons." Reality is composed of holons?

KW: Is that far out? Is this already confusing? No? Well, Arthur Koestler coined the term "holon" to refer to an entity that is itself a *whole* and simultaneously a *part* of some other whole. And if you start to look closely at the things and processes that actually exist, it soon becomes obvious that they are not merely wholes, they are also parts of something else. They are whole/parts, they are holons.

For instance, a whole atom is part of a whole molecule, and the whole molecule is part of a whole cell, and the whole cell is part of a whole organism, and so on. Each of these entities is neither a whole nor a part, but a whole/part, a holon.

And the point is, everything is basically a holon of some sort or another. There is a two-thousand-year-old philosophical squabble between atomists and wholists: which is ultimately real, the whole or the part? And the answer is, neither. Or both, if you prefer. There are only whole/parts in all directions, all the way up, all the way down.

There's an old joke about a King who goes to a Wiseperson and asks how it is that the Earth doesn't fall down. The Wiseperson replies, "The Earth is resting on a lion." "On what, then, is the lion resting?" "The lion is resting on an elephant." "On what is the elephant resting?" "The elephant is resting on a turtle." "On what is the . . . ?" "You can stop right there, Your Majesty. It's turtles all the way down."

Turtles all the way down, holons all the way down. No matter how far down we go, we find holons resting on holons resting on holons. Even subatomic particles disappear into a virtual cloud of bubbles within bubbles, holons within holons, in an *infinity* of probability waves. Holons all the way down.

Q: And all the way up, as you say. We never come to an ultimate Whole.

KW: That's right. There is no whole that isn't also simultaneously a part of some other whole, indefinitely, unendingly. Time goes on, and today's wholes are tomorrow's parts. . . .

Even the "Whole" of the Kosmos is simply a *part* of the next moment's whole, *indefinitely.* At no point do we have *the* whole, because there is no whole, there are only whole/parts forever.

So the first tenet says that reality is composed neither of things nor processes, neither wholes nor parts, but whole/parts, or holons—all the way up, all the way down.

Q: So reality is not composed of, say, subatomic particles.

KW: Yikes. I know that approach is common, but it is really a profoundly reductionistic approach, because it is going to *privilege* the material, physical universe, and then everything else—from life to mind to spirit—has to be *derived* from subatomic particles, and this will never, never work.

But notice, a subatomic particle is itself a holon. And so is a cell. And so is a symbol, and an image, and a concept. What all of those entities are, before they are anything else, is a holon. So the world is not composed of atoms or symbols or cells or concepts. It is composed of holons.

Since the Kosmos is composed of holons, then if we look at what *all holons have in common,* then we can begin to see what evolution in all the various domains has in common. Holons in the cosmos, bios, psyche, theos—how they all unfold, the common patterns they all display.

Q: What all holons have in common. That is how you arrive at the twenty tenets.

KW: Yes, that's right.

Agency and Communion

Q: So tenet 1 is that the Kosmos is composed of holons. Tenet 2 is that all holons share certain characteristics.

KW: Yes. Because every holon is a whole/part, it has two "tendencies" or two "drives," we might say—it has to maintain both its *wholeness* and its *partness*.

On the one hand, it has to maintain its own wholeness, its own identity, its own autonomy, its own *agency*. If it fails to maintain and preserve its own agency, or its own identity, then it simply ceases to exist. So one of the characteristics of a holon, in any domain, is its agency, its capacity to maintain its own wholeness in the face of environmental pressures which would otherwise obliterate it. This is true for atoms, cells, organisms, ideas.

But a holon is not only a whole that has to preserve its agency, it is also a part of some other system, some other wholeness. And so, in addition to having to maintain its own autonomy as a *whole*, it simultaneously has to fit in as a *part* of something else. Its own existence depends upon its capacity to fit into its environment, and this is true from atoms to molecules to animals to humans.

So every holon has not only its own agency as a whole, it also has to fit with its *communions* as part of other wholes. If it fails at either—if it fails at agency or communion—it is simply erased. It ceases to be.

Transcendence and Dissolution

Q: And that is part of tenet number 2—each holon possesses both agency and communion. You call these the "horizontal" capacities of holons. What about the "vertical" capacities of holons, which you call "self-transcendence" and "self-dissolution"?

KW: Yes. If a holon fails to maintain its agency and its communions, then it can break down completely. When it does break down, it decomposes into its subholons: cells decompose into molecules, which break down into atoms, which can be "smashed" infinitely under intense pressure. The fascinating thing about holon decomposition is that holons tend to dissolve in the reverse direction that they were built up. And this decomposition is "self-dissolution," or simply decomposing into subholons, which themselves can decompose into their subholons, and so on.

But look at the reverse process, which is the most extraordinary: the building-up process, the process of new holons emerging. How did inert molecules come together to form living cells in the first place?

The standard neo-Darwinian explanation of chance mutation and natural selection—very few theorists believe this anymore. Evolution clearly operates in part by Darwinian natural selection, but this process simply selects those transformations that have *already* occurred by mechanisms that absolutely nobody understands.

Q: For example?

KW: Take the standard notion that wings simply evolved from forelegs. It takes perhaps a hundred mutations to produce a functional wing from a leg—a half-wing will not do. A half-wing is no good as a leg and no good as a wing—you can't run and you can't fly. It has no adaptive value whatsoever. In other words, with a half-wing you are dinner. The wing will work only if these hundred mutations *happen all at once,* in one animal—and also these *same* mutations must occur *simultaneously* in another animal of the opposite sex, and then they have to somehow find each other, have dinner, a few drinks, mate, and have offspring with real functional wings.

Talk about mind-boggling. This is infinitely, absolutely, utterly mind-boggling. Random mutations cannot even begin to explain this. The vast majority of mutations are lethal anyway; how are we going to get a hundred nonlethal mutations happening simultaneously? Or even four or five, for that matter? But once this incredible transformation has occurred, then natural selection will indeed select the better wings from the less workable wings—but the wings themselves? Nobody has a clue.

For the moment, everybody has simply agreed to call this "quantum evolution" or "punctuated evolution" or "emergent evolution"— radically novel and emergent and incredibly complex holons come into existence in a huge leap, in a quantum-like fashion—with no evidence whatsoever of intermediate forms. Dozens or hundreds of simultaneous nonlethal mutations have to happen at the same time in order to survive at all—the wing, for example, or the eyeball.

However we decide these extraordinary transformations occur, the fact is undeniable that they do. Thus, many theorists, like Erich Jantsch, simply refer to evolution as "self-realization through self-transcendence." Evolution is a wildly *self-transcending* process: it has the utterly amazing capacity to go beyond what went before. So evolution is in part a process of transcendence, which incorporates what went before and then adds incredibly novel components. The drive to self-transcendence thus appears to be built into the very fabric of the Kosmos itself.

Four Drives of All Holons

Q: And that is the fourth "drive" of all holons. So we have agency and communion, operating "horizontally" on any level, and then "vertically" we have the move to a higher level altogether, which is self-transcendence, and the move to a lower level, which is self-dissolution.

KW: Yes, that's right. Because all holons are whole/parts, they are subjected to various "pulls" in their own existence. The pull to be a whole, the pull to be a part, the pull up, the pull down: agency, communion, transcendence, dissolution. And tenet 2 simply says that all holons have these four pulls.

So that's an example of how the twenty tenets start. There is nothing magical about the number "twenty." These are just some of the common patterns I have focused on. The rest of the twenty tenets look at what happens when these various forces play themselves out. The self-transcending drive produces life out of matter, and mind out of life. And the twenty tenets simply suggest some of these types of common patterns found in the evolution of holons wherever they appear—matter to life to mind, to maybe even higher stages. Maybe even spiritual stages, yes?

Q: So there is indeed some sort of unity to evolution.

KW: Well, it certainly seems so. The *continuous* process of self-transcendence produces *discontinuities*, leaps, creative jumps. So there are both discontinuities in evolution—mind cannot be reduced to life, and life cannot be reduced to matter; and there are continuities—the common patterns that evolution takes in all these domains. And in that sense, yes, the Kosmos hangs together, unified by a single process. It is a uni-verse, one song.

Creative Emergence

Q: That one song you call Spirit-in-action, or God-in-the-making, which is a point I want to come back to later. But for now, tenet number 3 states simply: Holons emerge.

KW: Yes. As we were saying, evolution is in part a self-transcending process—it always goes beyond what went before. And in that novelty, in that emergence, in that creativity, new entities come into being, new patterns unfold, new holons issue forth. This extraordinary process builds unions out of fragments and wholes out of heaps. The Kosmos, it seems, unfolds in quantum leaps of creative emergence.

Q: Which is why one level cannot be reduced to its lower components, or why a holon cannot be reduced to its subholons.

KW: Yes. I mean, you can analyze the whole into its constituent parts, and that's a completely valid endeavor. But then you have parts, not the whole. You can take a watch apart and analyze its parts, but they won't tell you the time of day. It's the same with any holon. The wholeness of the holon is not found in any of its parts, and that puts an end to a certain reductionistic frenzy that has plagued Western science virtually from its inception. Particularly with the systems sciences, the vivid realization has dawned: we live in a universe of creative emergence.

Q: Although there are still reductionists around, the tide does seem to have turned. You hardly have to explain anymore why reductionism, in and by itself, is "bad." And nonreductionism means, in some sense, that the Kosmos is creative.

KW: Amazing, isn't it? As "ultimate categories"—which means concepts that we need in order to think about anything else at all—Whitehead listed only three: creativity, one, many. (Since every holon is actually a one/many, those categories really come down to: creativity, holons.)

But the point is, as Whitehead put it, "The ultimate metaphysical ground is the *creative advance into novelty.*" New holons creatively emerge. Creativity, holons—those are some of the most basic categories that we need to think of before we can think about anything else at all!

So yes, that's tenet 3: holons emerge. And each holon has these four basic capacities—agency, communion, self-dissolution, self-transcendence—and so off we go, creating a Kosmos.

Q: This gets a little ahead of the story, so I don't want to pursue it too much right now. But you link creativity and Spirit.

KW: Well, what is creativity but another name for Spirit? If, as Whitehead said, creativity is an *ultimate*—you have to have it before you can have anything else—what is an "ultimate metaphysical ground" if not Spirit? For Spirit, I also use the Buddhist term "Emptiness," which we can talk about. But Spirit or Emptiness gives rise to form. New forms emerge, new holons emerge—and it's not out of thin air.

We already saw that many scientists *agree* that self-transcendence (or novel emergence) is built into the very fabric of the universe. By any other name, what is that self-transcending creativity? Spirit, yes? We are obviously talking in very general terms here, but so far it appears that we have: Spirit, creativity, holons.

Q: There has also been a recent warming in some scientific circles to a more spiritual or idealistic reading of creation.

KW: In a certain sense. The Big Bang has made Idealists out of almost anybody who thinks. First there was absolutely nothing, then Bang! Something. This is beyond weird. Out of sheerest Emptiness, manifestation arises.

This is a bit of a nightmare for traditional science, because it puts a time limit on the chance mutations that were supposed to explain the universe. Remember the thousand monkeys and Shakespeare—an example of how chance could give rise to the ordered universe?

Q: Given enough time, the randomly typing monkeys would manage to type out a Shakespeare play.

KW: Given enough time! One computation showed that the chance for monkey power to produce a single Shakespeare play was one in ten thousand million million million million million million. So maybe that would happen in a billion billion years. But the universe doesn't have a billion billion years. It only has twelve billion years.

Well, this changes everything. Calculations done by scientists from Fred Hoyle to F. B. Salisbury consistently show that twelve billion years isn't even enough to produce a *single enzyme* by chance.

In other words, something other than chance is pushing the universe. For traditional scientists, chance was their salvation. Chance was their god. Chance would explain all. Chance—plus unending time—would produce the universe. But they don't have unending time, and so their god fails them miserably. That god is dead. Chance is not what explains the universe; in fact, chance is what the universe is laboring mightily to overcome. Chance is exactly what the self-transcending drive of the Kosmos overcomes.

Q: Which is another way of saying that self-transcendence is built into the universe, or, as you put it, self-transcendence is one of the four drives of any holon.

KW: Yes, I think so. There is a formative drive, a telos, to the Kosmos. It has a direction. It is going somewhere. Its ground is Emptiness; its drive is the organization of Form into increasingly coherent holons. Spirit, creativity, holons.

Q: Now the "religious creationists" have made quite a big deal out of this. They say it fits with the Bible and Genesis.

KW: Well, they have seized upon the increasingly obvious truth that the traditional scientific explanation does not work very well. Creativity, not chance, builds a Kosmos. But it does not follow that you can then equate creativity with your favorite and particular God. It does not follow that into this void you can postulate a God with all the specific characteristics that make you happy—God is the God of only the Jews, or only the Hindus, or only the indigenous peoples, and God is watching over me, and is kind, and just, and merciful, and so on. We have to be very careful about these types of limited and anthropomorphic characteristics, which is one of the reasons I prefer "Emptiness" as a term for Spirit, because it means unbounded or unqualifiable.

But the fundamentalists, the "creationists," seize upon these vacancies in the scientific hotel to pack the conference with their delegates. They see the opening—creativity is an *absolute*—and they equate that absolute with their mythic god, and they stuff this god with all the characteristics that promote their own egoic inclinations, starting with the fact that if you don't believe in this particular god, you fry in hell forever, which is not exactly a generous view of Spirit.

So it is a good idea to start simple, I think, and be very careful. There is a spiritual opening in the Kosmos. Let us be careful how we fill it. The simplest is: Spirit or Emptiness is unqualifiable, but it is not inert and unyielding, for it gives rise to manifestation itself: new forms emerge, and that creativity is ultimate. Emptiness, creativity, holons.

Let's leave it there for the time being, okay? We can come back to this topic as things unfold.

Holarchy

Q: Fair enough. So we just looked at tenet number 3, "Holons emerge." Tenet number 4 is: Holons emerge holarchically. Holarchy?

KW: Koestler's term for natural hierarchy. Hierarchy today has a very bad reputation, mostly because people confuse dominator hierarchies with natural hierarchies.

A natural hierarchy is simply an order of increasing wholeness, such as: particles to atoms to cells to organisms, or letters to words to sentences to paragraphs. The whole of one level becomes a part of the whole of the next.

In other words, natural hierarchies are composed of holons. And thus, said Koestler, "hierarchy" should really be called "holarchy." He's absolutely right. Virtually all growth processes, from matter to life to mind, occur via natural holarchies, or orders of increasing holism and wholeness—wholes that become parts of new wholes—and that's natural hierarchy or holarchy.

Q: It's the dominator hierarchies that freak people out.

KW: With good reason, yes. When any holon in a natural holarchy usurps its position and attempts to dominate the whole, then you get a pathological or dominator hierarchy—a cancerous cell dominates the body, or a fascist dictator dominates the social system, or a repressive ego dominates the organism, and so on.

But the cure for these pathological holarchies is not getting rid of holarchy per se—which isn't possible anyway—but rather in arresting the arrogant holon and integrating it back into the natural holarchy, or putting it in its rightful place, so to speak. The critics of hierarchy—their names are legion—simply confuse these pathological holarchies with holarchies in general, and so they toss the baby with the bathwater.

Q: They claim in getting rid of hierarchies they are being holistic, because everything is treated equally and thus joined together.

KW: It appears to be just the opposite. The only way you get a holism is via a holarchy. When holists say "the whole is greater than the sum of its parts," that means the whole is at a *higher* or *deeper* level of organization than the parts alone—and that's a hierarchy, a holarchy. Separate molecules are drawn together into a single cell only by properties that supersede the molecules alone—the cell is holarchically arranged. And without holarchy, you simply have heaps, not wholes. You are a heapist, not a holist.

Q: But many feminists and many ecophilosophers claim that any sort of hierarchy or "ranking" is oppressive, even fascist. They say that all such value ranking is "old paradigm" or "patriarchal" or oppressive, and it ought to be replaced with a *linking*, not a *ranking*, worldview. They're very aggressive with this point; they hurl rather harsh accusations.

KW: This is a bit disingenuous, because you can't avoid hierarchy. Even the antihierarchy theorists that you mention *have their own hierarchy*, their own *ranking*. Namely, they think linking is *better* than ranking. Well, that's a hierarchy, a ranking of values. But because they don't own up to this, then their hierarchy becomes unconscious, hidden, denied. Their hierarchy denies hierarchy. They have a ranking system that says ranking is bad.

Q: You call this a "performative contradiction."

KW: Yes, the point is that the antihierarchy stance is self-contradictory. These theorists have a hierarchy; it's just hidden or concealed. With this stealth hierarchy they attack all other hierarchies, and they claim that they themselves are "free" of all that nasty ranking. So they rancorously denounce others for doing precisely what they themselves are doing. It's an altogether unpleasant affair.

Q: But hierarchy has been put to many abuses, as you yourself have explained at length.

KW: Yes, and in that regard I very much agree with these critics. But the point is not to get rid of hierarchies or holarchies altogether—that's impossible. Trying to get rid of ranking is itself a ranking. Denying hierarchy is itself a hierarchy. Precisely because the Kosmos is composed of holons, and holons exist holarchically, you can't escape these nested orders. Rather, we want to tease apart *natural* holarchies from *pathological* or *dominator* holarchies.

Q: So holarchies really are inescapable.

KW: Yes, because holons are inescapable. All evolutionary and developmental patterns proceed by holarchization, by a process of increasing orders of wholeness and inclusion, which is a type of *ranking* by *holistic* capacity. This is why the basic principle of holism is holarchy: the higher or deeper dimension provides a principle, or a "glue," or a pattern, that unites and *links* otherwise separate and conflicting and isolated parts into a coherent unity, a space in which separate parts can recognize a common wholeness and thus escape the fate of being merely a part, merely a fragment.

So linking is indeed important, but linking is itself set within ranking and holarchy, and can exist only because of holarchy, which provides the higher or deeper space in which the linking and joining can occur. Otherwise heaps, not wholes.

And when a particular holon usurps its position in any holarchy—when it wants to be only a whole, and not also a part—then that natural or normal holarchy degenerates into a pathological or dominator holarchy, which by any other name is illness, pathology, disease—whether physical, emotional, social, cultural, or spiritual. And we want to "attack" these pathological hierarchies, not in order to get rid of hierarchy per se, but in order to allow the normal or natural hierarchy to emerge in its place and continue its healthy growth and development.

The Way of All Embrace

Q: Okay, here is what we have so far. The Kosmos is composed of holons, all the way up, all the way down. All holons have four fundamental capacities—agency and communion, transcendence and dissolution. Holons emerge. Holons emerge holarchically.

KW: Yes, those are the first four tenets.

Q: So now we have tenet 5: Each emergent holon transcends but includes its predecessor(s).

KW: For example, the cell transcends—or goes beyond—its molecular components, but also includes them. Molecules transcend and include atoms, which transcend and include particles. . . .

The point is that since all holons are whole/parts, the wholeness *transcends* but the parts are *included*. In this transcendence, heaps are converted into wholes; in the inclusion, the parts are equally embraced and cherished, linked in a commonality and a shared space that relieves each of the burden of being a fragment.

And so yes, evolution is a process of transcend and include, transcend and include. And this begins to open onto the very heart of Spirit-in-action, the very secret of the evolutionary impulse.

2

The Secret Impulse

Q: The secret impulse of evolution?

KW: A molecule transcends and includes atoms. *Transcends*, in that it has certain emergent or novel or creative properties that are not merely the sum of its components. This is the whole point of systems theory and holism in general, that new levels of organization come into being, and these new levels cannot be reduced in all ways to their junior dimensions—they transcend them. But they also *include* them, because the junior holons are nonetheless components of the new holon. So, transcends and includes.

Q: So the higher has the essentials of the lower, plus something extra.

KW: Yes, that's another way of putting it, which Aristotle first pointed out—all of the lower is in the higher but not all of the higher is in the lower, which is what *invariably* establishes hierarchy or holarchy. Cells contain molecules, but not vice versa. Molecules contain atoms, but not vice versa. Sentences contain words, but not vice versa. And it is this *not vice versa* that establishes a hierarchy, a holarchy, an order of increasing wholeness.

Higher and Lower

Q: There is so much bitter argument over a level being "higher" or "lower" than another. And yet you have suggested a simple rule for establishing higher and lower in any sequence.

KW: Well, take any evolutionary development, say, atoms to molecules to cells to organisms. This is a sequence of increasing wholeness, increasing holons, each of which transcends and includes its predecessor. Now if, in a type of thought experiment, you "destroy" any particular type of holon, then all of the *higher* holons will also be destroyed, but none of the *lower* holons will be destroyed. And this simple thought experiment can help you spot what is higher, and what is lower, in any sequence.

So, for example, if you destroyed all the molecules in the universe, then all of the higher levels—cells and organisms—would also be destroyed. But none of the lower holons—atoms and subatomic particles—none of them would be destroyed.

Q: Yes, I see. So "higher" and "lower" organization is not merely a relative "value judgment."

KW: That's right. It truly is not an invention of patriarchal obnoxiousness or fascist ideology. If you destroy any particular type of holon, then all of the higher holons are also destroyed, because they depend in part on the lower holons *for their own components*. But the lower holons can get along perfectly well without the higher: atoms can exist just fine without molecules, but molecules cannot exist without atoms. A simple rule, but it helps us see what is higher, and what is lower, in terms of any holarchy.

This rule works for any developmental sequence, for any holarchy—moral development, language acquisition, biological speciation, computer programs, nucleic acid translations. It works by virtue of the simple way that wholes depend upon parts, but not vice versa. And "not vice versa," as we were saying, is holarchy, or an order of increasing wholeness.

Q: This is how you demonstrate that the biosphere is higher than the physiosphere.

KW: Yes, if you destroy the biosphere—that is, if you destroy all life forms—then the cosmos or physiosphere could and would still exist. But if you destroy the physiosphere, the biosphere is instantly destroyed as well. This happens because the biosphere transcends and includes the physiosphere, and not vice versa. And so yes, the physiosphere is a lower level of structural organization than the biosphere. That is the meaning of higher and lower organization. And the bios is *higher*, the cosmos is *lower*.

Q: In the same way, the noosphere is higher than the biosphere.

KW: In exactly the same way. The noosphere begins with the capacity to form any mental images, and this capacity begins with certain mammals, such as horses. But for this example, I'll confine the noosphere to more highly developed minds and human cultural productions, just to show what's involved—we get the same results either way.

The biosphere existed perfectly well for millions of years before human minds showed up, before the noosphere emerged. And if you destroyed that noosphere, the biosphere would and could still exist. But if you destroy the biosphere, then you destroy all human minds as well, because the biosphere is a part of the noosphere—and not vice versa. So yes, the biosphere is a lower level of structural organization than the noosphere. The noosphere transcends and includes the biosphere, it is not merely a part of the biosphere. That's reductionism.

Q: So the physiosphere is part of the higher wholeness of the biosphere, which is part of the higher wholeness of the noosphere, and not the other way around.

KW: Yes.

Depth and Span

Q: But why do so many people picture it backward?

KW: Probably because people confuse size or *span* with *depth*. And people think that great span means great depth, and this is precisely backward.

Q: So what exactly do "depth" and "span" refer to?

KW: The number of levels in any holarchy is referred to as its *depth*, and the number of holons on any given level is referred to as its *span*.

Q: So if we say atoms have a depth of one, then molecules have a depth of two, cells a depth of three.

KW: Yes, along those lines. Exactly what we want to call a "level" is somewhat arbitrary. It's like a three-story house. We can count each floor as a level, which is what we usually do, so the house would have a *depth* of *three*—three levels. But we could also count each step in the stairs as a level. Maybe there are twenty steps between floors—we would then say that the house has sixty levels, or a depth of sixty.

But the point is that, although these scales are relative or arbitrary, the relative placements are *not* arbitrary. Whether we say the house has three levels or sixty levels, the second floor is still higher than the first floor. As long as we use the same relative scale, then no problems arise, just as we can use Fahrenheit or Celsius to measure water temperature, as long as we are consistent.

So we could say quarks have a depth of one, atoms a depth of two, crystals a depth of three, molecules a depth of four, and so on. The depth is real, no matter what relative scale we decide to use.

Q: So depth and span.

KW: What confuses people is that evolution actually produces *greater depth* and *less span* on succeeding levels. And people tend to confuse collective *bigness* or *size* or *span* with *depth*, and so they get the order of significance totally backward.

Q: Evolution produces greater depth, less span. That is actually tenet number 8 (we're skipping some of them). So could you give an example of this tenet?

KW: There are fewer organisms than cells; there are fewer cells than molecules; there are fewer molecules than atoms; there are fewer atoms than quarks. Each has a *greater* depth, but *less* span.

The reason, of course, is that because the higher transcends and includes the lower, there will always be less of the higher and more of the lower, and there are no exceptions. No matter how many cells there are in the universe, there will always be more molecules. No matter how many molecules in the universe, there will always be more atoms. No matter how many atoms, there will always be more quarks.

So the greater depth always has less span than its predecessor. The *individual* holon has more and more depth, but the *collective* gets smaller and smaller. And since many people think bigger is better, they tend to confuse the direction of significance, they invert the order of being. They turn reality on its head and end up worshipping bigger as better.

Q: A holon transcends and includes its predecessors—it has *greater* depth—but the population size of the greater depth becomes *smaller*. The so-called pyramid of development.

KW: Yes. Figure 2-1 is from Ervin Laszlo's *Evolution: The Grand Synthesis*, which is generally considered to be a clear and accurate summary of the modern scientific view of evolution, such as it is. But you can see the pyramid of evolution very clearly. Where matter is favorable, life emerges; where life is favorable, mind emerges. (I would add, where mind is favorable, Spirit emerges.)

In the diagram, you can actually see that the vertical depth becomes greater, but the horizontal span becomes less. Interestingly, the perennial philosophy reached the same conclusion, in its own way.

Q: The perennial philosophy being . . . ?

KW: We might say it's the core of the world's great wisdom traditions. The perennial philosophy maintains that reality is a Great Holar-

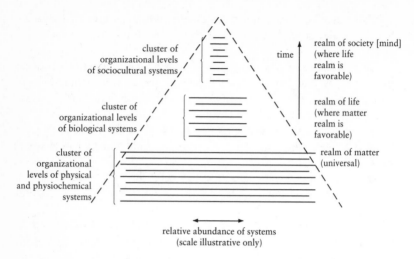

FIGURE 2-1. *The realms of evolution. From Ervin Laszlo,* Evolution: The Grand Synthesis *(Boston: Shambhala, 1987), p. 55.*

chy of being and consciousness, reaching from matter to life to mind to Spirit. Each dimension transcends and includes its junior dimension in a nested holarchy, often represented by concentric circles or spheres. This "transcend and include" is indicated in figure 2-2.

Each level includes its predecessor and then adds its own emergent qualities, qualities that are not found in the previous dimension. So each succeeding dimension is "bigger" in the sense of greater embrace, greater depth. And we will see that an individual holon's *identity* actually *expands* to include more and more of the Kosmos—precisely as shown in figure 2-2.

But since the actual *span* of the succeeding holons becomes *less* and *less*—the number of holons at each higher level becomes smaller—then this same diagram is often drawn in exactly the opposite fashion, as in figure 2-3. Greater depth means fewer holons reach that depth—means less span—and so the actual population size becomes smaller and smaller, as indicated in figure 2-3, which is the perennial philosophy's version of the pyramid of development.

Q: So we need to remember both of these progressions—greater depth, less span.

KW: Yes. In discussing evolution, perhaps we can keep both of these diagrams in mind. The first diagram indicates "transcend and in-

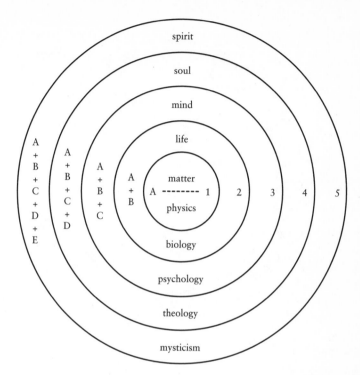

FIGURE 2-2. *Greater depth.*

clude"—an actual increase in embrace, inclusion, identity, enfolding—
which gets "larger" in the sense of "deeper": it contains or *enfolds* more
and more levels or dimensions of reality internal to it, as part of its very
makeup, its very being, its compound individuality, and so it is more
significant: it *signifies* or indicates that more and more of the Kosmos is
internal to it, just as a molecule internally contains atoms, actually enfolds them in its own being.

But the second diagram reminds us that the number of holons that
actually realize these deeper dimensions becomes smaller and smaller.
Figure 2-2 is depth, figure 2-3 is span. The one gets bigger, the other gets
smaller. Greater depth, less span.

Kosmic Consciousness

Q: But the highest level—Spirit. Isn't Spirit everywhere? It's not a
level, it's everywhere.

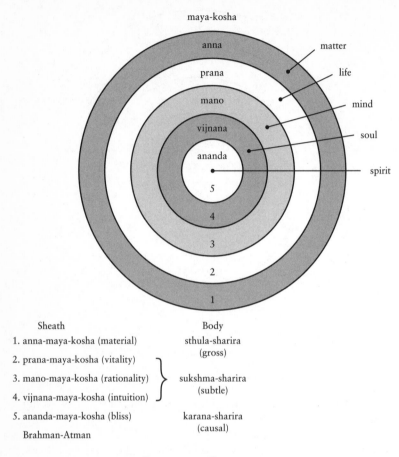

Figure 2-3. *Less span.*

KW: Each level transcends and includes its predecessor. Spirit transcends all, so it includes all. It is utterly beyond this world, but utterly embraces every single holon in this world. It permeates all of manifestation but is not merely manifestation. It is ever-present at every level or dimension, but is not merely a particular level or dimension. Transcends all, includes all, as the groundless Ground or Emptiness of all manifestation.

So Spirit is both the highest "level" in the holarchy, but it's also the paper on which the entire holarchy is written. It's the highest rung in the ladder, but it's also the wood out of which the entire ladder is made. It is both the Goal and the Ground of the entire sequence. I think this will become more obvious as we proceed.

Q: I don't want to get ahead of the story, but this also leads to an environmental ethics.

KW: Yes, the point of a genuine environmental ethics is that we are supposed to transcend and include all holons in a genuine embrace. Because human beings contain matter and life and mind, as components in their own makeup, then of course we must honor all of these holons, not only for their own *intrinsic worth*, which is the most important, but also because they are components in our own being, and destroying them is *literally* suicidal for us. It's not that harming the biosphere will eventually catch up with us and hurt us from the outside. It's that the biosphere is literally internal to us, is a part of our very being, our compound individuality—harming the biosphere is internal suicide, not just some sort of external problem.

So we can have a profoundly ecological view without being *merely* ecological, or reducing everything to the simple biosphere. We need an approach that transcends and includes ecology—precisely because the noosphere transcends and includes the biosphere, which transcends and includes the physiosphere. We don't need an approach that simply privileges ecology in a regressive flattening to one-dimensional life, to the flatland web of life.

Q: But many ecophilosophers and ecofeminists refer to mystical oneness with all nature, to what Bucke called "cosmic consciousness," where all beings are seen in an equal light, with no hierarchy at all, no higher or lower, just the great web of life.

KW: Yes, that type of mystical experience of equality is common in the higher stages of human development, and it is important to honor that.

But there are two very different issues here. Human identity can indeed expand to include the All—let's call it Kosmic consciousness, the *unio mystica*—just as in figure 2-2. Individual identity expands to Spirit and thus embraces the Kosmos—transcends all, includes all. And that is fine. But the number of humans actually realizing that supreme identity is very, very small. In other words, this very great depth has a very small span. As always, greater depth, less span.

But in that experience, the conscious identity is indeed an identity with the All, with the Kosmos. And in that identity, all beings, high or low, sacred or profane, are indeed seen to be perfect manifestations of

Spirit, precisely as they are—no lower, no higher. The *ultimate depth* is an ultimate oneness with the All, with the Kosmos.

But this *realization* is *not* given *equally* to all beings, even though all beings are equally manifestations of Spirit. This *realization* is the result of a developmental and evolutionary process of growth and transcendence.

And the web-of-life theorists usually focus on the equality of being and miss the holarchy of realization. They think that because an ant and an ape are both perfect manifestations of the Divine—which they are—then there is no difference in depth between them, which is reductionistic in the most painful fashion.

So we want our environmental ethics to honor all holons without exception as manifestations of Spirit, and also, at the same time, be able to make pragmatic distinctions in intrinsic worth, and realize that it is much better to kick a rock than an ape, much better to eat a carrot than a cow, much better to subsist on grains than on mammals.

If you agree with those statements, then you are acknowledging gradations in depth, gradations in intrinsic value—you are acknowledging a holarchy of value. Many ecophilosophers agree with those statements, but they can't say why, because they have a hierarchy that denies hierarchy—they have only the flatland web of life and bioequality, which is not only self-contradictory, it paralyzes pragmatic action and cripples intrinsic values.

The Spectrum of Consciousness

Q: Okay, I very much want to come back to all of that (in Part Three), but we need to stay on course. We were talking about the direction of evolution, the telos of the Kosmos, which is not random chance, but directionality.

KW: Evolution has a direction, yes, a principle of order out of chaos, as it is commonly phrased. In other words, a drive toward greater depth. Chance is defeated, depth emerges—the intrinsic value of the Kosmos increases with each unfolding.

Q: That's actually tenet 12, which is the last tenet I want to discuss. In that tenet, you give various indicators of directionality in evolution, which I'll just list. Evolution has a broad and general *tendency* to move in the direction of: increasing complexity, increasing differentiation/integration, increasing organization/structuration, increasing relative autonomy, increasing telos.

KW: Yes, those are some of the typically accepted—that is, scientifically accepted—directions of evolution. This doesn't mean that regression and dissolution don't occur—they do (dissolution is one of the four capacities of any holon). And it doesn't mean that every short-term development must follow those directions. As Michael Murphy says, evolution meanders more than it progresses. But over the long haul, evolution has a broad telos, a broad direction, which is particularly obvious with increasing differentiation—an atom to an amoeba to an ape!

But all of those scientific descriptions can generally be summarized as: the basic drive of evolution is to increase depth. This is the self-transcending drive of the Kosmos—to go beyond what went before, and yet include what went before, and thus increase its own depth.

Q: Now you also tie this in with consciousness. Because you add, "the greater the depth of a holon, the greater its degree of consciousness."

KW: Yes. Consciousness and depth are synonymous. All holons have some degree of depth, however minor, because there is no bottom. And with evolution, depth becomes greater and greater—consciousness becomes greater and greater. However much depth atoms have, molecules have more. And cells have more depth than molecules. And plants have more than cells. And primates more than plants.

There is a spectrum of depth, a spectrum of consciousness. And evolution unfolds that spectrum. Consciousness unfolds more and more, realizes itself more and more, comes into manifestation more and more. Spirit, consciousness, depth—so many words for the same thing.

Q: Since depth is everywhere, consciousness is everywhere.

KW: Consciousness is simply what depth looks like from the inside, from within. So yes, depth is everywhere, consciousness is everywhere, Spirit is everywhere. And as depth increases, consciousness increasingly awakens, Spirit increasingly unfolds. To say that evolution produces greater depth is simply to say that it unfolds greater consciousness.

Q: You use "unfolds and enfolds."

KW: Spirit is *unfolding* itself in each new transcendence, which it also *enfolds* into its own being at the new stage. Transcends and includes, brings forth and embraces, creates and loves, Eros and Agape, unfolds and enfolds—different ways of saying the same thing.

So we can summarize all this very simply: because evolution *goes beyond* what went before, but because it must *embrace* what went before, then its very nature is to transcend and include, and thus it has an inherent directionality, a secret impulse, toward increasing depth, increasing intrinsic value, increasing consciousness. In order for evolution to move at all, it must move in those directions—there's no place else for it to go!

Q: The general point being. . . ?

KW: Well, several. For one, because the universe has direction, we ourselves have direction. There is meaning in the movement, intrinsic value in the embrace. As Emerson put it, we lie in the lap of immense intelligence, which by any other name is Spirit. There is a theme inscribed on the original face of the Kosmos. There is a pattern written on the wall of Nothingness. There is a meaning in its every gesture, a grace in its every glance.

We—and all beings as such—are drenched in this meaning, afloat in a current of care and profound value, ultimate significance, intrinsic awareness. We are part and parcel of this immense intelligence, this Spirit-in-action, this God-in-the-making. We don't have to think of God as some mythic figure outside of the display, running the show. Nor must we picture it as some merely immanent Goddess, lost in the forms of her own production. Evolution is both God and Goddess, transcendence and immanence. It is immanent in the process itself, woven into the very fabric of the Kosmos; but it everywhere transcends its own productions, and brings forth anew in every moment.

Q: Transcends and includes.

KW: Indeed. And we are invited, I believe, to awaken as this process. The very Spirit in us is invited to become self-conscious, or even, as some would say, superconscious. Depth increases from subconscious to self-conscious to superconscious, on the way to its own shocking recognition, utterly one with the radiant All, and we awaken as that oneness.

What do you think? Is that crazy? Are the mystics and sages insane? Because they all tell variations on this same story, don't they? The story of awakening one morning and discovering that you are one with the All, in a timeless and eternal and infinite fashion.

Yes, maybe they are crazy, these divine fools. Maybe they are mumbling idiots in the face of the Abyss. Maybe they need a nice understanding therapist. Yes, I'm sure that would help.

But then, I wonder. Maybe the evolutionary sequence really is from matter to body to mind to soul to spirit, each transcending and including, each with a greater depth and greater consciousness and wider embrace. And in the highest reaches of evolution, maybe, just maybe, an individual's consciousness does indeed touch infinity—a total embrace of the entire Kosmos—a Kosmic consciousness that is Spirit awakened to its own true nature.

It's at least plausible. And tell me: is that story, sung by mystics and sages the world over, any crazier than the scientific materialism story, which is that the entire sequence is a tale told by an idiot, full of sound and fury, signifying absolutely nothing? Listen very carefully: just which of those two stories actually sounds totally insane?

I'll tell you what I think. I think the sages are the growing tip of the secret impulse of evolution. I think they are the leading edge of the self-transcending drive that always goes beyond what went before. I think they embody the very drive of the Kosmos toward greater depth and expanding consciousness. I think they are riding the edge of a light beam racing toward a rendezvous with God.

And I think they point to the same depth in you, and in me, and in all of us. I think they are plugged into the All, and the Kosmos sings through their voices, and Spirit shines through their eyes. And I think they disclose the face of tomorrow, they open us to the heart of our own destiny, which is also already right now in the timelessness of this very moment, and in that startling recognition the voice of the sage becomes your voice, the eyes of the sage become your eyes, you speak with the tongues of angels and are alight with the fire of a realization that never dawns nor ceases, you recognize your own true Face in the mirror of the Kosmos itself: your identity is indeed the All, and you are no longer *part* of that stream, you *are* that stream, with the All unfolding not around you but in you. The stars no longer shine out there, but in here. Supernovas come into being within your heart, and the sun shines inside your awareness. Because you transcend all, you embrace all. There is no final Whole here, only an endless process, and you are the opening or the clearing or the pure Emptiness in which the entire process unfolds—ceaselessly, miraculously, everlastingly, lightly.

The whole game is undone, this nightmare of evolution, and you are exactly where you were prior to the beginning of the whole show. With a sudden shock of the utterly obvious, you recognize your own Original Face, the face you had prior to the Big Bang, the face of utter Emptiness that smiles as all creation and sings as the entire Kosmos—and it is all undone in that primal glance, and all that is left is the smile, and the reflection of the moon on a quiet pond, late on a crystal clear night.

3

All Too Human

Q: The superconscious is a little ahead of our story! We have basically just covered evolution up to the emergence of human beings, the blossoming of the noosphere. You point out that each of the major stages of the evolution of human consciousness also follows the twenty tenets. So there is an overall continuity to evolution, from physiosphere to biosphere to noosphere.

KW: Which makes sense, doesn't it? And as evolution moves into the noosphere, then—based on the work of numerous researchers, such as Jean Gebser, Pitirim Sorokin, Robert Bellah, Jürgen Habermas, Michel Foucault, Peter Berger, to name a few—we can outline the predominant "worldviews" of the various epochs of human development. These stages, these worldviews, may be summarized as archaic, magic, mythic, rational, and existential.

Q: Which you also correlate with the major stages of technological/ economic development.

KW: Yes, which are: foraging, horticultural, agrarian, industrial, and informational. (You can see these on figure 5-2 on page 119.)

Q: In each of those stages, you outline the types of economic production, the worldview, the modes of technology, the moral outlook, the legal codes, the types of religion . . .

KW: And here is where we also begin to look at the status of men and women in each of those stages. Because the relative status of men and women has varied tremendously across these stages, and the idea is to search for various factors that contributed to these changes.

Q: Which includes the "patriarchy."

KW: Well, yes. Based on the exciting work of recent feminist researchers, such as Kay Martin, Barbara Voorhies, Joyce Nielsen, and Janet Chafetz, we can fairly well reconstruct the relative status of men and women in each of these five or so major evolutionary stages of human development.

If we pull all of these sources together, we have: the five or six major stages of techno-economic evolution, as outlined, for example, by Gerhard Lenski; the relative status of men and women in each of those stages, as outlined by Chafetz and Nielsen and others; and the correlation with worldviews, as outlined by Gebser and Habermas.

Using these sources—and numerous others we needn't go into—we can reach some fairly sturdy conclusions about the relative status of men and women in each of these stages, and, more important, we can isolate the factors that contributed to these differences in status.

Foraging

Q: Let's give a few examples here, to see exactly what you mean.

KW: In foraging societies (also called hunting and gathering), the roles of men and women were sharply delineated and sharply separated. Men, indeed, did most of the hunting, and women most of the gathering and child rearing. An astonishing 97 percent of foraging societies follow that rather rigid pattern.

But because there were few possessions—the wheel hadn't even been invented—there was little emphasis placed on either the male or female value sphere. Men's work was men's work, and women's work was women's, and never the twain shall cross—there were very strong taboos about that, especially about menstruating women—but that didn't seem to be parlayed into any major sort of difference in status.

Because of this, these societies are eulogized by some feminists, but none of those feminists, I think, would really enjoy the rigidity of the gender roles. Um, just the opposite, I think.

Q: These societies emerged when?

KW: Foraging societies first emerged somewhere between a million and four hundred thousand years ago. As Habermas points out, what separated the first humans from apes and hominids was not an economy or even tools, but rather the invention of the role of the father—what he calls "the familialization of the male." By participating in both the productive hunt and the reproductive family, the father bridged these two value spheres, and marked off the beginning point of specifically human evolution. Since the pregnant female did not participate in the hunt, this job fell to the male, whether he wanted it or not (mostly not, I would guess).

But with the familialization of the male, we would see the beginning of the single, great, enduring, and nightmarish task of all subsequent civilization: the taming of testosterone.

Fuck it or kill it, but now in service of the family man. This is very funny, don't you think? In any event, the tribal structure has this family or kinship lineage, and different tribes, with different kinship lineages, have very, shall we say, testy relations with each other. You are on the fucking side or you are on the killing side.

The "carrying capacity" of these early foraging tribes was around forty people. The average life span, Lenski reports, was around 22.5 years. We are, of course, talking about the original tribal structure, and not about indigenous peoples today, who have been subjected to hundreds of thousands of years of further types of various development. But the basic tribal structure itself means a small group based specifically on kinship lineage, and a foraging tribe means one whose subsistence is based on pre-agriculture hunting and gathering.

The ecomasculinists (deep ecologists) are particularly fond of this period.

Q: They like these societies because they were ecologically sound.

KW: Some primal tribal societies were ecologically sound, and some definitely were not. Some tribes practiced cut and slash and burn, and some were responsible for the extinction of numerous species. As Theodore Roszak points out in *The Voice of the Earth*, a "sacred" outlook toward nature did not in any way guarantee an ecologically sound culture.

Men and women, everywhere and at all times, have despoiled the environment, mostly out of *simple ignorance*. Even the highly revered Mayan culture disappeared largely through depleting the surrounding rain forests. Modernity's ignorance about the environment is much more serious, simply because modernity has many more powerful means to destroy the environment. Tribal ignorance, on the other hand, was usually milder; but ignorance is ignorance, and is certainly nothing to emulate. The *lack* of means in foraging societies does not simply equate with the *presence* of wisdom.

So it's true that some people today eulogize the primal tribal societies because of their "ecological wisdom" or their "reverence for nature" or their "nonaggressive ways." But I don't think the evidence supports any of those views in a sweeping and general fashion. Rather, I eulogize the primal tribal societies for entirely different reasons: We are all the sons and daughters of tribes. The primal tribes are literally our roots, our foundations, the basis of all that was to follow, the structure upon which all subsequent human evolution would be built, the crucial ground floor upon which so much history would have to rest.

Today's existent tribes, and today's nations, and today's cultures, and today's accomplishments—all would trace their lineage in an unbroken fashion to the primal tribal holons upon which a human family tree was about to be built. And looking back on our ancestors in that light, I am struck with awe and admiration for the astonishing creativity—the *original* breakthrough creativity—that allowed humans to rise above a given nature and begin building a noosphere, the very process of which would bring Heaven down to Earth and exalt the Earth to Heaven, the very process of which would eventually bind all peoples of the world together in, if you will, one global tribe.

But in order for that to occur, the original, primal tribes had to find a way to transcend their *isolated* tribal kinship lineages: they had to find a way to go trans-tribal, and agriculture, not hunting, provided the means for this new transcendence.

Horticultural

Q: So foraging eventually gave way to agriculture. You point out that there are two very different types of farming cultures— horticultural and agrarian.

KW: Yes, horticultural is based on a hoe or simple digging stick. Agrarian is based on a heavy, animal-drawn plow.

Q: Sounds like a very small distinction.

KW: It is actually quite momentous. A digging stick or simple hoe can be used quite easily by a pregnant woman, and thus mothers were as capable as fathers of doing horticulture. Which they did. In fact, about 80 percent of the foodstuffs in these societies were produced by women (the men still went off and hunted, of course). Small surprise, then, that about one-third of these societies have female-only deities, and about one-third have male-and-female deities, and women's status in such societies was roughly equal with men's, although their roles were still, of course, sharply separated.

Q: These were matriarchal societies.

KW: Well, matrifocal. *Matriarchal* strictly means mother-ruled or mother-dominant, and there have never been any strictly matriarchal societies. Rather, these societies were more "equalitarian," with roughly equal status between men and women; and many such societies did indeed trace ancestry through the mother, and in other ways have a "matrifocal" arrangement. As I said, about one-third of these societies had female-only deities, particularly the Great Mother in her various guises, and conversely, *virtually every known Great Mother society is horticultural.* Almost any place you see the Great Mother religion, you know there is a horticultural background. This began roughly around 10,000 BCE in both the East and West.

Q: This is often the favorite period of the ecofeminists.

KW: Yes, these societies and a few maritime ones. Where the ecomasculinists love the foraging societies, the ecofeminists are quite fond of horticultural, Great Mother societies.

Q: Because they lived in harmony with the seasonal currents of nature, and in other ways were ecologically oriented.

KW: Yes, as long as you performed that annual ritual human sacrifice to keep the Great Mother happy and the crops growing, all was well with nature. Average life expectancy, according to Lenski's research, was about twenty-five years, which is pretty natural as well.

You see, it's the same problem as with the ecomasculinists, who eulogize the previous foraging tribes because they were supposed to be in touch with unadulterated nature. But what is "unadulterated nature"? The ecofeminists claim that these early farming societies were living with the seasonal currents of nature, in touch with the land, which was pure nature not interfered with by humans. But the ecomasculinists vociferously condemn farming of any sort as the first rape of nature, because you are no longer just gathering what nature offers; you are planting, you are artificially interfering with nature, you are digging into nature and scarring her face with farming technology, you are starting to rape the land. The heaven of the ecofeminists is the beginning of hell according to the ecomasculinists.

So yes, the ecomasculinists maintain, horticulture belongs to the Great Mother, and it was under the auspices of the Great Mother that the horrible crime of farming began, the massive crime that tore into the earth and first established human arrogance over the ways of the gentle giant of nature. And eulogizing this period is simply human arrogance at its very worst, the argument goes.

Q: You don't eulogize either foraging or horticultural, it seems.

KW: Well, evolution keeps moving, yes? Who are we to point to one period and say everything past that period was a colossal error, a heinous crime? According to whom, exactly? If we really are in the hands of the Great Spirit or the Great Mother, do we really think She doesn't know what She's doing? Tell you the truth, that seems like arrogance to me.

In any event, we're three or four major technological epochs down the line, and I doubt evolution will run backward for us.

Q: You refer often to "the dialectic of progress."

KW: Yes, the idea is that every stage of evolution eventually runs into its own inherent limitations, and these may act as triggers for the self-transcending drive. The inherent limitations create a type of turmoil, even chaos, and the system either breaks down (self-dissolution) or escapes this chaos by evolving to a higher degree of order (self-transcendence)—so-called order out of chaos. This new and higher order escapes the limitations of its predecessor, but then introduces its own limitations and problems that cannot be solved on its own level.

In other words, there is a price to be paid for every evolutionary step forward. Old problems are solved or defused, only to introduce new and sometimes more complex difficulties. But the retrogressive Romantics— whether the ecomasculinists or the ecofeminists—simply take the *problems* of the subsequent level and compare them with the *accomplishments* of the previous level, and thus claim everything has gone downhill past their favorite epoch. This is pretty perverse.

I think we all want to honor and acknowledge the many great accomplishments of past cultures the world over, and attempt to retain and incorporate as much of their wisdom as we can. But the train, for better or worse, is in motion, and has been from day one, and trying to drive by looking only in the rearview mirror is likely to cause even worse accidents.

Q: You point out that our epoch, too, will only pass.

KW: No epoch is finally privileged. We are all tomorrow's food. The process continues. And Spirit is found in the process itself, not in any particular epoch or time or place.

Agrarian

Q: I want to come back to that in a moment. We were talking about horticultural societies and the eventual shift to agrarian. Even though both are farming, this shift from hoe to plow was actually momentous.

KW: Quite extraordinary. Where a digging stick can easily be handled by a pregnant woman, an animal-drawn plow cannot. As Joyce Nielsen and Janet Chafetz have pointed out, those women who attempt to do so suffer significantly higher rates of miscarriage. In other words, it was to women's Darwinian advantage *not* to plow. And thus, with the introduction of the plow, a massive, absolutely massive shift in culture began.

First, virtually all of the foodstuffs were now produced solely by men. Men didn't want to do this, and they did not "take away" or "oppress" the female workforce in order to do so. *Both men and women decided* that heavy plowing was male work.

Women are not sheep; men are not pigs. This "patriarchy" was a conscious co-creation of men and women in the face of largely brutal circumstances. For the men, this certainly was no day at the beach, and was not nearly as much fun as, gosh, big-game hunting, which men had largely to give up. Furthermore, according to researchers such as Lenski and Chafetz, the men in these "patriarchal" societies had it considerably worse than the women, according to any number of objective "life quality" scales, starting with the fact that men alone were conscripted for defense, and men alone were asked to put life in jeopardy for the State. The idea that the patriarchy was an ole boys' club that was nothing but fun, fun, fun for men is based on rather poor research infected with much ideology, it seems.

For what we really learn from these various societies is that when the sexes are heavily *polarized*—that is, when their value spheres are sharply divided and compartmentalized—then both sexes suffer horribly.

Q: Which is what happened with the patriarchy?

KW: The polarization of the sexes, yes. Agrarian societies have the most highly sexually polarized structure of any known societal type (along with herding). This was not a male plot, nor a female plot for that matter, but was simply the best that these societies could do under the technological form of their organization at that time.

Thus, when men began to be virtually the sole producers of foodstuffs, then—no surprise—the deity figures in these cultures switched from female-oriented to almost exclusively male-oriented. Over 90 percent of agrarian societies, *wherever they appear*, have solely male primary deities.

Q: In *Sex, Ecology, Spirituality* you say, "Where females work the field with a hoe, God is a Woman; where males work the field with a plow, God is a Man."

KW: Well, that's a quick summary, yes. God and Goddess might have more profound and more transpersonal meanings—which we can talk about later—but for the *average mode* of human consciousness at that time, those mythic images usually represented much more prosaic realities. They represented, in many cases, the bedrock techno-economic realities of the given society: who put food on the table.

Q: Where God is a Man—this is one of the meanings of "patriarchy."

KW: Yes, and patriarchy, father rule, is correctly named. And here we briefly touch base with Marx: Because of the *social relations* that began to organize themselves around the *basic forces of production*—in this case, the plow—men then began to dominate the *public* sphere of government, education, religion, politics. And women dominated the *private* sphere of family, hearth, home. This division is often referred to as male production and female reproduction. Agrarian societies began to arise around 4000–2000 BCE, in both East and West, and this was the dominant mode of production until the industrial revolution.

Just as far-reaching was the fact that advanced farming created a massive surplus in foodstuffs, and this freed a great number of individuals—a great number of males—to pursue tasks other than food-gathering and food-creating, and now on a very large scale. That is, farming technology freed some men from production, but women were still largely tied to reproduction. This allowed a series of highly specialized classes to arise: men that could devote their time, not just to subsistence endeavors, but to extended cultural endeavors. Mathematics was invented, writing was invented, metallurgy—and specialized warfare.

The production of a surplus freed men, under the "kill it" part of testosterone, to begin building the first great military Empires, and across the globe, beginning around 3000 BCE, came the Alexanders and Caesars and Sargons and Khans, massive Empires that, paradoxically, began unifying disparate and contentious tribes into binding social orders. These mythic-imperial Empires would, with the rise of rationality and industrialization, give way to the modern nation-state.

And likewise, with agrarian farming a class of individuals would be freed to ponder their own existence. And thus, with these great agrarian cultures came the first sustained *contemplative* endeavors, endeavors that no longer located Spirit *merely* in the biosphere "out there" (magical, foraging to early horticultural) and not merely in the mythic Heavens "up there" (mythology, late horticultural to early agrarian), but rather located Spirit "in here," through the door of deep subjectivity, the door of interior awareness, the door of meditation and contemplation. And thus arose the great axial sages, whose . . .

Q: Axial?

KW: Karl Jaspers's term for this incredibly significant period in history, beginning around the sixth century BCE in both East and West, a period that produced the great "axial sages," Gautama Buddha, Lao Tzu, Parmenides, Socrates, Plato, Patanjali, Confucius, the sages of the Upanishads, and so forth.

Q: All men.

KW: Well, agrarian is *always* all men. And one of the great tasks of spirituality in the postmodern world is to complement and balance this male-oriented spirituality with its correlative female forms. We don't want to simply toss out everything these great wisdom traditions have to teach us, because that would be catastrophic. It would be like saying we refuse to use the wheel because a man invented it.

But indeed, virtually all of these great traditions arose in an atmosphere where men spoke to God directly and women spoke to God only through their husbands.

Industrial

Q: I want to come back to that issue of male and female spirituality, because it involves what you call "Ascending" and "Descending" spirituality, or God and Goddess spirituality, and how we might balance these two approaches.

But first, to finish with agrarian and the shift to industrial. How does this relate to "modernity"?

KW: Both "modernity" and "postmodernity" are used in a bewildering variety of ways. But "modernity" usually means the events that were set in motion with the Enlightenment, from Descartes to Locke to Kant, and the concomitant technical developments, which moved from feudal agrarian with a mythic worldview to industrialization and a rational worldview. And "postmodernity" usually means, in the broadest sense, the whole sweep of post-Enlightenment developments, which also includes postindustrial developments.

Q: So we are at the beginning of modernity, the shift from agrarian to industrialization. . . .

KW: Industrialization, for all of its horrors and all of its nightmarish secondary effects, was first and foremost a technological means to secure subsistence *not* from human muscle working on nature, but from machine power working on nature. As long as agrarian societies demanded physical human labor for subsistence (plowing), those societies *inevitably* and *unavoidably* placed a premium on *male* physical strength and mobility. No known agrarian society has anything even vaguely resembling women's rights.

But within a century of industrialization—which removed the emphasis on male physical strength and replaced it with gender-neutral engines—the women's movement emerged for the *first time in history* on any sort of large scale. Mary Wollstonecraft's *Vindication of the Rights of Women* was written in 1792; it is the first major feminist treatise anywhere in history.

It is not that all of a sudden, women became smart and strong and determined after a million years of oppression, dupedom, and sheepdom. It is that the social structures had evolved, for the first time in history, to a point that physical strength did not overwhelmingly determine power in culture. Biology was no longer destiny when it came to gender roles. Within a mere few centuries—a blink in evolutionary time—women had acted with lightning speed to secure legal rights to own property, to vote, and to "be their own persons," that is, to have a property in their own selves.

Q: The data seem to support this view, correct?

KW: The empirical evidence presented by the feminist researchers that I mentioned indicates that, as Chafetz puts it, the status of women in late industrial societies is *higher* than in any other surplus-producing society in history—including the horticultural.

Women who vocally condemn late industrial (and informational) society and glowingly eulogize Great Mother horticultural societies seem to be out of touch with a good deal of evidence, or they very selectively choose a few nice items about yesterday and ignore the rest of yesterday's nightmare, and compare that "Eden" with nothing but the very worst of modernity. This is a very suspect endeavor.

None of which means further gains aren't required in today's world, for both men and women. Remember, the polarization of the sexes is brutally hard on each. Men and women both need to be liberated from the horrendous constraints of agrarian polarization. Industrialization began this liberation, began to expand gender roles beyond biological givens—transcend and include—but we need to continue developing this freedom and transcendence.

Q: For example?

KW: For example, when men are no longer automatically expected to be the primary producers and the primary defenders, we might see the average life expectancy of men rise a little bit more toward the female level. And see women less restricted to roles involving merely reproduction, or home and hearth. The brutalities were equal and shared, so the liberation will be equally shared and beneficial, I think. If anything, the men have more to gain, which is why, in the United States, polls consistently showed that a majority of men favored the Equal Rights Amendment but a majority of women opposed it, so it didn't pass, unfortunately.

Q: What about industrialization and the eco-crisis? Surely that is one of the major downsides of modernity, of the "dialectic of progress."

KW: Indeed. But it's an extremely tricky situation. The primary cause of any ecological devastation is, as we were saying, simple ignorance. It is only with scientific knowledge of the biosphere, of the precise ways in which all holons in the biosphere are interrelated, including the biological holons of the human being—it is only with that knowledge that men and women can actually attune their actions with the biosphere. A simple or sacred respect for nature will not do. A sacred outlook on nature did not prevent numerous tribes from despoiling the environment out of simple and innocent ignorance, and did not prevent the Mayans from devastating the rain forests, and it will not prevent us from doing the same thing, again out of ignorance.

Roszak points out that it is modern science, and modern science alone—the ecological sciences and systems sciences, for example—that can directly show us how and why our actions are corroding the biosphere. If the primal tribes knew that by cut and burn they would ruin their habitat and endanger their own lives—if they actually knew that with a scientific certainty—then they would at least have thought about it a little more carefully before they began their bio-destruction. If the Mayans knew that in killing the rain forests they were killing themselves, they would have stopped immediately, or at least paused considerably. But ignorance is ignorance; whether innocent or greedy, sacred or profane, ignorance destroys the biosphere.

Q: But the means have changed.

KW: That's the second point, indeed. Ignorance backed by primal or tribal technology is capable of inflicting limited damage. You can only do so much damage to the biosphere with a bow and arrow. An atomic bomb is something else. The *same* ignorance backed by industry is capable of killing the entire world. So we have to separate those two issues— the ignorance and the means of inflicting that ignorance—because with modernity and science we have, for the first time in history, a way to overcome our ignorance, at precisely the same time that we have created the means to make this ignorance absolutely genocidal on a global scale.

Q: So it's good news, bad news.

KW: The predicament of modernity, yes. Finally, we know better. At the same time, if we don't act on this knowledge, then finally, we all die. Brings new meaning to the Confucian curse, "May you live in interesting times."

4

The Great Postmodern Revolution

Q: Now we just ran through the techno-economic base of each epoch. What about the corresponding *worldviews*?

KW: The general point is fairly simple: different stages of consciousness growth present a different view of the world. The world looks different—is different—at each stage. As new cognitive capacities unfold and evolve, the Kosmos looks at itself with different eyes, and it sees quite different things.

For convenience, I generally call these worldviews archaic, magic, mythic, rational, and existential, with higher stages possible. You can see these on figure 5-2.

Q: So these are different ways that we look at the world?

KW: Yes, but we have to be very careful here. This might seem to be splitting hairs, but it really is very important: it's not that there is a single, pregiven world, and we simply look at it differently. Rather, as the Kosmos comes to know itself more fully, *different worlds* emerge.

It's like an acorn growing to an oak. An oak isn't a different picture of the same unchanging world present in the acorn. The oak has components in its own being that are quite new and different from anything found in the acorn. The oak has leaves, branches, roots, and so on, none of which are present in the acorn's actual "worldview" or "worldspace." Different worldviews create different worlds, enact different worlds, they aren't just the same world seen differently.

The Postmodern Watershed

Q: I understand the distinction, but it does seem a bit of hairsplitting. Why exactly is this distinction important?

KW: It's crucially important, because in many ways it's the great watershed separating the modern and postmodern approaches to knowledge. We want to take into account this extraordinary revolution in human understanding.

And, in fact, there is simply no way to carry these types of discussions forward unless we talk about the momentous differences between the modern and postmodern approaches to knowledge. But it's not all dull and dry. In many ways, it's even the key to locating Spirit in the postmodern world.

Q: Okay, so modern and postmodern . . .

KW: You've heard of all the "new paradigm" approaches to knowledge?

Q: Well, only that everybody seems to want the new paradigm. Or *a* new paradigm, anyway.

KW: Yes, well, the *old* paradigm that everybody *doesn't* want is the Enlightenment paradigm, which is also called the modern paradigm. It has dozens of other names, all pronounced with scorn and disgust: the Newtonian, the Cartesian, the mechanistic, the mirror of nature, the reflection paradigm.

By whatever name, that paradigm is now thought to be hopelessly outdated or at least severely limited, and everybody is in an absolute dither to get the new and therefore postmodern, or post-Enlightenment, paradigm.

But in order to understand just what a postmodern paradigm might look like, we need to understand the beast that it is desperately trying to replace.

Q: We need to understand the fundamental Enlightenment paradigm.

KW: Yes. And the fundamental Enlightenment paradigm is known as the *representation paradigm*. This is the idea that you have the self or the subject, on the one hand, and the empirical or sensory world, on the other, and all valid knowledge consists in making *maps* of the empirical world, the single and simple "pregiven" world. And if the map is accurate, if it correctly represents, or corresponds with, the empirical world, then that is "truth."

Q: Hence, the representation paradigm.

KW: Yes. The map could be an actual map, or a theory, or a hypothesis, or an idea, or a table, or a concept, or some sort of representation—in general, some sort of map of the objective world.

All of the major Enlightenment theorists, whether they were holistic or atomistic or anything in between—they all subscribed to this representation paradigm, to the belief in a single empirical world that could be patiently mapped with empirical methods.

And please remember that—whether the world was atomistic or holistic is completely beside the point. What they all agreed on was the mapping paradigm itself.

Q: But what's wrong with that representation paradigm? I mean, we do it all the time.

KW: It's not that it's wrong. It's just very narrow and very limited. But the difficulties of the representation paradigm are rather subtle, and it took a very long time—several centuries, actually—to realize what the problem was.

There are many ways to summarize the limitations of the representation paradigm, the idea that knowledge consists basically in making maps of the world. But the simplest way to state the problem with maps is: *they leave out the mapmaker*. What was being utterly ignored was the fact that the mapmaker might itself bring something to the picture!

Q: All of this reflecting and mapping left out the mapmaker.

KW: Yes. And no matter how different the various *postmodern* attacks were, *they were all united in an attack on the representation paradigm*. They all perfectly assaulted the reflection paradigm, the "mirror of nature" paradigm—the idea that there is simply a single empirical world or empirical nature, and that knowledge consists solely in mirroring or reflecting or mapping this one true world. All "post-Enlightenment" or "postmodern" parties agreed that this "mirror of nature" idea was utterly, hopelessly, massively naive.

Beginning especially with Kant, and running through Hegel, Schopenhauer, Nietzsche, Dilthey, Heidegger, Foucault, Derrida—all the great "postmodern" theorists—in all of them we find a powerful attack on the mapping paradigm, because it fails to take into account the self that is making the maps in the first place.

This self did not just parachute to earth. It has its own characteristics, its own structures, its own development, its own *history*—and all of those influence and govern what it will see, and what it *can* see, in that supposedly "single" world just lying around. The parachutist is up to its neck in contexts and backgrounds that determine just what it can see in the first place!

So the great postmodern discovery was that neither the self nor the world is simply pregiven, but rather they exist in contexts and backgrounds that have a history, a development.

Q: That evolve.

KW: That evolve, yes. The mapmaker is not a little disembodied, ahistorical, self-contained monad, antiseptic and isolated and untouched by the world it maps. The self does not have an unchanging *essence* so much as it has a *history*, and the mapmaker will make *quite different maps* at the various stages of its own history, its own growth and development.

So in this developmental process, the subject will picture the world quite differently, based not so much on what is actually "out there" in some pregiven world, but based in many ways on what the *subject itself brings to the picture*.

Q: Kant's "Copernican revolution": the mind forms the world more than the world forms the mind.

KW: Not in all ways, but in many important ways, yes. And Hegel then added the crucial point, the point that, in one way or another, defines all postmodern theories: the mind, the subject, can *"only be conceived as one that has developed."*

Nietzsche, for example, would turn this into genealogy, the investigation of the history of a worldview that we simply took for granted, that we assumed was simply the case for people everywhere, but in fact turns out to be quite limited and historically situated. And one way or another, all postmodern roads lead to Nietzsche.

Q: So the overall point is . . .

KW: The subject is not some detached, isolated, pregiven, and fully formed little entity that simply parachutes to earth and then begins innocently "mapping" what it sees lying around out there in the "real" world, the "real" territory, the pregiven world.

Rather, the subject is *situated* in contexts and currents of its own development, its own history, its own evolution, and the "pictures" it makes of "the world" depend in large measure not so much on "the world" as on this "history."

Q: Yes, I see. And this relates to our present discussion, how?

KW: Well, one of the things we want to do is *trace the history of these worldviews*. They are part of evolution in the human domain— which means, the various forms of Spirit-in-action as it unfolds through the human mind. At each of these stages, the Kosmos looks at itself with new eyes, and thus brings forth new worlds not previously existing.

Two Paths in Postmodernity

Q: So these worldviews develop.

KW: Yes. And the overall idea that worldviews develop—that neither the world nor the self is simply pregiven—that is the great postmodern discovery.

Faced with this discovery of "not pregiven," a theorist can then take *one of two routes* through this new and confusing postmodern landscape, where nothing is foundational.

The first, and probably most common, is to go the route of extreme *constructivism*—which is the *strong version* of "not pregiven." That is, because worldviews are not pregiven, you can claim that they are all arbitrary. They are simply "constructed" by cultures based on nothing much more substantial than shifting tastes.

So we have all these books with titles like the social construction of sex, the social construction of food, the social construction of labor, the social construction of clothing, and so on. I keep expecting to see something like the social construction of the large intestine.

Everything is "socially constructed"—this is the mantra of the extremist wing of postmodernism. They think that different cultural worldviews are entirely arbitrary, anchored in nothing but power or prejudice or some "ism" or another—sexism, racism, speciesism, phallocentrism, capitalism, logocentrism, or my favorite, phallologocentrism. Wow! Does that puppy come with batteries or what?

Q: Do those approaches have any merit at all?

KW: They do. It's only that the strong constructivist approach is simply too strong, too extremist. Worldviews just aren't that arbitrary; they are actually *constrained* by the currents in the Kosmos, and those currents *limit* how much a culture can arbitrarily "construct." We won't find a consensus worldview, for example, where men give birth or where apples fall upward. So much for arbitrary worldviews. They are not "merely constructed" in the sense of totally relative and arbitrary. Even Derrida now concedes this elemental point.

A diamond will cut a piece of glass, no matter what words we use for "diamond," "cut," and "glass," and no matter what culture we find them in. It is not necessary to go overboard and deny the pre-existence of the sensorimotor world altogether! And that sensorimotor world—the cosmos and the bios—constrains the worldviews "from below," so to speak.

Further, cultural construction is limited and *constrained* by the currents in the noosphere itself. The noosphere develops, it evolves. That is, it also follows the twenty tenets, and those currents most definitely constrain and limit the construction.

So in these and many other ways, the real currents in the Kosmos constrain worldviews and prevent them from being merely collective hallucinations. Worldviews, as we'll see, are anchored in validity claims, and these claims work because the currents are real.

Q: Isn't Foucault often associated with this extreme constructivism?

KW: Yes, he started down this road, only to find that it is a dead end.

Q: In what way?

KW: If the constructivist stance is taken too far, it defeats itself. It says, all worldviews are arbitrary, all truth is relative and merely culture-bound, there are no universal truths. But that stance itself claims to be universally true. It is claiming everybody's truth is relative *except mine*, because mine is absolutely and universally true. I alone have the universal truth, and all you poor schmucks are relative and culture-bound.

This is the performative contradiction hidden in all extreme multicultural postmodern movements. And *their* absolute truth ends up being very ideological, very elitist in the worst sense, it seems. Foucault even called his own early attempts in this direction "arrogant," a point most of his American followers have ignored, unfortunately.

This extreme constructivism is really just a postmodern form of nihilism: there is no truth in the Kosmos, only those notions that men force on others. This nihilism looks into the face of the Kosmos and sees an unending hall of mirrors, which finally show it nothing but its own egoic nastiness reflected to infinity. This is a major movement in American universities.

Q: Extreme constructivism. So that is one path taken in postmodernity.

KW: Yes. That's the strong version, which is too strong, too constructivist.

The other is the more moderate approach, a more moderate constructivism, and the most common version of that is now developmental or evolutionary. In its numerous and quite varied forms—Hegel, Marx, Nietzsche, Heidegger, Gebser, Piaget, Bellah, late Foucault, Habermas.

This approach recognizes that world and worldview are not altogether pregiven, but rather develop in history. And so it simply *investigates the actual history* and unfolding of these worldviews, not as a series of merely arbitrary flailings-around, but rather as an evolutionary or developmental pattern, governed in part by the currents of evolution itself.

Q: Governed by the twenty tenets.

KW: In my particular version of developmentalism, yes, but that's my particular take.

But the important point is, in many of these developmental or evolutionary approaches, each worldview gives way to its successor because certain *inherent limitations* in the earlier worldview become apparent. This generates a great deal of disruption and chaos, so to speak, and the system, if it doesn't simply collapse, *escapes this chaos* by *evolving* to a more *highly organized* pattern. These new and higher patterns solve or defuse the earlier problems, but then introduce their own recalcitrant problems and inherent limitations that *cannot* be solved on their own level—the same process of evolution we see in the other domains as well.

Q: You mentioned these worldviews as archaic, magic, mythic, rational, and existential, with the possibility of higher stages yet to come.

KW: Yes, that's one way to summarize them, in a very general fashion. We can discuss the specifics of these worldviews later, if you like. But for now, as I said, I correlate these "mental" worldviews with the "material" modes of production at each stage of human evolution. So corresponding with those worldviews that you just mentioned, we have, respectively: foraging, horticultural, agrarian, industrial, informational. So I'll often refer to them conjointly as mythic-agrarian, or rational-industrial, and so on, understanding that there are all sorts of overlaps and hybrids (see figure 5-2).

Q: In a sentence . . .

KW: The worldview is the mind, the base is the body, of Spirit. These bodyminds evolve, and bring forth *new worlds* in the process, as Spirit unfolds its own potential, a radiant flower in Kosmic spring, not so much Big Bang as Big Bloom.

And at each stage of development the world looks different because the world *is* different—and there is the great postmodern revelation.

On the Edge of Tomorrow

Q: I have two technical questions. How exactly do the best of the postmodern approaches overcome the so-called Cartesian dualism?

KW: The representation paradigm was dualistic in this sense: the subject doing the mapping was not really a part of the world that was being mapped. Or so it was thought. The alien mapmaker simply stood back from the pregiven world and mapped it, as if the two entities had virtually nothing in common.

Most "new paradigm" approaches still fall into this dualistic trap, because it is a very, very subtle trap. Most new paradigm approaches think that simply getting a *more accurate map* will solve the problem. If we had a nice holistic and systems map, instead of a nasty atomistic and mechanistic map, that would heal the dualism.

But, as Hegel (among others) forcefully pointed out, that doesn't solve the real problem at all, but merely continues it in subtler ways. It still assumes that the thought process is so basically different from the real world that the thought process can either reflect that world accurately and holistically, or reflect it inaccurately and atomistically. But that belief *is* itself the hidden Cartesian dualism.

Rather, said Hegel, we must realize that thoughts are not merely a reflection on reality, but are also a movement of that very reality itself. Thought is a performance of that which it seeks to know, and not a simple mirror of something unrelated to itself. The mapmaker, the self, the thinking and knowing subject, is actually a product and a performance of that which it seeks to know and represent.

In short, thought is itself a movement of that which it seeks to know. It's not that there is a map on the one hand and the territory on the other—that's the nasty Cartesian dualism—but rather that the map is itself a performance of the territory it is trying to map.

This nondualistic approach doesn't deny the representation paradigm altogether; but it does say that at a much deeper level, thought itself *cannot* deviate from the currents of the Kosmos, because thought is a product and performance of those very currents. And the task of philosophy, as it were, is not simply to clarify the maps and *correct* their deviations from reality, but to *elucidate* these deeper currents from which thought couldn't deviate even if it wanted to!

Q: In simpler terms?

KW: In Zen there is a saying, "That which one can deviate from is not the true Tao." In other words, in some ways our knowledge is indeed a matter of correcting our inaccurate maps; but also, and at a much deeper level, there is a Tao, a Way, a Current of the Kosmos, from which we have not deviated and could never deviate. And part of our job is to find this deeper Current, this Tao, and express it, elucidate it, celebrate it.

And as long as we are caught in merely trying to correct our maps, then we will miss the ways in which both correct and incorrect maps are equally expressions of Spirit.

Thus, the "new paradigm" approaches, such as many of the ecophilosophers', are constantly telling us that we have deviated from nature, which is true enough. But however true that is, I believe it suggests that these theorists have not understood the true Tao, from which we do not, and could never, deviate. And it was this much deeper truth that the genuine Nondual traditions, East and West, attempted to elucidate— which is the real overcoming of the Cartesian dualism!

Might this become clearer when we talk about higher levels of development?

Q: Actually, that's my second technical question. If worldviews have evolved from archaic to magic to mythic to rational and existential, who's to say there aren't higher worldviews down the road?

KW: Yes, that's important, isn't it? To paraphrase the man, "There are more things in heaven and earth than are dreamt of in our worldview."

Magic never in its wildest dreams thought that it would be trumped by mythic. And the mythic gods and goddesses never imagined that reason could and would destroy them. And here we sit, in our rational worldview, all smug and confident that nothing higher will sweep out of the heavens and completely explode our solid perceptions, undoing our very foundations.

And yet surely, the transrational lies in wait. It is just around the corner, this new dawn. Every stage transcends and includes, and thus inescapably, unavoidably it seems, the sun will rise on a world tomorrow that in many ways transcends reason. . . .

And so, to quote another famous theorist, "Fasten your seatbelts, it's going to be a bumpy night."

Transcendence and Repression

Q: So how can you tell if there is any sort of advantage to one worldview or another?

KW: Transcends and includes. As the higher stages of consciousness emerge and develop, they themselves include the basic components of the earlier worldview, then add their own new and more differentiated perceptions. They transcend and include. Because they are more inclusive, they are more adequate.

So it's not that the earlier worldview is totally wrong and the new worldview is totally right. The earlier one was adequate, the new one is more adequate. If it's not more adequate, then it won't be selected by evolution, it won't catch the currents of the Kosmos; it will go by the wayside, flotsam and jetsam on the shores of what might have been.

Of course, this doesn't mean that a "higher" worldview is without its own problems—just the contrary. Wherever there is the possibility of *transcendence*, there is, by the very same token, the possibility of *repression*. The higher might not just transcend and include, it might transcend and repress, exclude, alienate, dissociate.

And so, in following the emergence of worldviews, we have to keep a constant watch for possible *repressions* and *dissociations* that have occurred, and are still occurring, in the historical process.

The point is that *the animal that can transcend can also repress*—at any level. The Mayans had already moved from foraging to horticulture, and that meant *not only* that they could begin to bind various contentious tribes into a larger and solidified social structure—and *not only* that they could, via farming, free a class of priests to begin developing mathematics and astronomy and a sophisticated calendar—*but also* that they, in a way foragers never could, begin to deplete the rain forests. They transcended mere foraging, only to go too far and dissociate themselves in certain crucial ways from the biosphere, which was altogether suicidal.

They didn't differentiate and integrate, they dissociated and alienated. They didn't transcend and include, they repressed and denied. Since the biosphere is an internal component of the human holon, they secured their own destruction.

So this theme—transcendence versus repression—is an altogether crucial theme of historical development, and we want to watch carefully for signs of repression at each stage of human evolution, individual and collective. And this includes, of course, the massive problems with rational-industrialization.

Q: So each new worldview faces its own grave problems.

KW: *Creates* its own grave problems. The solution of the old problem is the creation of a new one—they come into being together, although the new problems usually surface only as the worldview approaches its own demise. This is the wonder, and this the nightmare, of worldviews.

And we are at the point where the mental, rational, industrial worldview is running into the grave problems *inherent* in its own organization. We have run up against our own limitations. We have met the enemy, and of course it is us. The *modern* is struggling to give way to the *post-modern*.

The phase-specific, phase-appropriate modern worldview, having served its purposes, is now living in its own fumes. We are breathing our own exhaust. And how we handle this, how we collectively handle this, will determine whether a new and more adequate worldview emerges to defuse these problems, or whether we are buried in our own wastes.

Spirit has run up against its own limitations at this stage in its unfolding. This extraordinary modern flower blossomed in its glorious spring, and now can do nothing but watch its own leaves fall dead on the ground of a rising tomorrow. And what indeed will bloom in that new field?

5

The Four Corners of the Kosmos

Q: So is it at least fair to say that you believe we are approaching the end limit of the rational-industrial worldview?

KW: Only if we are very careful about how to interpret that. The rise of modernity—and by "modernity" I mean specifically the rational-industrial worldview, and roughly, the Enlightenment in general—served many useful and extraordinary purposes. We might mention: the rise of democracy; the banishing of slavery; the emergence of liberal feminism; the widespread emergence of empirical sciences, including the systems sciences and ecological sciences; an increase in average life span of almost three decades; the introduction of relativity and perspectivism in art and morals and science; the move from ethnocentric to worldcentric morality; and in general the undoing of dominator social hierarchies in numerous significant ways.

Those are rather extraordinary accomplishments, don't you think? The antimodernist critics who do nothing but condemn modernity, while basking in these many benefits, are being quite unfair, it seems to me.

On the other hand, the giddy promoters of modernity as nothing but a great progress report ignore the recalcitrant problems that modernity has never solved and likely can never solve.

Q: The inherent problems or limitations built into modernity.

KW: Built into the rational-industrial worldview, yes.

Q: So moving "beyond modernity"—going "postmodern"—requires what, exactly?

KW: Well, in simple terms, to transcend and include modernity—or rational-industrialization—would mean, for the *transcend* part, that we have to (1) be open to modes of consciousness that move beyond mere rationality, and (2) embed them in modes of techno-economic structures that move beyond industrialization. In other words, a change of consciousness embedded in a change of institutions. Either one alone will probably not work.

Q: So, trans-rational and trans-industrial.

KW: Yes, remembering that both rationality and industry will be *included* as well, but now as mere components in a more balanced, more inclusive, more integrated stance that will incorporate—and limit—rationality and industry. What we might call sustainable rationality, sustainable industry.

But in some ways, rationality and industry, left to their own devices, have become cancers in the body politic, runaway growths that are malignant in their effects. They overstep their limits, overrun their functions, and drift into various dominator hierarchies of one sort or another. To transcend modernity is to negate or limit these overpowering facets, while including their benign and beneficial aspects. The coming transformation will transcend and include these features of modernity, incorporating their essentials and limiting their power.

And, of course, this new and wonderful transformation, which everybody seems to be yearning for, will nevertheless bring its own recalcitrant problems and brutal limitations. It will defuse some of the problems of rational-industrialization, which is wonderful, but it will create and unleash its own severe difficulties.

And so, if this is specifically what we mean by a coming transformation—as opposed to some utopian new age—then yes, I believe this transformation is definitely under way.

The Four Quadrants

Q: So part of the coming transformation will involve both a change in consciousness and a change in institutions.

KW: I believe so, yes. It will actually involve a new worldview, set in a new techno-economic base, with a new mode of self-sense, possessing new behavioral patterns.

Q: Okay, that gets us directly into what you call *the four quadrants* (see figure 5-1). But before we talk about these four quadrants, I'm curious, how did you arrive at this concept? I haven't seen it before, and I was wondering how you came up with it.

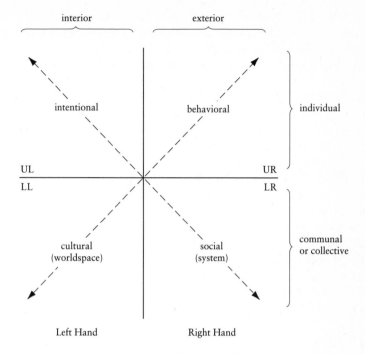

FIGURE 5-1. *The four quadrants.*

KW: You mean the mental steps I went through to arrive at the four quadrants?

Q: Yes.

KW: Well, if you look at the various "new paradigm" theorists—from holists to ecofeminists to deep ecologists to systems thinkers—you find that all of them are offering various types of holarchies, of hierarchies. Even the anti-hierarchy ecophilosophers offer their own hierarchy, which is usually something like: atoms are parts of molecules, which are parts of cells, which are parts of individual organisms, which are parts of families, which are parts of cultures, which are parts of the total biosphere. That is their defining hierarchy, their defining holarchy, and except for some confusion about what "biosphere" means, that is a fairly accurate holarchy.

And likewise, orthodox researchers offer their own hierarchies. We find hierarchies in moral development, in ego development, in cognitive development, in self needs, in defense mechanisms, and so on. And these, too, seem to be largely accurate. We also find developmental holarchies in everything from Marxism to structuralism to linguistics to computer programming—it's simply endless.

In other words, whether it's realized or not, most of the maps of the world that have been offered are in fact holarchical, for the simple reason that holarchies are impossible to avoid (because holons are impossible to avoid). We have literally hundreds and hundreds of these holarchical maps from around the world—East and West, North and South, ancient and modern—and many of these maps included the mapmaker as well.

So at one point I simply started making lists all of these holarchical maps—conventional and new age, Eastern and Western, premodern and modern and postmodern—everything from systems theory to the Great Chain of Being, from the Buddhist vijnanas to Piaget, Marx, Kohlberg, the Vedantic koshas, Loevinger, Maslow, Lenski, Kabbalah, and so on. I had literally hundreds of these things, these maps, spread out on legal pads all over the floor.

At first I thought these maps were all referring to the same territory, so to speak. I thought they were all different versions of an essentially similar holarchy. There were just too many similarities and overlaps in all of them. So by comparing and contrasting them all, I thought I might be able to find the single and basic holarchy that they were all trying to represent in their own ways.

The more I tried this, the more it became obvious that it wouldn't work. These various holarchies had some undeniable similarities, but they differed in certain profound ways, and the exact nature of these differences was not obvious at all. And most confusing of all, in some of these holarchical maps, the holons got *bigger* as development progressed, and in others, they became *smaller* (I didn't yet understand that evolution produces greater depth, less span). It was a real mess, and at several points I decided to just chuck it, forget it, because nothing was coming of this research.

But the more I looked at these various holarchies, the more it dawned on me that there were actually *four very different types* of holarchies, four very different types of holistic sequences. As you say, I don't think this had been spotted before—perhaps because it was so simple; at any event it was news to me. But once I put all of these holarchies into these four groups—and they instantly fell into place at that point—then it was very obvious that each holarchy in each group was indeed dealing with the same territory, but overall we had four different territories, so to speak.

Q: These four territories, these four different types of holistic sequences, you call the four quadrants.

KW: Yes, you can see these in figure 5-1. In figure 5-2, I've added some examples. I must emphasize that this figure only gives a very few examples from each quadrant, but you can get the general idea.

So the question then became, how did these four types of holarchies relate to each other? They couldn't just be radically different holistic sequences. They had to touch each other somehow.

Eventually it dawned on me that these four quadrants have a very simple foundation. These four types of holarchies are actually dealing

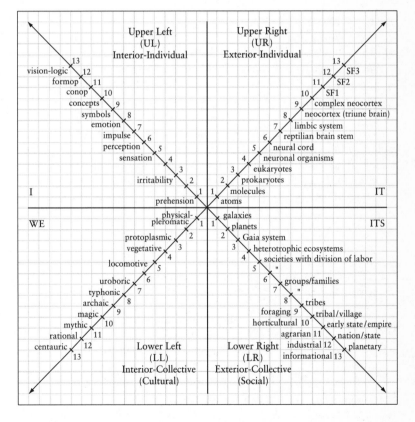

FIGURE 5-2. *Some details of the four quadrants.*

with the *inside* and the *outside* of a holon, in both its *individual* and *collective* forms—and that gives us four quadrants.

Inside and outside, singular and plural—some of the simplest distinctions we can make, and these very simple features, which are present in all holons, generate these four quadrants, or so I maintain. All four of these holarchies are dealing with real aspects of real holons—which is why these four types of holarchies keep insistently showing up on the various maps around the world.

It appears that these are some very bedrock realities, these four corners of the Kosmos.

Intentional and Behavioral

Q: Perhaps a few examples.

KW: Okay. The four quadrants are the *interior* and *exterior* of the *individual* and the *collective*, which you can see in figures 5-1 and 5-2.

We can start with the individual holon, in both its interior and exterior aspects. In other words, with the Upper-Left quadrant and the Upper-Right quadrant. Figure 5-3 is a little more detailed map of these two quadrants.

If you look at the Upper-Right column first, you can see the typical holarchy presented in any standard biology textbook. Each level transcends and includes its predecessor. Each level includes the basics of the previous level and then adds its own distinctive and defining characteristics, its own emergents. Each of these follows the twenty tenets, and so on.

prehension	atoms
irritability	cells (genetic)
rudimentary sensation	metabolic organisms (e.g., plants)
sensation	protoneuronal organisms (e.g., coelenterata)
perception	neuronal organisms (e.g., annelids)
perception/impulse	neural cord (fish/amphibians)
impulse/emotion	brain stem (reptiles)
emotion/image	limbic system (paleomammals)
symbols	neocortex (primates)
concepts	complex neocortex (humans)
UPPER LEFT	UPPER RIGHT

FIGURE 5-3. *The interior and the exterior of the individual.*

But notice that these are all *exterior* descriptions—it's what these holons look like from the outside, in an objective and empirical manner. Thus, in a scientific text, you will find the limbic system, for example, described in detail—its components, its biochemistry, when and how it evolved, how it relates to other parts of the organism, and so on. And you will probably find it mentioned that the limbic system is the home of certain very fundamental *emotions*, certain basic types of sex and aggression and fear and desire, whether that limbic system appears in horses or humans or apes.

But of those emotions, of course, you will not find much description, because emotions pertain to the *interior experience* of the limbic system. These emotions and the awareness that goes with them are what the holon with a limbic system *experiences from within*, on the *inside*, in its *interior*. And *objective* scientific descriptions are not much interested in that interior consciousness, because that interior space cannot be accessed in an objective, empirical fashion. You can only *feel* these feelings from within. When you experience a sort of primal joy, for example, even if you are a brain physiologist, you do not say to yourself, Wow, what a limbic day. Rather, you describe these feelings in intimate, personal, emotional terms, *subjective* terms: I feel wonderful, it's great to be alive, or whatnot.

So in the Upper-Left column, you can see a list of some of the basic types of *subjective* or *interior awareness* that go with these various *objective* or *exterior forms* listed in the Upper-Right column. "Irritability"—the capacity to actively respond to environmental stimuli—begins with cells. Sensations emerge with neuronal organisms, and perceptions emerge with a neural cord. Impulses emerge with a brain stem, and basic emotions with a limbic system. And so on.

This is also a holarchy, but a subjective or interior holarchy. Each level also transcends and includes it predecessor, each follows the twenty tenets, and so on. And this Left-Hand holarchy, like the Right-Hand, is based on extensive evidence already available, which we can discuss if you want.

But the main point is that this Left-Hand dimension refers to the inside, to the *interior depth* that is *consciousness* itself.

Q: You said earlier that depth is consciousness, or what depth looked like from within.

KW: Yes, exactly. The Left Hand is what the holon looks like from within; the Right Hand is what the same holon looks like from without. Interior and exterior. Consciousness and form. Subjective and objective.

Q: The Upper-Right quadrant is the one we are most familiar with, simply because it is part of the standard, objective, empirical, scientific map.

KW: Yes, and we can assume it's accurate enough, as far as it goes. It gives the typical holarchy for individual holons described in objective terms: atoms to molecules to cells (early cells, or prokaryotes, and advanced cells, or eukaryotes) to simple organisms (first with a neuronal net and then with a more advanced neural cord). Then to more complex organisms, reptiles to paleomammals to humans, the latter possessing a complex triune brain, which transcends and includes its predecessors, so that the triune brain has a *reptilian* stem and a *paleomammalian* limbic system, plus something new, a complex *neocortex* capable of abstract logic and linguistics and vision-logic (in figure 5-2, I have listed these more complex capacities as SF1, SF2, SF3, which we'll discuss later).

We don't have to agree with the exact placement of everything in figure 5-3, but most people would agree that *something* like that is occurring.

Cultural and Social

Q: So that is the upper half of the diagram, the individual. There is now the lower half, the collective.

KW: Yes. Individual holons exist only in *communities* of similar-depth holons. So we need to go through both of the columns in figure 5–3 and find the types of *communal* holons that are always associated with the *individual* holons.

Q: And this communal aspect also has an interior and an exterior, which are Lower Left and Lower Right.

KW: Yes.

Q: You call these "cultural" and "social."

KW: Yes, "cultural" refers to all of the *interior* meanings and values and identities that we share with those of similar communities, whether it is a tribal community or a national community or a world community. And "social" refers to all of the exterior, material, institutional *forms* of the community, from its techno-economic base to its architectural styles to its written codes to its population size, to name a few.

So in a very general sense, "cultural" refers to the shared collective *worldview* and "social" refers to the *material base* of that worldview. (Of course, right now I'm just talking about how these appear in human holons; we'll discuss nonhuman in a moment.) Social means any objective, concrete, material components, and especially the techno-economic base, so you see these listed as foraging, horticultural, agrarian, industrial; and the geopolitical structures of villages, states, world federation, and so on. These are all examples of the exterior forms of the collective, as you can see in figure 5-2.

Q: I think that's straightforward enough. But let's look at nonhuman holons. We usually don't think of them as having a common worldview or common worldspace—a common culture.

KW: If consciousness is depth, and depth goes all the way down, then shared depth or common depth also goes all the way down—culture goes all the way down.

Q: I'm sorry?

KW: In other words, if holons share outsides, they share insides.

Q: Their "culture," as it were.

KW: Yes. By the culture or worldspace of holons, I simply mean a shared space of what they *can* respond to: quarks do not respond to all stimuli in the environment, because they *register* a very narrow range of what will have meaning to them, what will *affect* them. Quarks (and all holons) respond only to that which *fits their worldspace*: everything else is a foreign language, and they are outsiders. The study of what holons *can* respond to is the study of shared worldspaces. It's the common world that all holons of a similar depth will respond to. That is their shared culture.

Q: Okay, perhaps an example.

KW: Nonhuman cultures can be very sophisticated. Wolves, for example, share an emotional worldspace. They possess a limbic system, the interior correlate of which is certain basic emotions. And thus a wolf orients itself and its fellow wolves to the world through the use of these basic emotional cognitions—not just reptilian and sensorimotor, but affective. They can hunt and coordinate in packs through a very sophisticated emotional signal system. They share this emotional worldspace.

Yet anything *outside* that worldspace is *not registered*. I mean, you can read *Hamlet* to them, but no luck. What you are, with that book, is basically dinner plus a few things that will have to be spat out.

The point is that a holon responds, and *can respond*, only to those stimuli that fall within its worldspace, its worldview. Everything else is nonexistent.

Q: Same with humans.

KW: Same with humans. By the time evolution reaches the neocortex, or the complex triune brain, with its interior correlates of images and symbols and concepts, these basic worldspaces have become articulated into rather sophisticated cognitive structures. These worldspaces *incorporate* the basic components of the previous worldspaces—such as cellular irritability and reptilian instincts and paleomammalian emotions—but then *add* new components that articulate or unfold new worldviews.

As we were saying earlier, the Kosmos looks different at each of these stages because the Kosmos *is* different at each of these stages. At each of these stages, the Kosmos looks at itself with new eyes, and thus brings forth new worlds not previously existing.

These cultural worldspaces are listed on the Lower Left. And you can see that they evolve from physical and vegetative and reptilian ("uroboric"—of the serpent) and limbic-emotional ("typhonic"), into more specifically hominid and then human forms: archaic, magic, mythic, rational, centauric (or existential), with possibly higher stages yet to come.

These worldviews are correlated with the *exterior* forms of the *social structures* that support each of those worldviews. For example, from the prokaryotic Gaia system to societies with a division of labor (in neural organisms) to groups/families of paleomammals to the more human forms of: *foraging* tribes to *horticultural* villages to *agrarian* empires to *industrial* states to *informational* global federation. Which is the list to date, as reconstructed from available evidence. These are all listed on the Lower Right.

Q: And these four quadrants are related to each other in exactly what fashion?

KW: I have some specific thoughts on this, but right now I don't want to push my own theory in this particular regard. I will settle for the orienting generalization that we cannot reduce these quadrants to each other without profound distortions. As usual, reductionism seems to be a bad idea. Let's just say they interrelate, or they interact, or they each have correlates in the others. When we talk about the different truths in each quadrant, I think you'll see what I mean.

An Example

Q: Why don't you take an example of a single thought, a single thought holon, and show how it has *correlates in all four quadrants*. I wonder if we could go through that example briefly.

KW: Okay. Let's say I have a thought of going to the grocery store. When I have that thought, what I actually experience is the thought itself, the interior thought and its meaning—the symbols, the images, the idea of going to the grocery store. That's Upper Left.

While I am having this thought, there are, of course, correlative changes occurring in my brain—dopamine increases, acetylcholine jumps the synapses, beta brainwaves increase, or whatnot. Those are observable behaviors in my brain. They can be empirically observed, scientifically registered. And that is Upper Right.

Now the internal thought itself only makes sense in terms of my cultural background. If I spoke a different language, the thought would be composed of different symbols and have different meanings. If I existed in a primal tribal society a million years ago, I would never even have the thought "going to the grocery store." It might be, "Time to kill the bear." The point is that my thoughts themselves arise in a *cultural background* that gives texture and meaning and context to my individual thoughts, and indeed, I would not even be able to "talk to myself" if I did not exist in a community of individuals who also talk to me.

So the cultural community serves as an *intrinsic background* to any individual thoughts I might have. My thoughts do not just pop into my head out of nowhere; they pop into my head out of a cultural background, and however much I might move beyond this background, I can never simply escape it altogether, and I could never have developed thoughts in the first place without it. The occasional cases of a "wolf boy"—humans raised in the wild—show that the human brain, left without culture, does not produce linguistic thoughts on its own. The self is far from the autonomous and self-generating monad the Enlightenment imagined.

In short, my individual thoughts only exist against a vast background of cultural practices and languages and meanings, without which I could form virtually no individual thoughts at all. And this vast background is my culture, my cultural worldview, my worldspace, which is the Lower Left.

But my culture itself is not simply disembodied, hanging in idealistic midair. It has *material components*, much as my own individual thoughts have material brain components. All *cultural* events have *social* correlates. These concrete social components include types of technology, forces of production (horticultural, agrarian, industrial, etc.), concrete institutions, written codes and patterns, geopolitical locations (towns, villages, states, etc.), and so on. And these material, social, empirically observable components—the actual *social system*—are crucial in helping to determine the types of cultural worldview.

So my supposedly "individual thought" actually has at least these four facets, these four aspects—intentional, behavioral, cultural, and social. And around the circle we go: the social system will have a strong influence on the cultural worldview, which will set limits to the individual thoughts that I can have, which will register in the brain physiology. And you can go around that circle in any direction you want. The quadrants are all interwoven. They are all mutually determining. They all cause, and are caused by, the other quadrants.

Q: Because all individual holons have these four facets.

KW: Yes, every holon has these four aspects, these four quadrants. It is not that an individual holon exists in one or another of these quadrants. It is that every individual holon has these four quadrants, these four aspects to its being. It's like a diamond with four facets, or four faces.

Of course, these four facets become very complicated and intermixed, but there are at least these four. These four seem to be the *minimum* that we need to understand any holon. And this especially holds for higher transformation, for higher states of consciousness, as I guess we'll see.

The Shape of Things to Come

Q: We started this discussion by talking about transformation in general, and any possible coming transformation in particular.

KW: This transformation is already proceeding, and if we want to consciously find these evolutionary currents operating in our own being as well—if we want to consciously join Spirit-in-action—then the four quadrants can help us orient ourselves more effectively, can help us become more conscious of the evolutionary currents already flowing around us and through us and in us.

We could say that Spirit manifests as all four quadrants. Spirit isn't just a higher Self, or just Gaia, or just awareness, or just the web of life, or just the sum total of all objective phenomena, or just transcendental consciousness. Rather, Spirit exists in and as all four quadrants, the four compass points, as it were, of the known Kosmos, all of which are needed to accurately navigate.

So what we will want to talk about, I suppose, is how this coming transformation—and the higher spiritual stages—will appear and manifest in all four quadrants. What is a higher Self? What is higher brain functioning? What is the transformation of the body as well as of the mind? What is a higher or deeper culture? How is it embedded in wider social systems? What is more highly developed consciousness? How is it anchored in new social institutions? Where is the sublime?

What would all of this look like? How can we help it along in all of these quadrants, and not just focus on Self, or just Gaia, or just the World Federation? For it appears that all of these will emerge together, or they will emerge not at all.

Q: It's a package deal.

KW: It seems to be a package deal, yes. Higher or deeper stages of consciousness development disclose deeper and wider patterns in self, in individual behavior, in culture, and in society—intentional, behavioral, cultural, and social—all four quadrants.

If we don't take all of those into account, then I think they might start the transformation without us. The transformation will occur, is occurring, but we'll be sitting in our favorite quadrant, explaining to people why we have the new paradigm, and transformation will sail on without us. We will abort our own full-quadrant participation in forces that are already in play. We will go limping into the future, all puzzles and grins, and these wider currents will not be activated in our own being. We'll be driftwood on the shore of this extraordinary stream. We will mistake our crutches for liberation, we will offer our wounds to the world, we will bleed into the future all smiles and glory.

I don't think that partial approach will ever work. It seems instead that we need an *integral* approach that will include all four quadrants, all four faces of Spirit. Perhaps the secret to higher transformation involves this more balanced, complete, and integral approach. What do you think?

6

The Two Hands of God

Q: I think that "the truth will set you free." But you started to suggest that each quadrant has a different type of truth! This does not look like we are moving toward an integral or inclusive view; it looks like we are moving into parts and fragments and lots of differences.

KW: Yes, but that's actually good news. By understanding these different truths, and acknowledging them, we can more sympathetically include them in an integral embrace. We can more expansively attune ourselves to the Kosmos. The final result might even be an attunement with the All, might even be Kosmic consciousness itself. Why not? But I think first we need to understand these various truths, so they can begin to speak to us, in us, through us—and we can begin to hear their voices and honor them, and thus invite all of them together into a rainbow coalition, an integral embrace.

These truths are behind much of the great postmodern rebellion. They are the key to the interior and transcendental dimensions; they speak eloquently in tongues of hidden gods and angels; they point to the heart of holons in general, and invite us into that interior world; they are antidote to the flat and faded world that passes for today. We might even say that these four types of truth are the four faces of Spirit as it shines in the manifest world.

Q: Tell me it's not complicated.

KW: More fun than a human should be allowed to have. But there is a very simple way to shake all of this down and summarize it; so it soon enough becomes very, very simple.

In the meantime, figure 6-1 (page 129) is a small sampling of different

76

LEFT-HAND PATHS	RIGHT-HAND PATHS
· Interpretive	· Monological
· Hermeneutic	· Empirical, positivistic
· Consciousness	· Form

	LEFT-HAND PATHS	RIGHT-HAND PATHS
INDIVIDUAL	Freud C. G. Jung Piaget Aurobindo Plotinus Gautama Buddha	B. F. Skinner John Watson John Locke Empiricism Behaviorism Physics, biology, neurology, etc.
COLLECTIVE	Thomas Kuhn Wilhelm Dilthey Jean Gebser Max Weber Hans-Georg Gadamer	Systems Theory Talcott Parsons Auguste Comte Karl Marx Gerhard Lenski

FIGURE 6-1. *Some representative theorists in each quadrant.*

theorists who have plugged in to a particular quadrant with its particular truth. It'll help if we discuss some examples of each.

Mind and Brain

Q: Okay, start with this. You have the mind—your lived experience, images, symbols, feelings, thoughts—listed on the Upper Left—and the brain on Upper Right. So you're saying that mind and brain are not the same.

KW: We can grant that they are intimately related. But for the moment, we can also grant that in many important ways they are quite different. We need to respect those differences and try to account for them.

For example, when brain physiologists study the human brain, they study all of its objective components—the neural makeup, the various synapses, the neurotransmitters such as serotonin and dopamine, the electrical brainwave patterns, and so on. All of those are *objective* or *exterior* aspects of the human being. Even though the brain is "inside" the human organism, the brain physiologist knows that brain only in an objective and exterior fashion.

But you yourself can't even see your brain as an object, unless you cut open your skull and get a mirror. That's the only way you can see your brain. But you can see and experience your *mind* directly, right now, intimately and immediately. The mind is what your awareness looks like *from within*; your brain is simply what it looks like *from without*, from the outside.

Q: And they don't look the same at all.

KW: No. Your brain looks like a big crumpled grapefruit. But your mind doesn't look like that at all. Your mind looks like your direct experience right now—images, impulses, thoughts. Perhaps we will ultimately decide that mind and brain are actually identical, or parallel, or dualist, or whatever, but we have to start with the undeniable fact they are phenomenologically quite different.

Q: But what about the idea that they really are the same thing, and we just haven't figured out how to show this?

KW: Let's look to an expert on the brain itself—say, a brain physiologist. The brain physiologist can know every single thing about my brain—he can hook me up to an EEG machine, he can use PET scans, he can use radioactive tracers, he can map the physiology, determine the levels of neurotransmitters—he can know what every atom of my brain is doing, and he still won't know a single thought in my mind.

This is really extraordinary. And if he wants to know what is going on in my *mind*, there is one and only one way that he can find out: *he must talk to me*. There is absolutely no other way that he, or anybody else, can know what my actual thoughts are without asking me, and talking to me, and communicating with me. And if I don't want to tell you, then you will never know the actual specifics of my individual thoughts. Of course, you can torture me and force me to tell—but that's the point: you force me to *talk*.

So you can know all about my brain, and that will tell you nothing about the specific contents of my mind, which you can find only by talking to me. In other words, you must engage in *dialogue*, not monologue—you must engage in *intersubjective* communication, and not simply study me as an *object* of empirical investigation—as an object of the empirical gaze—which will get you nowhere.

As we will see in greater detail as we go along, all of the Right-Hand dimensions can be accessed with this empirical gaze, this "monological" gaze, this objectifying stance, this empirical mapping—because you are only studying the exteriors, the surfaces, the aspects of holons that can be *seen* empirically—the Right-Hand aspects, such as the brain.

But the Left-Hand aspects, the *interior* dimensions, can only be accessed by communication and interpretation, by "dialogue" and "dialogical" approaches, which are not *staring* at exteriors but *sharing* of interiors. Not objective but intersubjective. Not surfaces but depths.

So I can study your brain forever, and I will never know your mind. I can know your brain by objective study, but I can only know your mind by talking to you.

The Left- and Right-Hand Paths

Q: This takes us directly to the differences between the Left- and Right-Hand paths.

KW: Yes. From virtually the inception of every major knowledge quest, East and West alike, the various approaches have fallen into one or another of these two great camps, interior versus exterior, Left versus Right. We find this in psychology (Freud vs. Watson), in sociology (Weber vs. Comte), in philosophy (Heidegger vs. Locke), in anthropology (Taylor vs. Lenski), in linguistics (hermeneutics vs. structuralism)—and even in theology (Augustine vs. Aquinas)!

Occasionally you find an approach that emphasizes both the Left- and Right-Hand dimensions, which of course would be my recommendation, but mostly you find a bitter war between these two equally important, but rarely integrated, approaches. So I think it's crucial to understand the contributions that both of these paths have made to our understanding of the human condition, because both of them are truly indispensable.

And, as we'll soon see, it seems almost impossible to understand higher and spiritual developments without taking both of these paths into account.

The Monological Gaze: The Key to the Right-Hand Paths

Q: Let's take them one at a time. The Right-Hand paths . . .

KW: Everything on the Right Hand, all the aspects on the Right half of figure 5-2, are objects or exteriors that can be seen empirically, one way or another, with the senses or their extensions—microscopes, telescopes, photographic equipment, whatnot. They are all *surfaces* that can be *seen*. They all have simple location. You don't have to *talk* to any of them. You just observe their *objective behavior*. You look at the behavior of atoms, or cells, or populations, or individuals, or societies, or ecosystems.

Q: You also call this "monological."

KW: Yes, all the Right-Hand aspects are basically monological, which means they can be seen in a monologue. You don't have to try to get at their interiors, at their consciousness. You do not need a *dialogue*, a mutual exchange of depth, because you are looking only at exteriors.

If you are getting a CAT scan of your brain, the lab technicians will talk to you only if it's unavoidable. "Would you mind moving your head over here, dearie?" The technicians couldn't care less about your interior depths, because they only want to capture your exterior surfaces, even if those exteriors are "inside" you—they're just more objects. When the lab technicians take this objective picture of your brain, do they see the real you? Do they see *you* at all?

No, you are being treated merely as an *object* of the *monological gaze*, not as a *subject* in *communication*—which is what makes empirical medicine so dehumanizing in itself. The lab technician just wants your Right Hand, not your Left Hand, not your consciousness, your feelings, your meanings, your values, your intentions, your hopes, your fears. Just the facts, ma'am. Just the exteriors. And that's fine. That's completely acceptable. That's your brain.

But you can never, and will never, see a mind that way.

Q: Feminists are always complaining about being the object of the male gaze.

KW: It's the same thing. Women often complain about being made into an object, a sexual object, in this case, of the male gaze. But it's the same general phenomenon, the same monological gaze: you are reduced from a subject in communication to an object of observation, a slab of meat, an object with no depth. "He never talks to me." And women understandably react to this. Men, on the other hand, are reduced to passive objects whenever they have to ask for directions, and of course, they'd rather die on the spot.

There is nothing wrong with these Right-Hand and empirical and scientific paths; it's just that they are not the whole story. Living life only according to the Right Hand is like living life perpetually under the gaze of a lab technician. It's all empiricism, all monological gaze, all behaviorism, all shiny surfaces and monochrome objects—no interiors, no depth, no consciousness.

I don't want to get too much ahead of the story, but we can now briefly mention that the downside of the Enlightenment paradigm was that, in its rush to be empirical, it inadvertently collapsed the Left-Hand dimensions of the Kosmos into the Right-Hand dimensions—it collapsed interior depths into observable surfaces, and it thought that a *simple mapping* of these empirical exteriors was all the knowledge that was worth knowing. This left out the mapmaker itself—the consciousness, the interiors, the Left-Hand dimensions—and, a century or two later, it awoke in horror to find itself living in a universe with no value, no meaning, no intentions, no depth, no quality—it found itself in a disqualified universe ruled by the monological gaze, the brutal world of the lab technician.

And that, of course, began the postmodern rebellion.

Interpretation: The Key to the Left-Hand Paths

Q: That's part of our next discussion (see chapter 7). We were talking about the differences between the Left- and Right-Hand paths.

KW: Yes, as we were saying, if you look at figure 5-2, every holon on the Right Hand can be empirically seen, one way or another. They all have *simple location*, because these are the physical-material correlates of all holons. And so with every Right-Hand aspect, you can physically point right at it and say, "There it is." You can put your finger right on them, so to speak. There is the brain, or there is a cell, or there is the town, or there is the ecosystem. Even subatomic particles exist as probabilities of being found in a given location at a given time!

But nothing on the Left Hand can be seen in that simple fashion, because *none of the Left-Hand aspects have simple location.* You can point to the brain, or to a rock, or to a town, but you cannot simply point to envy, or pride, or consciousness, or value, or intention, or desire. Where is desire? Point to it. You can't really, not the way you can point to a rock, because it's largely an *interior* dimension, so it doesn't have *simple location.*

This doesn't mean it isn't real! It only means it doesn't have simple location, and therefore you can't see it with a microscope or a telescope or any sensory-empirical device.

Q: So how can these interior depths be accessed or "seen"?

KW: This is where *interpretation* enters the picture. All Right-Hand paths involve perception, but all Left-Hand paths involve interpretation.

And there is a simple reason for this: surfaces can be seen, but depth must be interpreted. As you and I talk, you are not just looking at some surface, some smiling face, some empirical object. You want to know what's going on inside me. You are not just watching what I do, you want to know what I feel, what I think, what's going on within me, in my consciousness.

So you ask me some questions. "What's happening? What do you think about this? How do you feel about this?" And I will tell you some things—we will talk—and you have to figure out what I mean, you have to *interpret* what I mean. With each and every sentence, you have to interpret the meaning. What does he mean by that? Oh, I understand, you mean this. And so on.

And there is no other way to get at my interior except by interpretation. We must talk, and you must interpret. This seems unavoidable. Even if you were a great psychic and could totally read my mind, you would still have to figure out what my thoughts mean—you still have to interpret what you read.

Q: Very different from the monological gaze.

KW: Yes, this is quite different from simply staring at some surfaces with simple location and reporting what you see, whether those surfaces are rocks or cells or ecosystems or brain components. Depth does not sit on the surface waiting to be seen! Depth must be communicated, and communication must be interpreted.

Just so, everything on the Left half of figure 5-2 requires some sort of interpretation. And interpretation is absolutely *the only way* we can get at each other's depth.

So we have a very simple distinction between the Right and the Left: *surfaces can be seen, but depth must be interpreted.*

Q: That's a clear distinction!

KW: Yes. And this is why, as we'll see, the Right-Hand paths are always asking, "What does it *do*?," whereas the Left-Hand paths are always asking, "What does it *mean*?"

This is incredibly important, because it gives us two very different approaches to consciousness and how we understand consciousness. There are important contributions to be made by both of these paths, but they need to be integrated or balanced. And this in turn will determine how we approach the higher stages of consciousness development itself, in both individual and collective transformation—it will bear directly on our spiritual evolution.

We are dealing, so to speak, with the Right and Left Hands of God, of how Spirit actually manifests in the world, and to fully grasp that manifestation, we definitely need both hands!

What Does That Dream Mean?

Q: Perhaps some examples of these two paths. Start with psychology.

KW: Psychoanalysis is basically an interpretive or Left-Hand approach, and classical behaviorism is a Right-Hand or empirical approach.

In psychoanalysis, the title of Freud's first great book says it all: *The Interpretation of Dreams*. Dreams are an interior event. They are composed of symbols. The symbols can only be understood by interpretation. What does the dream *mean*? One of Freud's great discoveries was that the dream is not incoherent, but rather it possesses a meaning, a hidden meaning that can be interpreted and brought to light.

So the simplest way to summarize Freud is that the "talking cure"— the *dialogue* cure!—not monological, but dialogical—means that we must learn to interpret our own depths more adequately. We are plagued by symptoms, such as anxiety or depression, that are baffling to us. Why am I so depressed? What is the meaning of this? And thus, in the course of psychoanalysis—or really, any depth psychotherapy—I will learn to look at my dreams, or at my symptoms, or my depression, or my anxiety, in a way that makes sense of them. I will learn how to interpret them in a way that sheds light on my own interior.

Perhaps I will find that I have a hidden rage at my absent father, and this rage was disguised as symptoms of depression. I had unconsciously *misinterpreted* this anger as depression. And so in therapy, I will learn to reinterpret this depression more accurately; I will learn to translate "sad" as "mad." I will get in touch with this angry aspect of my own depth, an aspect that I had tried to hide from myself by misinterpreting it, mistranslating it, disguising it.

The more adequately I interpret my depth—the more I can see that "sad" is really "mad"—then the more my symptoms will ease, the more the depression will lift. I am more faithfully interpreting my inner depths, and so those depths stop sabotaging me in the forms of painful symptoms.

Q: So that's an example of an interpretive or Left-Hand approach for individuals. That's an Upper-Left quadrant approach.

KW: Yes. And it applies not just to psychoanalysis. All "talking therapies"—from aspects of cognitive therapy to interpersonal therapy to Jungian therapy to Gestalt therapy to transactional analysis—are all fundamentally based on this single principle, namely, the attempt to find *a more adequate interpretation for one's interior depth*. A more adequate way to find the *meaning* of my dreams, my symptoms, my depths, my life, my being.

My life is not simply a series of flatly objective events laid out in front of me like so many rocks with simple location that I am supposed to stare at until I see the surfaces more clearly. My life includes a deeply subjective component that I must come to understand and interpret to myself. It is not just surfaces; it has depths. And while surfaces can be seen, depths must be interpreted. And the more adequately I can interpret my own depths, then the more transparent my life will become to me. The more clearly I can see and understand it, the less it baffles me, perplexes me, pains me in its opaqueness.

Q: So what about the individual therapies that aim at the Upper-Right quadrant? What about the exterior approaches to the individual?

KW: The Upper-Right quadrant approaches, such as behaviorism or biological psychiatry—at their extreme, they want absolutely nothing to do with interpretation and depth and interiors and intentions. They couldn't care less about what's going on "inside," in the "black box." Many of them don't even think it exists. They are interested solely in observable, empirical, exterior behavior.

So with behaviorism, you simply find the observable response you want to increase or decrease, and you selectively reinforce or extinguish it. Your interiors are of no consequence; your consciousness is not required. With behaviorism, the therapist will engineer operant conditionings that will reinforce the desired response and extinguish the undesirable ones.

Similarly, with purely biological psychiatry, the therapist will administer a drug—Prozac, Xanax, Elavil—that will bring about a stabilization of behavioral patterns. Many psychiatrists will administer the drug within the first consultation, and then just periodically check with you, say once a month, to make sure it's having the desired effect. Of course, some medical psychiatrists will engage in a bit of the talking cure, but many don't, and we are giving "pure examples" of the Upper Right.

And with this pure biological psychiatry, as with pure behaviorism, your presence is not required. That is, there is no attempt to get at the meaning of the symptoms. There is no extensive interpretation of your predicament. There is no attempt to increase your own self-understanding. There is no attempt to explore your interior depths and come to a clearer understanding of your own being.

Q: Nonetheless, I take it that you are not condemning these exterior approaches in themselves.

KW: No, that would miss the point from the other direction. Every holon has these four aspects, these four quadrants. Empiricism and behaviorism are a superior approach to the exteriors of holons. They are basically correct as far as they go. I *fully* endorse them as far as they go.

The problem, of course, is that they don't go very far. And thus you often have to condemn them in the same breath, because they usually deny not only the importance but the very *existence* of the other quadrants. You are depressed, not because you lack values or meanings or virtues in your life, but because you lack serotonin, even though stocking your brain to the hilt with serotonin won't do a thing to develop your values.

In other words, my depression can be interiorly caused by an absent father, the exterior correlate of which might be a low level of serotonin in my brain, and Prozac can to some degree correct that serotonin imbalance. Which is fine, and sometimes extremely helpful. But Prozac will not in any way help me to understand my interior pain, to *interpret* it in a way that it takes on meaning for me and helps me to become transparent to myself. And if you are not interested in that, if you are not interested in understanding your own depth, then Prozac alone will suit your purposes.

But if you desire to see into your own depths and interpret them more adequately, then you will have to *talk* to somebody who has seen those depths before and helped others interpret them more adequately. In this intersubjective dialogue with a therapeutic helper, you will hold hands and walk the path of more adequate interpretations, you will enter a circle of intersubjective depth, and the more clearly you can interpret and articulate this depth, the less baffling you will become to yourself, the clearer you will become to yourself, the more transparent you will be.

And eventually, as we'll see, you might even become transparent to the Divine, liberated in your own infinite depth. But in any event, none of this, at any level, will open to you if you insist on hugging only the surfaces.

Social Science versus Cultural Understanding

Q: What about the collective? What about Lower-Left and Lower-Right approaches? The *cultural* and *social*? One is interpretive, the other is empirical?

KW: Yes. Like psychology, sociology has, almost from its inception, divided into two huge camps, the interpretive (Left Hand) and the naturalistic or empirical (Right Hand). The one investigates culture or cultural meanings, and attempts to get at those meanings *from within*, in a sympathetic *understanding*. The other investigates the social system or social structures and functions *from without*, in a very positivistic and empirical fashion. And so, of course, the former asks, What does it mean?; the latter, What does it do?

Q: Take them one at a time.

KW: Understanding the *cultural* meanings is an *interpretive* affair. You have to learn the language, you have to immerse yourself in the culture, you have to find out what the various practices mean. And these are the hermeneutic cultural sciences—Wilhelm Dilthey, Max Weber, Martin Heidegger, Hans-Georg Gadamer, Paul Ricoeur, Clifford Geertz, Mary Douglas, Karl-Otto Apel, Charles Taylor, Thomas Kuhn, to name a prominent few.

These approaches all involve sympathetic resonance, sharing, talking—they are dialogical, interpretive. They want to get at the interior meaning, and not just the exterior behavior. They want to get inside the black box. They want to get at the Left-Hand dimensions. And the *only* way you can get at depth is via interpretation.

But the *empirical* social sciences mostly want to study the *behavior* of societies in a detached fashion: the birthrates, the modes of production, the types of architecture, the suicide rates, the amount of money in circulation, the demographics, the population spread, the types of technology, and so on—all exterior behaviors, no interior intentions. Most of those statistics can be gathered without ever having to talk to any of the cultural natives. No nasty black boxes here.

So these approaches are mostly monological, empirical, behavioral. You are looking at the *behavior* of a "social action system," you are not inquiring into the interior meaning or depth of the culture. And to the extent that you do investigate meaning or values, you make them almost totally subservient to the social system. And these are the standard positivistic, naturalistic, empirical social sciences—August Comte, Karl Marx, Talcott Parsons, Niklas Luhmann, Gerhard Lenski, and so on.

Q: You give an example of the Hopi Rain Dance. About how the Left- and Right-Hand approaches differ.

KW: The Left-Hand approach, the interpretive approach, wants to know what is the meaning of the Rain Dance? When the native peoples engage in the Dance, what does it mean for them? Why do they value it? And as the interpretive investigator becomes a "participant observer," then he or she begins to understand that the Rain Dance is largely a way to celebrate the sacredness of nature, and a way to ask that sacredness to bless the earth with rain. And you know this is so because this is what you are told by the practitioners themselves as you continue your attempts at mutual understanding.

The Right-Hand paths want little to do with this. They look instead at what the *function* of the Dance is in the overall *behavior* of the *social system*. They are not so much interested in what the natives *say* the meaning is. Rather, they look at the behavior of the Dance in the overall observable system. And they conclude that the Dance, despite what the natives say, is actually functioning as a way to create social cohesion in the social action system. In other words, the Dance provides social integration.

Q: As I understand it, you are saying both are correct.

KW: Yes. They are the Left- and the Right-Hand approaches to the same communal holon. The Left Hand seeks to understand what the Dance means, its interior meaning and value, which can only be understood by *standing within* the culture. And the Right Hand seeks to understand what the Dance *does*, its overall *function* in the observable *behavior* of the social system, which can only be determined by *standing outside* the system in a detached and impartial fashion. Left- and Right-Hand paths.

Hermeneutics

Q: Interpretation is the meaning of "hermeneutics."

KW: Yes. Hermeneutics is the art and science of interpretation. Hermeneutics began as a way to understand interpretation itself, because when you interpret a text, there are good ways and bad ways to proceed.

In general, the Continental philosophers, particularly in Germany and France, have carried on the interpretive aspects of philosophy, and the Anglo-Saxon philosophers in Britain and North America have shunned interpretation and focused mostly on pragmatic and empiric-analytic studies. This old war between the Left- and the Right-Hand paths!

This is why Thomas Kuhn caused such an uproar with his notion of paradigms—the idea that "objective scientific theories" are actually sunk in background contexts that govern their interpretations. And why Charles Taylor caused a sensation with the publication of his seminal essay, "Interpretation and the Sciences of Man," which demonstrated that background contexts of interpretation are necessary to understand cultural movements. This could only be shocking to Anglo-Saxon philosophers, whose paradigm of knowledge is the monological gaze: I see the rock.

So even though "hermeneutics" is a fancy word, please remember it. It's the key to the entire Left-Hand dimensions. The Left Hand is composed of depth, and interpretation is the *only way* to get at depth. As Heidegger would say, interpretation goes all the way down. And mere empiricism is virtually worthless in this regard.

Q: But empiricists say interpretation is not objective and thus not "really real."

KW: It's like studying *Hamlet*. If you take a text of *Hamlet* and study it empirically, then you will find that it is made of so much ink and so much paper. That's all you can know about *Hamlet* empirically—it's composed of seven grams of ink, which is made of so many molecules, which have so many atoms—all of the things you can find in the Upper-Right quadrant.

But if you want to know the *meaning* of *Hamlet*, then you have to read it. You have to engage in intersubjective understanding. You have to *interpret* what it means.

True, this is not a merely objective affair. But neither is it subjective fantasy. This is very important, because empiric-scientific types are always claiming that if something isn't empirically true, then it isn't true at all. But interpretation is not subjective whim. There are *good* and *bad* interpretations of *Hamlet*. *Hamlet* is not about the joys of war, for example. That is a bad interpretation; it is wrong.

Q: So there are validity criteria for interpretations.

KW: Yes. The fact that the Left-Hand dimensions have this strong interpretive aspect does not mean they are merely arbitrary or ungrounded, or that they are nothing but subjective and idiosyncratic fantasies. There are good and bad interpretations, felicitous interpretations and false or distorted interpretations, interpretations that are more adequate and those that are less adequate.

And this can be determined by a community of those who have looked into the same depth. As I said, the meaning of *Hamlet* is *not*

"Have a nice day." That interpretation can be easily *rejected* by a community of those who have read and studied the text—that is, by a community of those who have entered the interior of *Hamlet*, by those who share that depth.

Even if you bring your own individual interpretations to *Hamlet*, which is fine, those interpretations are grounded in the realities and contexts of your actual lifeworld. Either way, the point is that interpretation does not mean wildly arbitrary!

This interpretive knowledge is just as important as empirical knowledge. In some ways, more important. But, of course, it's a bit trickier and requires a bit more sophistication than the head-banging obviousness of the monological gaze. But there is, alas, a type of mind that believes only those things with simple location actually exist, even though that belief itself does not have simple location. . . .

All Interpretation Is Context-Bound

Q: You point out that the crucial feature of interpretation is that it is always *context-bound*.

KW: Yes. The primary rule of interpretation is that all meaning is context-bound. For example, the meaning of the word "bark" is different in the phrases "the bark of a tree" and "the bark of a dog." The important point is that the context helps determine which interpretation is correct.

And that context itself exists in yet further contexts, and so off we go in the "hermeneutic circle." The reason, of course, is that there are only holons, and holons are nested indefinitely: holons within holons, contexts within contexts, endlessly.

So all meaning is context dependent, and contexts are boundless. We earlier mentioned that one of the prime aims of postmodernism was to emphasize the importance of interpretation. Jonathan Culler has, in fact, summarized all of deconstruction (one of the most influential of the postmodern movements, founded by Jacques Derrida) in this way: "One could therefore identify deconstruction with the twin principles of the *contextual determination of meaning* and the *infinite extendability of context.*" In other words, all meaning is context dependent, and contexts are boundless. We arrived at this truth by looking at the four quadrants and the nature of holons; Derrida did so by an investigation of language, which is a vivid example of holons within holons indefinitely. (Of course, deconstruction can be taken too far, into extreme constructivism, but we needn't take that route.) The point is simply that by emphasizing the endlessly holonic nature of reality, we are in general agreement with the best of the postmodern insights.

Nested holons—contexts forever—simply means that we always need to be sensitive to background contexts in understanding meaning. And the more of these contexts we can take into account, then the richer our interpretations will be—all the way up, all the way down.

Nonhuman Interpretation

Q: So this interpretive component applies to nonhumans as well? It applies to nonhuman holons?

KW: If you want to know their *interiors*, yes, absolutely. If you want to get at the interior of any holon, what else are you going to do?

When you interact with your dog, you are not interested in just its exterior behavior. Since humans and dogs share a similar limbic system, we also share a *common emotional worldspace* ("typhonic"). You can sense when your dog is sad, or fearful, or happy, or hungry. And most people interact with those interiors. They want to share those interiors. When their dog is happy, it's easy to share that happiness. But that requires a sensitive *interpretation* of what your dog is feeling. Of course, this is not verbal or linguistic communication; but it is an *empathic resonance* with your dog's interior, with its depths, with its degree of consciousness, which might not be as great as yours, but that doesn't mean it's zero.

So you empathically interpret. And the dog does the same with you— you each *resonate* with the other's interior. In those moments, you share a common worldspace—in this case, a common emotional worldspace. You, of course, will elaborate it conceptually, which a dog can't do. But the basic emotions are similar enough, and you know it. You interpret your dog's interior feelings, and relate with those feelings. That's the whole point of getting a dog, isn't it?

Of course, the lower a holon, or the less depth it has, then the less consciousness it has, the less interior it has—and the less you can easily interpret and share. Of course, some people get on famously with their pet rocks, which I suppose shows you something.

Q: So because both you and the dog share some sort of *common background*—in this case, the emotional worldspace—then you can interpret each other to some degree.

KW: That's right. The common worldspace provides the *common context* that allows the interpretation, the sharing. As we said, all interpretation requires a context, and in this case, it is the context of the emotional worldspace, which is the common culture we share with dogs.

Of course, we also share all lower worldspaces—the physical (such as gravity), the vegetative (life), the reptilian (hunger). Since we also contain a reptilian stem, we can also share with lizards, but it becomes less fun, doesn't it? Down to pet rocks, with shared mass and gravity. Less depth, less to share. Really, all you and your pet rock can share is, you fall at the same speed.

Q: So when we reach specifically human contexts . . .

KW: Yes, when it comes specifically to humans, then *in addition* to the earlier backgrounds—cellular, reptilian-stem, mammalian-limbic—we *also* have complex cognitive and conceptual and linguistic backgrounds. And we ground our mutual interpretations in these *common cultural backgrounds* (the Lower Left). There is no other way for communication to occur.

Q: And these backgrounds evolve.

KW: Yes, all four quadrants evolve, all follow the twenty tenets. With respect to the cultural background—the Lower-Left quadrant—we saw it evolve in humans from archaic to magic to mythic to rational to existential, on the way to possibly higher worldviews. And each of these worldviews governs the *types* of ways that we *can* interpret the Kosmos.

So how indeed will you and I interpret the Kosmos? Will we interpret it magically? Will we interpret it mythically? Will we interpret it rationally? Or start to go transrational altogether?

But you can start to see why there isn't simply a pregiven world just lying around waiting to be reflected with the monological gaze.

Q: No wonder the human sciences have always divided into these two camps, Right Hand versus Left—surfaces can be seen, but depth must be interpreted.

Spiritual Interpretation

Q: But how is interpretation important in spiritual transformation or spiritual experience?

KW: Give an example.

Q: Say I have a direct experience of interior illumination—a blinding, ecstatic, mind-blowing experience of inner light.

KW: The experience itself is indeed direct and immediate. You might even become one with that light. But then you come out of that state, and you want to tell me about it. You want to talk to me about it. You want to talk to yourself about it. And here you must *interpret* what this deep experience was. What was this light? Was it Jesus Christ? Was it Buddha-mind? Was it an archetype? An angel? Was it an alien UFO? Was it just some brain state gone haywire? What was it? God? Or a piece of undigested meat? The Goddess? Or a food allergy?

You must interpret. And if you decide it was some sort of genuine spiritual experience, then of what flavor? Allah? Keter? Kundalini? Savikalpa-samadhi? Jungian archetype? Platonic form? This is not some unimportant or secondary issue. This is not some theoretical hair splitting. This is not some merely academic concern. Quite the contrary. How you interpret this experience will govern how you approach others with this illumination, how you share it with the world, how you fit it into your own self system, and the ways you can even speak about it to others and think about it yourself. And it will determine your future relation to this light!

And like all interpretations—whether of *Hamlet* or of the inner light—there are *good* and there are *bad* interpretations. And in this interpretation, will you do a good job or a bad job?

In other words, even if this experience of light was transmental, or beyond words altogether, still you are a compound individual. Still you are composed not only of this spiritual component—which is perhaps what the light was; you are also composed of mind and body and matter. And mentally you must orient yourself to this experience. You must interpret it, explain it, make sense of it. And if you can't *interpret it adequately*, it might very likely drive you insane. You will not be able to integrate it with the rest of your being because you cannot adequately interpret it. You don't know what it *means*. Your own extraordinary depth escapes you, confuses you, obscures you, because you cannot interpret it adequately.

Q: So interpretation is an important part of even spiritual or transmental experiences.

KW: Yes, definitely. Many people today are having just these types of spiritual or transmental experiences—experiences from the higher or deeper stages of consciousness evolution. But they *don't know how to interpret them*. They have these extraordinary intuitions, but they sometimes unpack the intuitions in an inadequate or incomplete fashion. And these inadequate interpretations tend to abort further transformation, derail it, sabotage it.

Q: So examples of "bad" interpretations would be, what? How can we tell if an interpretation is bad?

KW: Remember, one of the basic rules of interpretation is that all meaning is *context-bound*. So in any attempt to interpret these types of spiritual experiences, we want to make sure that the context against which we interpret the experience is as full and complete as possible. In other words, we want to make sure that we have checked our interpretation against *all four quadrants*. We want an "all-quadrants" view, an interpretation from the context of the Kosmos in all its dimensions.

What is happening now is that many people are trying to interpret these experiences based on the realities of just one quadrant—and sometimes just one level in one quadrant! This diminishes the other quadrants and cripples the fullness of the interpretation, cripples the fullness of the experience itself.

Q: For example?

KW: Many people interpret these spiritual experiences basically in terms of only the Upper-Left quadrant—they see the experience in terms of a higher Self, or higher consciousness, or archetypal forms, or enneagram patterns, or care of the soul, or the inner voice, or transcendental awareness, and so forth. They tend to ignore the cultural and social and behavioral components. So their insights are limited in terms of how to relate this higher Self to the other quadrants, which are then often interpreted rather narcissistically as mere extensions of their Self. The new age movement is replete with this type of Self-only interpretation.

Others see these experiences as basically a product of brain states— the Upper Right. They attempt to interpret these experiences as coming solely or predominantly from theta brain wave states, or massive endorphin release, or hemispheric synchronization, and so on. This also devastates the cultural and social components, not to mention the interior states of consciousness itself. It is hyperobjective and merely technological.

Others—especially the "new paradigm" ecological theorists— attempt to interpret these experiences mostly in terms of the Lower-Right quadrant. The "ultimate reality" for them is the empirical web of life, or Gaia, or the biosphere, or the social system, and all holons are reduced to being merely a strand in the great web. These approaches poorly understand the interior stages of consciousness development, and reduce all Left-Hand components to Right-Hand strands in the empirical web. This mistakes great span for great depth and therefore collapses vertical depth to horizontal expansion. This results in various forms of what many critics have called ecofascism.

Others attempt to interpret these experiences merely in terms of collective cultural consciousness and a coming worldview transformation—the Lower-Left quadrant. This overlooks what individual consciousness can do at any given point, and denies the importance of social structures and institutions in helping to support and embed these experiences. And so on.

Q: All of which tend to be very partial.

KW: All of these "one-quadrant" interpretations have a moment of truth to them, and an important moment at that. But because they don't adequately include the other quadrants, they cripple the original experience. They unpack this spiritual intuition very poorly, in very fragmented terms. And these fragmented interpretations do not help facilitate further spiritual intuitions. Fragmented interpretations tend to abort the spiritual process itself.

Q: So the point is. . . .

KW: Since Spirit-in-action manifests as all four quadrants, then an adequate interpretation of a spiritual experience ought to take all four quadrants into account. It's not just that we have different levels—matter, body, mind, soul, and spirit—but that each of these manifests in four facets—intentional, behavioral, cultural, and social.

Q: So a balanced or *integral* view would include all of that—all of the levels and all of the quadrants.

KW: Yes, I think so. A truly integral view would be "all-level, all-quadrant." This integral view becomes especially important as we look at the higher or deeper stages of human growth and development—at the further stages of consciousness evolution. If there is indeed a transformation in our future, it lies in these higher or deeper stages, and it looks like these can only be accessed in their richness and fullness if we honor and appreciate the different types of truth that will unfold to set us free.

Q: As for an "all-level, all-quadrant" view, many people seem to understand the "all-level" part. They realize that there is some sort of spectrum of consciousness from matter to body to mind to soul to spirit, although they might not use exactly those terms. But I'm not sure many people understand the "all-quadrant" part. The example you gave about how people tend to interpret spiritual illumination in terms of just one quadrant confirms that. I'd like to come back to the levels of consciousness evolution (see Part Two). But right now perhaps we could focus on the all-quadrant part. Because, as you say, it might be the case that the higher levels will not fully unfold without understanding all four quadrants in a balanced, integral, and inclusive fashion.

KW: These levels and quadrants are simply aspects of the Kosmos, aspects of our very own being. So the whole point, I think, is that we want to find ourselves in sympathetic attunement with all aspects of the Kosmos. We want to find ourselves at home in the Kosmos. We want to touch the truth in each of the quadrants. We begin to do so by noticing that each speaks to us with a different voice. If we listen carefully, we can hear each of these voices whispering gently their truths, and finally joining in a harmonious chorus that quietly calls us home. We can fully resonate with those liberating truths, if we know how to recognize and honor them.

From attunement to atonement to at-onement: we find ourselves in the overpowering embrace of a Kosmic sympathy on the very verge of Kosmic consciousness itself . . . if we listen very carefully.

7

Attuned to the Kosmos

Q: We must listen very carefully. You mean, to all four types of truth.

KW: Truth, in the broadest sense, means being *attuned* with the real. To be authentically in touch with the true, and the good and the beautiful. Yes?

And that implies that we can also be out of touch with the real. We can be lost, or obscured, or mistaken, or wrong in our assessments. We can be out of touch with the true, out of touch with the good, out of touch with the beautiful.

And so a collective humanity, in the course of its evolution, has discovered, through painful trial and error, the various ways that we can check our attunement with the Kosmos. Various ways to see if we are in touch with truth or lost in falsity. Whether we are honoring the good or obscuring it. Whether we are moved by the beautiful or promoting degradation.

Humanity, in other words, has painfully learned and labored hard to fashion a series of *validity claims*—tests that can help us determine if we are in touch with the real, if we are adequately attuned to the Kosmos in all of its rich diversity.

Q: So the validity claims themselves . . .

KW: The validity claims are the ways that we connect to Spirit itself, ways that we attune ourselves to the Kosmos. The validity claims force us to confront reality; they curb our egoic fantasies and self-centered ways; they demand evidence from the rest of the Kosmos; they force us outside of ourselves! They are the checks and balances in the Kosmic Constitution.

Q: As we were saying, befriending the four quadrants and their truths makes it more likely that the higher levels of consciousness will emerge in a more balanced and integral fashion. In order to get "all-level," we need first to get "all-quadrant."

KW: I believe that is very true.

Q: So perhaps we could go around the four quadrants and very briefly summarize this. The four truths, what they are, and the tests for their validity.

KW: These are listed in figure 7-1. And once we briefly review these, I promise I'll give that very, very simple way to summarize them all!

Propositional Truth

Q: Is there an easy definition of "truth"?

KW: Most people take truth to mean representational truth. Simple mapping or simple correspondence. I make a statement or a *proposition*

	INTERIOR Left-Hand Paths	EXTERIOR Right-Hand Paths
INDIVIDUAL	SUBJECTIVE *truthfulness* sincerity integrity trustworthiness	OBJECTIVE *truth* correspondence representation propositional
	I	it
	we	its
COLLECTIVE	*justness* cultural fit mutual understanding rightness INTERSUBJECTIVE	*functional fit* systems theory web structural-functionalism social systems mesh INTEROBJECTIVE

FIGURE 7-1. *Validity claims.*

that refers to or represents something in the concrete world. For example, I might say, "It is raining outside." Now we want to know if that is true or not. We want to know the validity or the "truth status" of that statement. So basically, we go and look outside. And if it is indeed raining, we say that the statement "It is raining outside" is a true statement.

Q: Or a true proposition.

KW: Yes. It's a simple mapping procedure. We check to see if the proposition *corresponds* with or fits the facts, if the map accurately reflects the real territory. (Usually it's more complicated, and we might try to disprove the map, and if we can never disprove it, we assume it is accurate enough.) But the essential idea is that with representational or propositional truth, my statement somehow refers to an *objective state of affairs*, and it accurately corresponds with those objects or processes or affairs.

Q: So propositional truth basically deals with just the exterior or objective or Right-Hand dimensions?

KW: Yes, that's right. Both the Upper-Right and Lower-Right quadrants contain the observable, empirical, exterior aspects of holons. We will subdivide these in a moment into the Upper and Lower versions, but the point is that all Right-Hand holons have *simple location*. These aspects can be easily seen, and thus with propositional truth, we tie our statements to these objects or processes or affairs. (This is also called the correspondence theory of truth.)

All of which is fair enough, and important enough, and I in no way deny the general importance of empirical representation. It's just not the whole story; it's not even the most interesting part of the story.

Truthfulness

Q: So an objective state of affairs—the brain, planets, organisms, ecosystems—can be represented with empirical mapping. These empirical maps are all variations on "It is raining." Objective propositions.

KW: Yes. But if we now look at the Upper Left—the actual *interior* of an individual holon—then we have an entirely different type of validity claim. The question here is not, Is it raining outside? The question here is, When I tell you it is raining outside, am I telling you the truth or am I lying?

You see, here it is not so much a question of whether the map matches the objective territory, but whether the mapmaker can be trusted.

And not just about objective truths, but especially about interior truths. I mean, you can always check and see if it is raining. You can do that yourself. But the *only* way you can know my interior, my depth, is by asking me, by *talking* to me, as we have seen. And when I report on my inner status, I might be telling you the truth, *but I might be lying.* You have no other way to get at my interior except in talk and dialogue and interpretation, and I might fundamentally distort, or conceal, or mislead—in short, I might lie.

So the way we tend to navigate in the Right Hand is by using the yardstick of propositional truth—or simply "truth" for short—but the way we navigate in the Upper Left is by using the yardstick of *truthfulness* or sincerity or honesty or trustworthiness. This is not so much a matter of *objective truth* but of *subjective truthfulness.* Two very different criteria—truth and truthfulness.

Q: So those are two different validity claims.

KW: Yes, that's right. And this is no trivial matter. Interior events are *located* in states of consciousness, not in objective states of affairs, and so you can't empirically nail them down with simple location. As we saw, they are accessed with communication and interpretation, not with the monological gaze.

And in this communication, *I might intentionally lie to you.* For various reasons, I might try to misrepresent my interior, I might try to make it appear to be something other than it really is. I might dash the entire Left-Hand dimensions against the wall of deceitfulness. I might lie to you.

Furthermore, and this is crucial, I might lie to myself. I might try to conceal aspects of my own depth from myself. I might do this intentionally, or I might do it "unconsciously." But one way or another, I might *misinterpret my own depth*, I might lie about my own interior.

And, in part, the "unconscious" is the locus of the all the ways I have lied to myself. I might have started lying to myself because of intense environmental trauma. Or maybe I learned it from my parents. Or maybe I had to do so as a defense mechanism against an even more painful truth.

But in any event, my unconscious is the locus of my insincerity, of my being less than truthful with myself, less than truthful about my subjective depth, my interior status, my deep desires and intentions. The unconscious is the locus of the lie.

Q: When we were talking about psychoanalysis and the interpretive therapies, you said their goal was to provide more truthful interpretations.

KW: Yes, that's exactly the same thing. The point of "depth psychology" and therapy is to help people *interpret* themselves more *truthfully*. The Left Hand, of course, is interpretation, and so it is no surprise that truthful or more adequate interpretation is the central therapeutic criterion.

The example we used was "sad" and "mad" about an absent father. What that means is that at some point early in my life, I started interpreting anger as depression. Perhaps I was enraged at my father for not being around. This rage, however, is very dangerous for a child. What if this rage could actually kill my father? Perhaps I had better not have this anger, because after all I love my father. So I'm angry at myself instead. I beat myself up instead. I'm rotten, no good, wretched to the core. This is very depressing. I started out mad, now I'm calling it sad.

One way or another, I have misinterpreted my interior, I have distorted my depth. I have started calling anger "sadness." And I carry this lie around with me. I cannot be truthful with myself because that would involve such great pain—to want to kill the father I love—so I would rather lie about the whole thing. And so this I do. My "shadow," my "unconscious," is now the locus of this lie, the focal point of this insincerity, the inner place that I hide from myself.

And because I lie to myself—and then forget it is a lie—then I will lie to you without even knowing it. I will probably even seem very sincere about it. In fact, if I have thoroughly lied to myself, I will honestly think I'm telling the truth. And if you give me a lie detector test, it will show that I'm telling the "truth." So much for empirical tests.

Finally, because I have misinterpreted my own depth, I will often misinterpret yours. I am cutting something off in my own depth—I am dissociating it, or repressing it, or alienating it—and so I will *distort interpretations* from that depth, both *in myself* and *in others*. My interpretations will be laced with lies, nested in insincerity. I will misinterpret myself, and I will often misinterpret you.

And you will probably notice this, notice that something is off base. I will say something so wacky, you'll have to respond, "That's not what I meant!" And you will think to yourself, "Where on earth did he get *that* one?"

Q: So these various interpretive therapies, such as psychoanalysis or Gestalt or Jungian, help you to contact and more truthfully interpret your depths.

KW: Yes, exactly. The idea is not to make some sort of more accurate map of the objective world, but to relax your resistances and sink into your interior depths, and learn to report those depths more truthfully, both to others and to yourself.

And this allows your *depth* to begin to match your *behavior*. Your words and your actions will match up. That is, your Left will match your Right. You will "walk your talk." And your left hand will know what your right hand doeth. We generally refer to this as integrity. You have the sense that the person won't lie to you, because they haven't lied to themselves.

Of course, if you live in the world of the lab technician—the empiricist, the behaviorist, the systems theorist, the cybernetic scurrying, the monological madness—you don't particularly care about interior truthfulness, because you don't particularly care about interiors, period. Not in their own terms, anyway. You just want monological truth, objective surfaces, empirical behavior, systems networks, and you don't care about interior depth and sincerity and truthfulness—in fact, there is nothing on the empirical maps that even vaguely corresponds with truthfulness!

Truthfulness, you see, doesn't have simple location, and it is not a merely empirical state of affairs, so it appears on none of the empirical maps. Not on a physicist's map, not on a biologist's map, not on a neurologist's map, not on a systems theory map, not on an ecosystem map. It is a Left-Hand, not a Right-Hand, affair!

And yet in that Left Hand exists your entire lifeworld, your actual awareness, your own depth. And if you are alive to depth at all, you will come to know that depth in yourself and in others through truthfulness and sincerity and trustworthiness.

The essential point is that the way to depth is blocked by deceit, blocked by deception. And the moment you acknowledge *interiors*, you must confront the primary roadblock to accessing those interiors: you must confront deception and deceit.

Which is precisely why we navigate in this domain by truthfulness. And yes, that is what all Left-Hand therapies work with. More truthful interpretations of your own inner depth.

Q: Different interpretive therapies do have different types of interpretations, however.

KW: Well, yes, and that's a long discussion. Perhaps I could just say that the different interpretive therapies differ primarily on *how deep* they are willing to go in their interpretations. Or how high they are willing to go. The Upper-Left quadrant is, as we were saying, a *spectrum of consciousness*—a spectrum of levels of developmental awareness.

And different therapies tend to plug into different levels of this spectrum, and use their favorite level as the basic reference point around which they will offer their interpretations.

As we saw, all interpretation is *context-bound*, and different therapies have their own favorite context within which they offer their interpretations. This doesn't mean that they are wrong, only that we have to identify their context, their favorite level. We have to situate their interpretations.

Freudians emphasize the emotional-sexual level; cognitive therapists emphasize the verbal; transpersonal therapists emphasize the spiritual. But they all primarily confront the distortions, the lies and self-deceptions with which we hide truthful aspects of these dimensions from ourselves—the lies and distortions that obscure our emotions, our self-esteem, our spiritual nature.

Q: So a full-spectrum model would be a type of composite story, including all the various levels of the spectrum of consciousness and the therapies that are most effective for each level.

KW: Yes, that is one of the tasks of a full-spectrum model, and many researchers are now hard at work on such a model (these are discussed in Part Two). An excellent introduction to this field is *Paths beyond Ego*, by Roger Walsh and Frances Vaughan.

But my basic point about these Left-Hand or interpretive therapies is that, once we strip them of their exclusiveness or their single-level partialness, then they all have something very important to teach us. They all have something to tell us about the various layers of the self—of consciousness—and about the *truthful interpretations* that can help us access these various dimensions.

Because the amazing fact is that truth alone will not set you free. Truthfulness will set you free.

Justness

Q: What about the Lower-Left quadrant?

KW: The crucial point is that the *subjective* world is *situated* in an *intersubjective* space, a cultural space, and it is this intersubjective space that *allows* the subjective space to arise in the first place. Without this cultural background, my own individual thoughts would have no meaning at all. I wouldn't even have the tools to interpret my own thoughts to myself. In fact, I wouldn't even have developed thoughts, I would be "wolf boy."

In other words, the *subjective* space is inseparable from the *intersubjective* space, and this is one of the great discoveries of the postmodern or post-Enlightenment movements.

So here, in the Lower Left, the validity claim is not so much *objective* propositional truth, and not so much *subjective* truthfulness, but *intersubjective fit*. This cultural background provides the *common context* against which my own thoughts and interpretations will have some sort of meaning. And so the validity criterion here involves the "cultural fit" with this background.

Q: So the aim of this validity claim is what, exactly? We have objective truth, we have subjective truthfulness, and we have intersubjective . . . what?

KW: The aim here is *mutual understanding*. Not that we necessarily *agree* with each other, but can we at least *understand* each other? Because if that can't happen, then we will never be able to exist in a common culture. Can you and I arrange our subjective spaces so that we see eye to eye? Can we find a common cultural background that allows communication to exist in the first place? Can we find a cultural fit, a common meaning, between ourselves? This must happen to some degree before any communication can occur at all!

Q: So the aim here is not so much the mapping of objective truth, and not simply being truthful, but reaching mutual understanding?

KW: Yes. This has many, many aspects. You and I are going to have to agree on some sort of morals and ethics if we are going to live in the same space. And we are going to have to find some sort of common law. And we are going to have to find some sort of identity that overlaps our individual selves and shows us something in common, some sort of collective identity, so that we can see something of ourselves in each other, and treat each other with care and concern.

All of that is involved in this *cultural fit*, this background of common meaning and appropriateness and justness. I have been describing this background as if it were some sort of contract that you and I consciously form, like a social contract, and sometimes it is. Sometimes we simply reach mutual agreement about, for example, the voting age or the speed limit on the highway. That is part of cultural fit, of how we agree on rules and common meanings that allow us all to fit together.

But much of cultural fit is not a conscious contract; much of it is so deeply background that we hardly know it's there. There are linguistic structures and cultural practices so deeply contextual that we are still trying to dig them up and understand them (one of Heidegger's main themes). But the point is, wherever they come from, there is no escaping these intersubjective networks that allow the subjective space to develop in the first place!

What is so remarkable about mutual understanding is not that I can take a simple word like "dog" and point to a real dog and say, "I mean that." What is so remarkable is that *you* know what *I* mean by that! Forget the simple empirical pointing! Instead, look at this intersubjective understanding. It is utterly amazing. It means you and I can inhabit each other's interior to some degree. You and I can *share* our *depth*. When we point to *truth*, and we are situated in *truthfulness*, we can reach *mutual understanding*. This is a miracle. If Spirit exists, you can begin to look for it here.

Q: So this is cultural fit or justness.

KW: Yes, justness, goodness, rightness. How do we reach the common good? What is right and appropriate for us, such that we can all inhabit the same cultural space with some sort of dignity and fairness? How do we arrange our subjective spaces so that they mesh in the common intersubjective space, the common worldspace, the common culture, upon which we have all depended for our own subjective being?

This is not a matter of arranging *objects* in the space of simple location! It is a matter of arranging *subjects* in the collective interior space of culture.

This is not simply truthfulness, and not simply the true, but the good.

Q: So, as you say, cultural fit or justness includes all sorts of items, from ethics and morals and laws, to group or collective identities, to background cultural contexts, and so on.

KW: Yes, all of which we have been summarizing as a common worldview or worldspace, which we also called "cultural," the Lower Left.

And remember, this cultural space exists for all holons, even though it might be simpler and less complex. So there is *intersubjectivity woven into the very fabric of the Kosmos at all levels*. This is not just the Spirit in "me," not just the Spirit in "it," not just the Spirit in "them"—but the Spirit in "us," in all of *us*.

And, as we will see when we return to environmental ethics, we want to arrive at a *justness* for all sentient beings: the deeper *good* for all of *us*.

Functional Fit

Q: What's the difference between Upper Right and Lower Right? You said they have a different validity claim.

KW: The Upper Right is exteriors of just *individuals*, the Lower Right is exteriors of *systems*. So the Upper Right is propositional truth in the very strictest sense: a proposition refers to a single fact. But in the Lower Right, the proposition refers to the social system, whose main validity claim is *functional fit*—how various holons fit together in the overall objective system.

Q: But doesn't the Lower Left also involve systems? You said that in cultural fit, it's how an individual fits with the whole cultural background. Isn't that also systems theory?

KW: No, it isn't, and the reason it isn't is basically the entire story of the postmodern revolt against Enlightenment modernity. In a sense, the entire post-Cartesian revolt points out dramatically why *systems theory* is just *more Cartesian dualism* in its worst aspects. Understanding why that is so is the very essence of the postmodern advance.

Q: Let's go into that, because it is certainly at odds with what the systems theorists themselves say. They say they are *overcoming* the fundamental Enlightenment paradigm.

KW: Just the opposite. The fundamental Enlightenment paradigm, as we have seen, was the representation paradigm—the mapping paradigm, the monological paradigm—and the systems theorists are just doing more of the same. They don't overcome it, they clone it.

It's true that both the Lower Right and Lower Left are dealing with "systems" in the broad sense, because the entire lower half is the communal or the collective. But the Lower Left describes that system *from within*, from the *interior*. It describes the consciousness, the values, the worldviews, the ethics, the collective identities. But the Lower Right describes the system in purely objective and exterior terms, from without. It doesn't want to know how collective values are intersubjectively shared in mutual understanding. Rather, it wants to know how their objective correlates *functionally fit* in the overall social system, which itself has simple location.

So open any good book on systems theory and you will find nothing about ethical standards, intersubjective values, moral dispositions, mutual understanding, truthfulness, sincerity, depth, integrity, aesthetics, interpretation, hermeneutics, beauty, art, the sublime. Open any systems theory text and you will find *none* of that even mentioned. All you will find are the objective and *exterior correlates* of all of that. All you will find in systems theory are information bits scurrying through processing channels, and cybernetic feedback loops, and processes within processes of dynamic networks of monological representations, and nests within nests of endless processes, all of which have *simple location*, not in an individual, but in the social system and network of objective processes.

All of which is true! And all of which *leaves out* the interiors in their own terms, the actual lived experiences and values and lifeworlds—it honors the Right Hand of the collective, but completely devastates the Left Hand.

Q: But why can't you simply say, as systems theorists do, that systems theory is the basic reality of which the subjective aspects are simply parts—all parts of the great web. That web covers everything, by definition.

KW: By exterior definition! That great web always has simple location. So with the systems approach, the split between the subjective and the objective is "healed" by *reducing* all subjects to objects in the "holistic" system. It reduces all subjective and intersubjective occasions to interobjective fit, functional fit, monological fit.

Well, that *is* the fundamental Enlightenment paradigm. This is why theorists from Taylor to Foucault to Habermas have pointed out that systems theory is just more of the same reductionistic nightmare—all of the Left Hand aspects are reduced to Right-Hand descriptions in the great system, the great web.

Q: What you call *subtle reductionism*.

KW: Yes, subtle reductionism. Gross reductionism we all know about: everything is reduced to atoms in the Upper Right. This is very gross. Subtle reductionism does not do that. In fact, it aggressively *fights* that! But it immediately gets caught in a subtle reductionism: all Left-Hand aspects are reduced to their correlates in the Right Hand. The Right Hand has extensive functional fit and a systems view, so it appears that you are being very holistic and all-inclusive, but you have just gutted the interiors of the entire Kosmos, you have just perfectly ruined the lifeworld of all holons.

Objective systems within systems within systems—atoms are parts of cells, which are parts of organisms, which are parts of ecosystems, which are parts of the biosphere, and so on. In other words, *functional fit*. The truth of the Lower Right is found in how the individual holons functionally fit into the holistic system, how each is a strand in the interrelated web, which is the primary reality. So the system theorist is always talking collective systems—Gaia, or ecosystems, or interrelated webs of interaction, or the web of life, or information flow charts as objectively mapped, or planetary federations and global networks, and so on. All in objective and monological terms.

All of which is true, but all of which totally leaves out the Left-Hand dimensions. So the systems theorists admirably fight gross reductionism, but they are totally caught in the monological madness of subtle reductionism, which is the real root of the Enlightenment nightmare, as recent scholarship has made more than clear.

Q: Systems theory does claim to be a monological science.

KW: Yes, and we don't argue with them. They are entirely correct. And that says it all.

Q: Is the difference between the Lower Left and cultural fit, versus the Lower Right and functional fit—would this be the same as the two approaches to the Rain Dance?

KW: Yes, very much. The Lower-Left approach studies the community by becoming a participant observer, and attempts to *understand* it *from within*. Remember, the validity criteria in the Lower Left is mutual understanding. And this you attempt to do by becoming a participant observer. You enter the interior meaning of the community. And you understand this meaning only by understanding its *cultural fit*—by understanding what the meaning of the Dance is, based on how it fits into the vast background of cultural and linguistic meanings and practices. And the participant observer, the hermeneutic interpreter, might find that, as we said, the Dance is part of a sacred ritual with nature. That is its interior meaning, which you *understand* by immersing yourself in this cultural background which will give you the common worldspace or *common context* against which you can now make *adequate interpretations*.

Now the standard systems scientist, or standard systems theorist, is not primarily interested in any of that, in any of the interior meaning. Rather, systems theory is interested in the *function* that the Dance performs in the overall *social system*. What the natives *say* this Dance means is not so important. What is really important is that the Dance is part of an objective social system, and this objective system in many ways determines what the individual participants are doing. The *real* function of the Dance is to provide autopoietic self-maintenance of the system. The Dance is thus part of the social system's attempt to maintain its social integration, its *functional fit*. It provides a common ritual around which social cohesion is organized. And this can be determined by observing the Dance from an *objective* stance, an "empirical" or positivistic stance—objective and monological. You can even make a monological flow chart of it, which, believe me, is not how the natives experience the Dance at all!

Q: But I suppose that, again, you do not think that one of those approaches is right and the other wrong.

KW: They are both correct, in my opinion. One approaches the sociocultural holon from within, the other from without. One is how *subjects* fit together in cultural space—how you and I reach mutual understanding or *intersubjectivity*; the other is how objects fit together in physical space, in the total objective system, in *interobjectivity*. The one uses hermeneutics, or interpretation of interior *depth*; the other uses empirical-analytic observation, or objective analysis of observable *behavior*. "What does it mean?" versus "What does it do?"

Both are entirely valid; they are each the correlates of the other. They are, in fact, the Left and Right Hands of Spirit as it manifests in the collective. But, alas, these two academic disciplines don't get along too well with each other, a cat fight we might as well avoid.

Conclusion: The Four Faces of Spirit

Q: Okay, so we have four different quadrants, each with a different type of truth, a different voice. And each has a different test for its truth—a different validity claim, as shown in figure 7-1.

KW: Yes. All of these are valid forms of knowledge, because they are *grounded* in the realities of the four facets of every holon. And therefore all four of these truth claims can be redeemed, can be confirmed or rejected by a community of the adequate. They each have a different validity claim which carefully guides us, through checks and balances, on our knowledge quest. They are all falsifiable in their *own domains*, which means false claims can be dislodged by further evidence from that domain. (So let us gently ignore the claims of any one quadrant that it alone has the only falsifiable test there is, so it alone has the only truth worth knowing!)

And over the centuries and millennia, humanity has, by very painful trial and error, learned the basic procedures for these tests for truth.

Q: Which is why they're so important.

KW: Definitely. These truths are the golden treasure of a collective humanity, hard won through blood and sweat and tears and turmoil in the face of falsity, error, deception, and deceit. Humanity has slowly and increasingly *learned*, over a million-year history, to separate truth from appearance, goodness from corruption, beauty from degradation, and sincerity from deception.

And ultimately, these four truths are simply the four faces of Spirit as it shines in the manifest world. The validity claims are the ways that we connect to Spirit itself, ways that we attune ourselves to the Kosmos. As we said at the beginning of this discussion, the validity claims force us to confront reality; they curb our egoic fantasies and self-centered ways; they demand evidence from the rest of the Kosmos; they force us outside of ourselves! They are the checks and balances in the Kosmic Constitution.

And so, following these paths to truth, we fit with the flow of the Kosmos, we are delivered into currents that take us outside of ourselves, beyond ourselves, and force us to curb our self-serving ways, as we fit into ever deeper and wider circles of truth. From attunement to atonement to at-onement: until, with a sudden and jolting shock, we recognize our own Original Face, the Face that was smiling at us in each and every truth claim, the Face that all along was whispering ever so gently but always so insistently: please remember the true, and please remember the good, and please remember the beautiful.

And so the whispering voice from every corner of the Kosmos says: let truth and truthfulness and goodness and beauty shine as the seals of a radiant Spirit that would never, and could never, abandon us.

8

The Good, the True, and the Beautiful

Q: I want to move into the higher or transpersonal stages. But before we do that, you said there was a very simple way to summarize the four quadrants, their truths and validity claims—all of that, a simple way to summarize it!

KW: Yes. Here are the basic divisions: Everything on the Right Hand can be described in "it" language. Everything in the Upper Left is described in "I" language. And everything on the Lower Left is described in "we" language.

Q: I, we, and it. That's simple enough.

The Big Three

Q: These three languages are listed on the inside corners of figure 7-1 (page 149) and on figure 5-2 (page 119).

KW: Yes. It-language is objective, neutral, value-free surfaces. This is the standard language of the empirical, analytic, and systems sciences, from physics to biology to ecology to cybernetics to positivistic sociology to behaviorism to systems theory.

In other words, it is monological. It is a monologue with surfaces, with "its." It-language describes objective exteriors and their interrelations, observable surfaces and patterns that can be seen with the senses or their instrumental extensions—whether those empirical surfaces are "inside" you, like your brain or lungs, or "outside" you, like ecosystems. Even information scurrying through channels can be described in it-language. Information, in fact, is defined as negative entropy, which is about as it-ish as you can get. Your presence is not required.

I-language, on the other hand, *is* your presence, your consciousness, your subjective awareness. Everything on the Upper Left is basically described in I-language, in the language of interior subjectivity. The subjective component of any holon is the I-component.

Of course, this "I" or self or subjectivity becomes greater with greater depth—there is more subjectivity in an ape than in a worm—but the point is, this I-component in any case cannot be described in it-language. That would reduce the subject to a mere object, and we all instinctively resist this, and resist it aggressively. Subjects are understood, objects are manipulated.

Q: The lab technician . . .

KW: Yes, that was one example. Your "I" is treated as an "it." Whether these objects are singular, or whether they are collective strands in the great and wonderful web, people instinctively know that this reduction is dangerous.

Q: And the third language?

KW: The third language, we-language, is the Lower Left, the cultural or intersubjective dimension. The Upper Left is how "I" see the world; the Lower Left is how "we" see it. It is the collective worldview that we of a particular time and place and culture inhabit. These worldviews evolve, of course, and so we find archaic, magic, mythic, rational, which we have already briefly mentioned.

So at the very minimum, we have these three fundamental languages, and they are quite different, addressing these different domains. And the failure to differentiate these languages has caused an enormous amount of confusion.

Q: You call these "the Big Three."

KW: Yes. The Big Three—this is just a simplified version of the four quadrants, since both Right-Hand quadrants are objective exteriors ("it" or "its"). So for simplicity's sake, the four quadrants can usually be treated as three, as the Big Three—I, we, and it.

So when we say that every individual holon has four quadrants—or, in simpler form, the Big Three—we also mean that every holon has these aspects or facets that can only be described in these different languages. And the reason we can't reduce any of these languages to the others is the same reason we can't reduce any of the quadrants to the others. So we can only describe a holon adequately and fully if we *use all three languages,* so as to describe all of its quadrants, and not simply privilege one quadrant or one language, which, of course, is what usually happens.

Q: So, the Big Three. You have pointed out an enormous number of correlations with these three—such as morals, science, and art; or Plato's the Good, the True, and the Beautiful.

KW: Yes. Here are just a few of the various forms of the Big Three:

I (Upper Left):	consciousness, subjectivity, self, and self-expression (including art and aesthetics); truthfulness, sincerity.
We (Lower Left):	ethics and morals, worldviews, common context, culture; intersubjective meaning, mutual understanding, appropriateness, justness.
It (Right Hand):	science and technology, objective nature, empirical forms (including brain and social systems); propositional truth (singular and functional fit).

Science—empirical science—deals with objects, with "its," with empirical patterns. Morals and ethics concern "we" and our intersubjective world. Art concerns the beauty in the eye of the beholder, the "I." And yes, this is essentially Plato's the Good (morals, the "we"), the True (in the sense of propositional truth, objective truths or "its"), and the Beautiful (the aesthetic dimension as perceived by each "I").

The Big Three are also Sir Karl Popper's three worlds—objective (it), subjective (I), and cultural (we). And the Big Three are Habermas's three validity claims: objective truth, subjective sincerity, and intersubjective justness.

And, of enormous historical importance, the Big Three showed up in Kant's immensely influential trilogy—*The Critique of Pure Reason* (objective science), *The Critique of Practical Reason* (morals), and *The Critique of Judgment* (aesthetic judgment and art).

Dozens of examples could be given, but that's the general picture of the Big Three.

Q: Okay, I want to very briefly return to the fundamental Enlightenment paradigm—to the whole movement of "modernity" itself—and I want you to explain it in terms of the Big Three.

This is important, I think, because all of the "new paradigm" approaches claim to be overcoming the Enlightenment paradigm, and you keep saying that most of them are still thoroughly caught in it. You keep saying, for example, that systems theory is still following the Enlightenment paradigm. So, in terms of the Big Three, what was the fundamental Enlightenment paradigm?

KW: Oh, that part is fairly easy. The fundamental Enlightenment paradigm reduced all I's and all we's to mere its. The mainstream Enlightenment thought that all of reality could be captured in it-language, which alone was supposed to be "really real." So it reduced the Big Three to the big flat one of it-language. In other words, it reduced all of the Left-Hand dimensions to their Right-Hand correlates—subtle reductionism. Is this clear?

Q: It rejected art and morals in favor of science?

KW: Yes, in a sense. But the best way to get a handle on the negative aspects of modernity and the Enlightenment is to first understand their *positive* contributions. Each stage of development, remember, has a "dialectic of progress"—in plain language, every new development is good news, bad news. And we have been stressing some of the bad news, but this really doesn't make much sense without first understanding the corresponding good news. So I'd like to briefly talk about that good news of modernity, or else we get caught in merely anti-modernist rhetoric, which is unhelpful.

The Good News: Differentiation of the Big Three

Q: Okay, out of curiosity, can this "good news" of modernity also be stated in terms of the Big Three?

KW: Yes. According to theorists from Weber to Habermas, the good news of modernity was that it managed, for the first time in history, to fully *differentiate* the Big Three on a large scale. That is, to differentiate art, morals, and science; or self, culture, and nature. These domains were no longer fused with each other, no longer syncretically fused and confused.

We moderns take this differentiation so much for granted that we tend to forget what was involved in the previous mythological worldview, where art and science and religious morals were all indiscriminately fused. Not integrated, just fused! Big difference.

Here is a good example. This was a highly regarded and widely accepted "refutation" of Galileo's discovery of the moons of Jupiter: "There are seven windows given to animals in the domicile of the head, through which the air is admitted to the tabernacle of the body, to enlighten, to warm, and to nourish it. What are these parts of the *microcosm*? Two nostrils, two eyes, two ears, and a mouth. So in the heavens, as in a *macrocosmos*, there are two favorable stars, two unpropitious, two luminaries, and Mercury undecided and indifferent. From this and many other similarities in nature, such as the seven metals, etc., which it were tedious to enumerate, we gather that the number of planets is necessarily seven."

Q: Seven bodily orifices means that there *must* be seven planets.

KW: Yes. In other words, the subjective space and the objective space are so poorly differentiated that what happens in one must govern what happens in the other. Likewise, the subjective and the cultural space were still poorly differentiated, so that if you disagreed with Church religion, with the cultural background, then you were not just a *heretic*, you were also a political *criminal*—you could be tried by the Church for *heresy* and by the State for *treason*, because these had not yet been differentiated.

In other words, in all of these cases, the I and the we and the it domains were not very clearly differentiated. It is not that they were *integrated*; they simply were *not yet differentiated*! Huge difference.

Now I realize that there are certain "new paradigm" theorists who want to see this mythic indissociation as some sort of holistic heaven, but I think not one of them would actually enjoy living in that atmosphere. Most of their "new paradigm" notions would be immediately charged with both heresy and treason—a situation for which mythic-imperial cultures the world over devised numerous and unpleasant remedies. In other words, I think they are either not very informed or not very sincere about all this eulogizing of the previous mythic worldview.

Q: So the Enlightenment or modernity differentiated the Big Three for the first time.

KW: Yes, on any sort of large scale. Kant's three *Critiques* being the perfect example in this regard.

This was truly a quantum leap in human capacity. And this is why this extraordinary differentiation of the Big Three—the differentiation of art, morals, and science—has been called, by Weber and Habermas, the *dignity* of modernity, and I agree entirely. "Dignity" because the I and the we and the it domains could pursue their own knowledge without violent intrusions, or even punishments, from the other domains. You could look through Galileo's telescope without being burned at the stake. And all of that was good news indeed.

This differentiation of the Big Three would have an enormous number of beneficial gains. Here are just a few:

- The differentiation of self (I) and culture (we) contributed directly to the rise of democracy, where each self had a vote and was not simply subsumed by the dominator mythic hierarchy of the church or state. The rise of the liberal democracies on a widespread scale.
- The differentiation of mind (I) and nature (it) contributed to the liberation movements, including the liberation of women and slaves, because biological might no longer made noospheric right. The rise of liberal feminism and abolition as widespread and effective cultural movements.
- The differentiation of culture (we) and nature (it) contributed to the rise of empirical science and medicine and physics and biology, because truth was no longer subservient to state and church mythology. The rise of ecological sciences. And on and on and on . . .

Q: So liberal democracy, feminism, the ecological sciences, the abolition of slavery—all part of the good news of modernity, and all related directly to the differentiation of the Big Three. So what about the bad news?

The Bad News: Dissociation of the Big Three

KW: We have seen that one of the twenty tenets is that evolution proceeds by *differentiation* and *integration*. The good news of modernity was that it learned to *differentiate* the Big Three; the bad news was that it had not yet learned how to *integrate* them.

So the *dignity* of modernity began to slide into the *disaster* of modernity: the Big Three didn't just differentiate, they tended to *dissociate*!

Which was very bad news indeed. Because they were dissociated—that is, because the Big Three were not harmoniously balanced and integrated—they were ripe for plunder by the more aggressive approaches of the it-domain.

And thus, for various reasons that we can talk about if you want, the *rapid and explosive advances in the it-domain*—the spectacular advances in the empirical and technical sciences—began to overshadow and overrun the advances in the I and the we domains. Science began to crowd out consciousness and aesthetics and morals.

The great and undeniable advances in the empirical sciences from the

Renaissance to the Enlightenment made it appear that all of reality could be approached and described in it-language, in objective scientific terms. And conversely, if something couldn't be studied and described in an objective, empirical fashion, then it wasn't "really real." The Big Three were reduced to the "Big One" of scientific materialism, scientific exteriors and objects and systems.

And so the it-approaches began to *colonize* the I and the we domains. All knowledge had to be objective it-knowledge, and so all of reality began to look like a bunch of its, with no subjects, no consciousness, no selves, no morals, no virtues, no values, no interiors, no depths. The Left-Hand dimensions of I and we were collapsed into the Right Hand of the Big It.

Q: The Big Three collapsed into the Big One of flatland.

KW: Yes, exactly. And this project can initially seem to make a great deal of sense, precisely because every holon does indeed have an objective or Right-Hand aspect! Every component on the Left Hand has its empirical and objective and Right-Hand correlates (as you can easily see on figure 5-2). Even if I have an out-of-the-body experience, it registers some sort of changes in the empirical brain!

And since empirical and monological studies are *infinitely easier* than that messy interpretation and intersubjective hermeneutics and empathetic mutual understanding, it initially *made all the sense in the world* to restrict knowledge to the empirical domain, to the Right-Hand dimensions. This is completely understandable, and even noble in its own way.

And this is what the fundamental Enlightenment paradigm did. The basic knowledge quest was for the rational Ego to simply map or mirror the entire world in it-language. What Rorty has aptly called "the mirror of nature."

Q: The mapping paradigm, the representation paradigm.

KW: Yes, which just happened to leave out the mapmaker and the interiors altogether. Interpretation is not required; the world is simply obvious and "pregiven." And you simply map this pregiven world, the world of simple location. You map the Right-Hand world.

In this sweeping Enlightenment agenda, nature was held to be a perfectly *harmonious and interrelated system*, a great it-system, and knowledge consisted in patiently and empirically mapping this it-system in it-language.

And this great harmonious it-system, this perfectly "holistic" system, was the fundamental Enlightenment grid, the bedrock of the radical Enlightenment.

Q: But the "new paradigm" theorists strongly maintain that what was fundamental about the Enlightenment paradigm was its *atomism*. And that they are going to overcome that by replacing it with *holism*, or systems theory.

KW: Yes, they do say that, and it is deeply confused. I don't know who started that nonsense, but it is nonsense indeed.

Q: I've marked a section in *Sex, Ecology, Spirituality* where you introduce this topic, and I want to read it for the audience.

These theorists claim, for example, that the great "negative legacy" of the Enlightenment was its atomistic and divisive ontology. But atomism was *not* the dominant theme of the Enlightenment. As we will see in great detail—and as virtually every historian of the period has made abundantly clear—the dominant theme of the Enlightenment was the "harmony of an interlocking order of being," a systems harmony that was behind everything from Adam Smith's great "invisible hand" to John Locke's "great interlocking order" to the Reformers' and the Deists' "vast harmonious whole of mutually interrelated beings."

To give only a few examples now, Charles Taylor represents the virtually uncontested conclusion of scholars that "For the mainstream of the Enlightenment, nature as the whole interlocking system of objective reality, in which all beings, including man, had a natural mode of existence which dovetailed with that of all others, provided the basic model, the blueprint for happiness and hence good. The Enlightenment developed a model of nature, including human nature, as a *harmonious whole whose parts meshed perfectly*," and the "unity of the order was seen as an interlocking set calling for actions which formed a harmonious whole." As Alexander Pope would have it, speaking for an entire generation: "Such is the World's great harmony, that springs from Order, Union, full Consent of things; Where small and great, where weak and mighty, made to serve [each other], not suffer; strengthen, not invade; Parts relate to Whole; All served, all serving; nothing stands alone."

Already the *Encyclopédie*, bastion of Enlightenment thought, had announced that "everything in nature is linked together," and Lovejoy points out that "they were wont to discourse with eloquence on the perfection of the Universal System as a whole."

KW: Yes, the dominant theme of the Enlightenment was this great "web of life" conception, a great interlocking order of beings, each mutually interwoven with all others. There were indeed a few atomistic cranks, as there have been from Democritus forward. But they did not represent the dominant and central themes of the mainstream Enlightenment, as these scholars make abundantly clear.

Q: So what was the real "negative legacy" of the Enlightenment?

KW: Well, as we were saying, this Enlightenment web-of-life conception was indeed holistic and interwoven, but it acknowledged only holarchies in the Right-Hand dimensions. It did not acknowledge the holarchies in the Left Hand on *their own terms*. It *collapsed* the Big Three into the Big One—collapsed the interwoven I and we and it . . . into a flatland system of just interwoven its.

And so, of the Big Three of consciousness, culture, and nature, only sensory nature now was real, and all real knowledge must therefore be a mere *reflection* of that *only* reality. The reflection paradigm. The mirror of nature. The collapse of the Kosmos.

Systems theory isn't a cure for this negative legacy of the Enlightenment, it is an intrinsic part of that nightmare!

Q: Part of flatland.

KW: Yes, what Mumford called the disqualified universe. It-language is essentially value-free, neutral. It has *quantity*, but no *quality*. So if you describe everything in terms of quantities and objective exteriors and network processes and systems variables, then you get no qualitative distinctions whatsoever—you get the *disqualified* universe.

Recall that everything on the Right Hand has simple location, which can be *bigger* or *smaller* but not *better* or *worse*. Open-mindedness is better than narrow-minded bigotry, but a rock is not better than a planet. Because the Right Hand has some sort of physical extension, it can fairly easily be quantified and counted—1, 2, 3, 4, 5. You get amounts, not morals. And while seven might be *larger* than three, it is not *better*. And thus, if you start treating the entire world as an object—holistic or otherwise—you strip it of all value. You have disqualified the Kosmos.

And when you are done with that, and you pause to look around, you find to your utter horror that you are standing in a flat and faded universe, with no meaning, no depth, no interpretation, no beauty, no goodness, no virtue, and nothing sublime. Just a bunch of holistic its in functional fit.

Q: Whitehead's famous remark: "a dull affair, soundless, scentless, colorless; merely the hurrying of material, endlessly, meaninglessly."

KW: Yes, to which he added, "Thereby, modern philosophy has been ruined." More to the point, the modern lifeworld has been ruined. Once you go from Left to Right, from interior to exterior, from mind to brain, from compassion to serotonin, you go from value to valueless, from virtue to virtueless, from worth to worthless.

And if you think the great it-domain is the *only* reality, then you will maintain that all values and all virtues are "merely subjective." That is, they are personal choices not anchored in any sort of substantive reality. You will not see that depth is intrinsic to the Kosmos. You will not see that value is intrinsic to the Kosmos. You will not see that consciousness is intrinsic to the Kosmos.

All of that is lost, denied, erased from the shiny monochrome world that you now triumphantly inhabit. And once you have carefully scrubbed the Kosmos clean of consciousness and virtue and value, you should not be surprised if your own lifeworld starts to look completely hollow and empty. To *complain* about this state of affairs is like murdering your parents and then complaining you're an orphan.

The Task of Postmodernity: Integration of the Big Three

Q: So overcoming the negative legacy of the Enlightenment means what, exactly?

KW: Well, to begin with, to overcome the negative aspects of the Enlightenment is *not* to replace monological atomism with monological holism, with flatland systems theory. Atomism and systems holism are both Right-Hand reductionism, one gross, one subtle, but nonetheless.

Nor should we seek our solutions by *regressing* to mythic or magic indissociation of the Big Three, where self and culture and nature were *not yet* differentiated. We must preserve the dignity of modernity, even while we attempt to overcome the disaster of modernity. The dignity was differentiation; the disaster was dissociation.

So if modernity managed to differentiate the Big Three on a widespread scale, it is up to postmodernity to integrate them. The very currents of evolution—the twenty tenets—demand this differentiation and integration, and we today are on the cusp of that demand.

Q: The demand of postmodernity. The demand of an *integral* view.

KW: Yes. This does not mean that everything called "postmodern" is therefore an attempt at this integration. Much of postmodern thought is extremist, nihilistic, narcissistic. But the more authentic currents of postmodernity, as I use the term—from Hegel to Heidegger to Habermas to Foucault to Taylor—are trying to get some balance back into the picture, largely by trying to honor science and morals and aesthetics equally, and not simply reduce one to the other in an orgy of theoretical violence.

So that is exactly what we will want to watch for: ways to integrate mind and culture and nature in the postmodern world. Which is to say, ways to honor Spirit in all four quadrants, to recognize the four faces of Spirit—or simply the Big Three—and thus attune ourselves to, and situate ourselves in, and give blessings for: the Good, and the True, and the Beautiful.

The Spiritual Big Three

Q: This is where we begin to touch on spiritual themes. You have tied the Big Three in to the notions of Buddha, Dharma, and Sangha. Buddha was a great spiritual realizer, Dharma is the truth he realized, and Sangha is the community of those who are attempting this realization.

KW: Yes, those are the Big Three as consciousness evolution continues into the higher or superconscious or transpersonal domains. Of course, this is using the Buddhist terms; others will do as well.

Q: Let's briefly go over them one at a time.

KW: Figure 5-2 only lists some of the milestones in average or collective consciousness up to the present, up to modern rationality (marked "formop" and "vision-logic" in the Upper Left).

But beyond those stages there lie transrational or transpersonal or more properly spiritual developments, which I suppose we'll talk about soon enough. And my point is that these higher developments also proceed *in all four quadrants*. Or, in simplified form, in the Big Three. This higher evolution occurs in the I, and the we, and the it domains.

And the ultimate I is Buddha, the ultimate We is Sangha, and the ultimate It is Dharma.

Q: For example . . .

KW: We can put this in several different ways.

When you are ultimately *truthful* with yourself, you will eventually realize and *confess* that "I am Buddha," I am Spirit. Anything short of that is a lie, the lie of the ego, the lie of the separate-self sense, the contraction in the face of infinity. The deepest recesses of your consciousness directly intersect Spirit itself, in the supreme identity. "Not I, but Christ liveth in me"—which is to say, the ultimate I *is* Christ. This is not a state you are bringing into existence for the first time, but simply a timeless state that you are recognizing and confessing—you are being ultimately *truthful* when you state, "I am Buddha," the ultimate Beauty.

And the ultimate cultural fit or justness is, "We are all members of the Community of Spirit." *All sentient beings*—all holons in fact—contain Buddha-nature—contain depth, consciousness, intrinsic value, Spirit—and thus we are all members of the council of all beings, the mystical church, the ultimate We. Which is ultimate ethics, the ultimate Good.

And the ultimate objective truth is that all beings are perfect manifestations of Spirit or Emptiness—we are all manifestations of the ultimate It, or Dharma. Which is the ultimate Truth.

The ultimate I, the ultimate We, and the ultimate It—Buddha, Sangha, Dharma.

Q: This is why understanding the four quadrants, or just the Big Three, is so important for understanding higher or spiritual developments. This is why we need an "all-level, all-quadrant" approach.

KW: I think so, yes. Spirit manifests in all four quadrants equally, and so all four quadrants (or simply the Big Three) ought to be taken into account in order for the realization of Spirit to be full and complete and unbroken.

Q: Buddha?

KW: Well, we haven't talked about these higher stages of the Upper-Left quadrant, but the essential point is that they disclose deeper or higher stages of consciousness, to the point that the individual "I" discovers its prior identity with Spirit, however you wish to conceive that. The Buddhists would say that the individual "I" discovers its prior nature as Emptiness, so that the isolated and alienated "I" relaxes into the radically open and empty and transparent ground of all manifestation. The Sufis call it the Supreme Identity, the identity of the soul and Godhead. In Zen we have the True Self that is no-self, or no individual self at all, this primordial Emptiness that is the transparency of all Form. In Christianity, "Let this consciousness be in you which was in Christ Jesus."

The evidence is simply that the individual self discovers a primordial and unqualifiable Ground, so that its own self intersects the Ground of the Kosmos at large. The ultimate Self that is no-self: that is the Buddha-nature or Buddha-mind or Christ-consciousness in each and every sentient being. The ultimate self, the ultimate I, is Buddha. That's Upper Left.

Q: Dharma?

KW: Dharma refers to Spirit as an *objective fact,* as an objective State of Affairs. The ultimate It of the Kosmos is the Dharma, the Truth, the objective isness or suchness or thusness of all holons. The very Condition of all conditions, the very Nature of all natures, the very Itness of all holons—this is the Dharma, the objective Truth, which is that all holons, just as they are, in their Itness, are perfect manifestations of Emptiness, of Spirit. And that is the ultimate Truth!

Q: And Sangha?

KW: *Sangha* means gathering or community. It is the "we" of Spirit. In mystical Christian terms, it is the Church, the mystical communion of Christ. It is the intersubjective circle of realization, the culture of the Divine. The Lower Left.

The point is that, precisely because Spirit manifests equally in all four quadrants, or equally in the Big Three, then we can describe Spirit *subjectively* as one's own Buddha-mind—the "I" of Spirit, the Beauty. And we can describe Spirit *objectively* as Dharma—the "It" of Spirit, the ultimate Truth. And we can describe Spirit *culturally* as Sangha—the "We" of Spirit, the ultimate Good.

These four quadrants, or the Big Three, are all facets of Spirit, facets of Emptiness. When Emptiness manifests, it does so as subject and object, each of which can be singular or plural. And that gives us the four quadrants, or simply the Big Three. So Spirit can be described—and must be described—with all three languages, I and we and it.

Each of those domains evolves. Which means, each unfolds its spiritual nature more and more, and thus realizes its spiritual nature more and more. And in the uppermost reaches of that evolution, the I and the We and the It increasingly become transparent to their own true nature. They each radiate the glory of the Ground that they are.

And in that radiant awareness, every I becomes a God, and every We becomes God's sincerest worship, and every It becomes God's most gracious temple.

PART TWO

THE FURTHER REACHES OF SPIRIT-IN-ACTION

9

The Evolution of Consciousness

Q: An integral approach is all-level, all-quadrant. We've looked at all-quadrant. Now I'd like to look at all-level. I want to discuss the evolution of consciousness itself, from the lowest to the highest stages, matter to body to mind to soul to spirit.

KW: One of the simplified maps of this overall evolution is figure 9-1 (page 179). The traditional "matter, body, mind, soul, and spirit" are listed on the right, and the slightly more expanded version we will be using is given on the left.

But let me first emphasize that we are now discussing just the Upper-Left quadrant, the interior stages of consciousness evolution. So we are not discussing, for example, the correlative changes in the Upper-Right quadrant. We aren't discussing changes in the brain stem, the limbic system, the neocortex, in brain wave patterns (alpha, beta, theta, or delta states), nor hemispheric synchronization, nor neurotransmitter imbalances with pathology, and so on.

Likewise, we aren't looking specifically at the larger cultural currents (Lower Left) or social structures (Lower Right) that are inseparable from individual consciousness development, even though these other quadrants are crucially important. What good does it do to adjust and integrate the self in a culture that is itself sick? What does it mean to be a well-adjusted Nazi? Is that mental health? Or is a maladjusted person in a Nazi society the only one who is sane?

All of those are crucial considerations. A malformation—a pathology, a "sickness"—in any quadrant will reverberate through all four quadrants, because every holon has these four facets to its being. So a society with an alienating mode of production (Lower Right)—such as slave wages for dehumanizing labor—will reflect in low self-esteem for laborers (Upper Left) and an out-of-whack brain chemistry (Upper Right) that might, for example, institutionalize alcohol abuse as self-medication. Similarly, a cultural worldview that devalues women will result in a tendency to cripple individual female potential and a brain chemistry that could definitely use some Prozac.

And so on around the four-quadrant circle. Cripple one quadrant and all four tend to hemorrhage. But in this discussion we'll temporarily ignore all that—ignore family therapy, ignore brain chemistry and brain states, ignore cultural and social analysis—so we can focus on the Upper-Left quadrant itself and discuss the levels of consciousness as they appear in an individual.

But don't imagine those other quadrants are unimportant! In fact, we are fast approaching an understanding that sees individual "pathologies" as but the tip of an enormous iceberg that includes worldviews, social structures, and cultural access to depth. Individual therapy is not unimportant, but in many ways it's almost secondary. But for now, yes, we can definitely focus on the Upper Left. [Note: This chapter discusses the evolution of consciousness in abstract terms; the next two chapters give many concrete examples. So if this chapter seems abstract, please read on. . . .]

Higher Stages of Development

Q: A brief summary of the Upper Left is given in figure 9-1.

KW: Yes. If you compare this with figure 5-2, you'll see that figure 5-2 goes up to "vision-logic," which is stage 6 in figure 9-1. The reason is that figure 5-2 only lists the stages of average consciousness up to this point in collective history. It doesn't list any of the higher or deeper stages shown in figure 9-1.

Q: So the immediate question is, does this mean that somebody who lived in the past, say in the mythic-agrarian age, did not have access to these higher stages?

KW: No, not at all. In any given era, some people are above the average, some below. The Lower-Left quadrant is simply the average level at that point.

Every society has a certain *center of gravity*, we might say, around which the culture's ethics, norms, rules, and basic institutions are organized, and this center of gravity provides the basic cultural cohesion and social integration for that society.

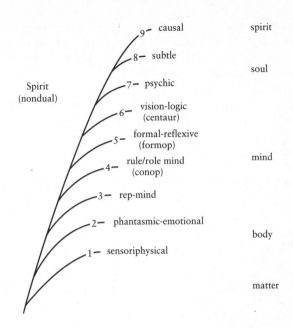

FIGURE 9-1. *The basic levels or spheres of consciousness.*

This cultural center of gravity acts like a magnet on individual development. If you are below the average level, it tends to pull you up. If you try to go above it, it tends to pull you down. The cultural center of gravity acts as a pacer of development—a magnet—pulling you up to the average expectable level of consciousness development. Beyond that, you're on your own, and lots of luck, because now the magnet will try to drag you down—in both cases, you're "outlawed."

Q: So there's a difference between average mode and most advanced mode for any culture.

KW: Yes, that's right. For example, say that five hundred years from now an anthropologist is studying America, and comes across the writings of Krishnamurti, and decides everybody in America was like Krishnamurti. This is silly, of course, but that is what many new age theorists are doing with past epochs. They take a representative of the *most advanced* mode of consciousness at the time—say, a shaman—and conclude that the *average mode* was also shamanic, that a hundred thousand years ago everybody was a shaman. Well, a hundred thousand years ago almost nobody was a shaman. A shaman—perhaps there was one per tribe—was a very rare and gifted soul, and most people did not share this shamanic awareness. In fact, most people were terrified of the power of the shaman, and they hadn't a clue as to the higher mode of awareness that the shaman accessed.

So yes, one of the things I have tried to do, in looking at these past epochs, is *first*, to define the average center of gravity—archaic, magic, mythic, rational, existential—and *second*, to look carefully at the most evolved individuals who rose above this average mode—often at great cost to themselves—and disclosed higher or deeper modes of awareness (the shaman, the yogi, the saint, the sage). These higher or deeper modes of awareness are what we are calling, in figure 9-1, the *psychic*, the *subtle*, the *causal*, and the *nondual* levels of superconscious development.

Ladder, Climber, View

Q: Those four higher stages of development are what I want to discuss. But are all of these stages really as "ladder-like" as figure 9-1 presents them? Are they really that discrete?

KW: Figure 9-1 does look like a ladder, which has confused many people, who think that developmental models are rigidly "linear." But this is a misunderstanding of what developmental models attempt to do.

The best way to think of figure 9-1 is as a series of concentric circles or nested spheres, with each higher level transcending and including its predecessor. It is an *actualization holarchy*, each stage of which *unfolds* and then *enfolds* its predecessors in a nested fashion. Figure 9-1 is simply one slice of that concentric pie. You could draw the whole figure as concentric circles, which is exactly what we did in figure 2-2, if you recall. In fact, figure 9-1 is simply a slightly expanded version of 2-2: *matter* (sensorimotor), *body* (emotional and vital), *mind* (rep-mind to vision-logic), *soul* (psychic and subtle), and *spirit* (causal and nondual). And, as we will see, this great holarchy of consciousness is the backbone of the world's great wisdom traditions, found universally and cross-culturally.

But more important, these nine levels or spheres only deal with a part of what is actually going on with consciousness development. Even if we call figure 9-1 a "ladder," there is still the *climber* of the ladder, and there are the *different views* from each rung, none of which is a simple linear step-by-step process!

Q: So ladder, climber, view. Start with the ladder—the levels or spheres.

Basic Levels: The Ladder

KW: These are depicted in figure 9-1. These nine levels or spheres are the *basic levels* of consciousness.

It's not necessary to remember any of these stages, but for reference, figure 9-1 includes: sensation and perception (sensoriphysical), impulse and image (phantasmic-emotional), symbols and concepts (rep-mind, short for representational mind), concrete rules (rule/role mind, or "conop," short for concrete operational), formal-reflexive ("formop"), and vision-logic (integrative). And then to the higher or transpersonal stages of psychic, subtle, and causal. (The paper on which the diagram is written is the "highest" stage, which is not really a stage at all but the nondual Ground of the whole display. Spirit is both the highest level—"causal"—and the Ground of all levels—"nondual.")

We can discuss all of those in a moment. They are just a few of the major milestones in consciousness development, stretching from matter to body to mind to soul to spirit. This list is by no means exhaustive, it's just a representative sample.

Q: Since these are actually nested spheres, why do you even draw them like a ladder?

KW: The ladder metaphor is useful because it indicates that the basic components of consciousness do emerge in fairly discrete stages, and if you destroy a lower rung, all the higher rungs go with it. Where the ladder metaphor fails badly is that each higher stage does not actually sit on top of the lower stage but rather *enfolds* it in its own being, much as a cell enfolds molecules which enfold atoms. As I said, it's a nested holarchy. But I myself often use the ladder metaphor because I want especially to emphasize the levels of growth involved.

For example, in development, images emerge before symbols, which emerge before concepts, which emerge before rules, and so on (as shown in figures 5-2, 5-3, and 9-1). This order is irreversible. No amount of social conditioning can alter that sequence, and we know of no societies where that order is altered. It is holarchical, it is cross-cultural, and as far as we can tell, there are no exceptions. Just as you must have words before you can have sentences, and you must have sentences before you can have paragraphs, so these basic holons build upon and incorporate their predecessors, which is why the order cannot be reversed: the higher rungs rest on the lower, and that is part of the usefulness of the ladder metaphor.

The Self: The Climber

Q: So those are the basic rungs in the ladder of awareness, or the holarchy of awareness.

KW: Yes. But that is not where the real action is, so to speak. Even if we rather crudely picture this development of basic levels as a "ladder," the real action involves the *climber* of the ladder. This climber is the *self*. Sometimes called the *self-system*. (Objectively, or in it-language, it is a self-system; subjectively, it is a person, a self, a self-sense. I use both.)

Q: So does this self or self-system have its own characteristics?

KW: Yes, the self, the climber, has specific characteristics and capacities that are *not found on the ladder itself.*

The reason is that the ladder is basically selfless—there is no inherent self-sense in any of its rungs. But the self appropriates these rungs, or *identifies* with them, and this generates various types of self-identity and various stages of self-growth, until the self falls off the ladder altogether in radical Emptiness—which is a bit ahead of the story. But the point is that the ladder and the climber of the ladder are quite different affairs!

As for the specific characteristics of the self, in *Transformations of Consciousness* I list these as identification, organization, will or attention, defense, metabolism, and navigation.

It's not necessary to go into those, but I might mention that "navigation," for example, involves the *four drives* that all holons, including the self-holon, possess—namely, agency and communion, self-transcendence and self-dissolution (regression). At each rung in the self's growth and development, it has these four basic choices about which way to go in its development. Too much or too little of any of those four drives, and the self gets into pathological trouble, and the *types* of pathology depend upon which of the nine basic rungs the trouble occurs at.

Q: So as the self negotiates or climbs these basic rungs, things can go wrong at any rung or stage.

KW: Yes, the self might be climbing the ladder of expanding consciousness, but the crucial point is that it can lose an arm or a leg at any rung!

If something goes wrong at any stage in this developmental unfolding, aspects of the self can get damaged or "left behind." This "getting left behind" is called repression, or dissociation, or alienation. The self can lose an arm or a leg at any stage, and this loss results in a pathology that is characteristic of the stage at which the loss occurred.

So we see pathology go from psychosis to borderline to neurosis to existential to spiritual, depending upon where the "accident" occurred.

I'll give some concrete examples of this in just a moment. The point for now is that not only are these basic levels growing and unfolding, but the self has to actually negotiate them, has to actually climb the developmental rungs of expanding awareness, and the self can take a bad step at any rung—and get very badly hurt.

A Fulcrum

Q: You call each of these steps a *fulcrum*.

KW: Yes, based on the very important line of research by such theorists and clinicians as Margaret Mahler, Otto Kernberg, Heinz Kohut, and Gertrude Blanck and Robert Blanck, not to mention Jung's pioneering work on individuation. A fulcrum simply describes the momentous process of differentiation and integration as it occurs in human growth and development.

One of Yogi Berra's malapropisms was: "When you come to a fork in the road, take it." Well, a fulcrum is simply a crucial fork in the developmental road, and the self has to deal with that fork. How it does so, in each case, influences its subsequent fate.

Q: So nine basic levels means there are nine corresponding fulcrums or steps for the self to negotiate.

KW: Yes, that's right. But it is really a very flowing and fluid affair. These milestones are just general markers along the way. The self must step up to each rung in the basic ladder, and that step is the fulcrum at that stage.

So every fulcrum has a 1-2-3 structure. *One*, the self evolves or develops or steps up to the new level of awareness, and it *identifies* with that level, it is "one with" that level. *Two*, it then begins to move beyond that level, or differentiate from it, or dis-identify with it, or transcend it. And *three*, it identifies with the new and higher level and centers itself there. The new rung is actually resting on the previous rungs, so they must be included and integrated in the overall expansion, and that *integration* or inclusion is the third and final subphase of the particular fulcrum. (These are summarized in fig. 9-2.)

So you can remember a fulcrum because all of them have this same 1-2-3 structure: identify, dis-identify, integrate; or fusion, differentiation, integration; or embed, transcend, include.

And if anything goes wrong with this 1-2-3 process, *at any rung*, then

Ladder	Climber	View
Basic rungs of aware-ness	Climber of the basic rungs	Changing view of self and other at each stage,
Once they emerge, they remain in existence as basic building blocks or holons of con-sciousness	Each step in the climb is a fulcrum, a 1-2-3 process of: (1) fusion/identifica-tion (2) differentiation/ transcendence (3) integration/inclu-sion	including a different: self-identity self-need moral sense

FIGURE 9-2. *Ladder, climber, view.*

you get a broken leg or whatnot. And the scar tissue of that disaster will depend on what the world looked like when you broke your leg. And generally, the lower the rung, the more severe the pathology.

New Worlds Emerge: Changing Views

Q: So we have the ladder and its basic rungs, and we have the self or the climber and its fulcrums—and that leaves the different views.

KW: Yes, at each rung in the developmental unfolding there is a dif-ferent view of the world—a different view of self and of others—a *differ-ent worldview.* The world looks different—is different!—at each rung in the developmental unfolding. As we have constantly seen, different worldspaces, different worlds, come into being as consciousness evolves—there is not simply a pregiven world that is monologically re-flected!

And here I would particularly emphasize that at each rung you get a different type of *self-identity*, a different type of *self-need*, and a different type of *moral stance* (see fig. 9-3). All of these are aspects of the different worlds that unfold at each rung or level or sphere of awareness.

So that's the thumbnail sketch. The ladder with its basic rungs of awareness; the climber with its fulcrums; and the different views of the world from each rung. Ladder, climber, view.

Q: So now some concrete examples.

KW: This model of consciousness development is based on the work of perhaps sixty or seventy theorists, East and West. (For a full discus-

LADDER Basic Level	CLIMBER	VIEW Maslow (self-needs)	Loevinger (self-sense)	Kohlberg (moral sense)
sensoriphysical	F-1	(physiological)	autistic / symbiotic	(premoral) / 0. magic wish
phantasmic-emotional	F-2		beginning impulsive	
rep-mind	F-3	safety	impulsive / self-protective	I. preconventional / 1. punishment/obedience / 2. naive hedonism
rule/role mind	F-4	belongingness	conformist / conscientious-conformist	II. conventional / 3. approval of others / 4. law and order
formal-reflexive	F-5	self-esteem	conscientious / individualistic	III. postconventional / 5. individual rights / 6. individual principles of conscience
vision-logic	F-6	self-actualization	autonomous / integrated	
psychic	F-7	self-transcendence		Kohlberg has suggested a higher, seventh stage:
subtle	F-8	self-transcendence		7. universal-spiritual
causal	F-9	self-transcendence		

FIGURE 9-3. *Some examples of ladder, climber, view.*

sion of this model, see *Integral Psychology.*) Figure 9-3 gives three of them: Abraham Maslow, Jane Loevinger, and Lawrence Kohlberg. I tend to use them as examples simply because they are so well known.

Q: So ground this for me. Take the example of the rule/role mind, and run across the table for each of the columns.

KW: The rule/role mind is the capacity that begins to develop in children around age seven or so. It is the capacity to form complex mental *rules* and to take social *roles*. The child begins to understand that he or she is not just a body with impulses and desires, but also a social self among other social selves, and the child must fit into these sociocultural roles. This is a difficult and trying period.

So the example works like this. As the *basic level* of the rule/role mind emerges, the child's self will face that new rung of awareness. So it must negotiate the *fulcrum* at that level, the 1-2-3 process of stepping up to a new level of awareness. So it will first step onto that rung—it will *identify* with that rung, identify with that capacity to follow the rules and the roles. In other words, it will identify with the rule/role mind (that's phase 1 in the fulcrum).

So the self at this point is a rule/role self. That is its central identity. That is its basic *self-sense*. It has a sense of conforming with these rules and roles, and therefore, as you can see in Loevinger's column, the self-sense at this stage is *conformist*. And for the same reason, the *basic need* of the self at this stage is for *belongingness*, which you can see in Maslow's column. And the self's *moral stance* at this stage therefore centers on the conventional approval of others, which you can see in Kohlberg's column.

Q: So that's across the table—ladder, climber, view.

KW: Yes, basically. This is all terribly simplified, I hope you understand, but that's the general idea.

Q: And if development continues?

KW: If development continues, then the self will eventually grow beyond these views, and *expand its awareness* once again. In order to do so, it has to step off its present rung, or dis-identify with it, or transcend it—this differentiation or transcendence is phase 2 of the fulcrum—and then *identify* with the next-higher rung—that's phase 3, which then begins the new fulcrum, and off we go again. Until, of course, developmental arrest sets in.

Q: Now about these changing views. They are generally stage-like themselves, correct? Loevinger and Kohlberg and Maslow give stages.

KW: Yes, but in a very general sense, which again has confused many critics. All developmentalists, with virtually no exceptions, have a stage-like list, or even a ladder-like list, a holarchy of growth and development—Kohlberg, Carol Gilligan, Heinz Werner, Jean Piaget, Habermas, Robert Selman, Erik Erikson, J. M. Baldwin, Silvano Arieti, Jenny Wade, Clare Graves, Robert Kegan, Susanne Cook-Greuter, John Broughton, Deirdre Kramer, Cheryl Armon—even the contemplative traditions from Plotinus to Padmasambhava to Chih-i and Fa-tsang. And they have this ladder-like holarchy because that is what fits their data. These stages are the result of empirical, phenomenological, and interpretive evidence and massive amounts of research data. These folks are not making this stuff up because they like ladders.

But there is an important point about these holarchies. Even in their stronger versions, such as Kohlberg's, the self at any given point in its development will tend to give around 50 percent of its responses from one level, 25 percent from the level above that, and 25 percent from the level below it. No self is ever simply "at" a stage. And further, there are all sorts of regressions, spirals, temporary leaps forward, peak experiences, and so on.

Q: So it's more of an average.

KW: Yes, it's a little bit like what we were saying about cultures—they have an average *center of gravity,* with some of their members falling above, and some below, that center.

In the same way, the self-system has its own center of gravity, so to speak, which means some components of its own interior can be above, some below, its own average awareness. The climber of the ladder, in other words, is more like a blob than a discrete entity—it sort of slops along the basic spheres of expanding consciousness. Development, as I said, is really a very fluid and flowing affair.

Pathology

Q: You said the self could get hurt at any rung—lose an arm or a leg.

KW: Yes, some aspects of the climber, the blob, can get stuck at lower rungs. And these little blobs get split off from the main blob and remain stuck at those lower stages.

Q: That's repression.

KW: In the most general sense, yes. We can use the moral stages as an example.

As you can see in figure 9-3, the lower and earlier stages of moral development are egocentric, narcissistic, me-only-oriented. They tend to be very impulsive and very hedonistic. These are Kohlberg's *preconventional* stages. The middle stages are called *conventional* because, as we just saw, they tend to be very conformist—my country right or wrong. The higher stages are called *postconventional*, because they begin to transcend conventional or conformist modes and center instead on universal pluralism and individual rights. Higher than this are the "post-postconventional," or spiritual stages, which we'll get to in a moment.

Now if for various reasons there is some sort of repeated and severe trauma during the earlier stages—say, in the preconventional stages, during the first three or four years of life—then here is what tends to happen:

Since the center of gravity of the self is at this preconventional, impulsive stage, then aspects of that *impulsive self* can be split off or *dissociated*. If this dissociation is extremely severe, then self-development will come to a screeching halt. But more often than not, the self will simply limp along down the road, dissociation and all. It will continue to develop, it will continue to climb the basic rungs in expanding awareness, however haltingly or however wounded. It might bleed all over the place, but it keeps climbing.

But an aspect of the *impulsive self* has nonetheless been split off and dissociated. That split-off aspect does *not* continue the climb, does not continue to grow and develop. Rather, it sets up shop in the basement. And it has a moral worldview of stage 1, since in this example that is where the dissociation occurred. It remains at moral stage 1, even as the rest of the self continues to grow and develop. So this split-off aspect is completely narcissistic, egocentric, self-absorbed, and altogether impulsive. It continues to *interpret* the world within the categories available to it at that primitive or archaic stage.

As the main blob of the self glops on up the ladder, this little blob remains behind, sabotaging the main self with neurotic or even psychotic symptoms. The main blob is getting a higher and wider view of the world, but the little blob is committed to its self-only, narcissistic, archaic worldview, its preconventional impulses and needs.

And the *internal conflict* between the main blob, which now might be at moral stage 3 or 4 or 5 . . . well, the internal conflict between the main blob and the little blob of stage 1 can be devastating. This is not an external conflict; it is a civil war. And that, by any other name, is pathology.

And, as we'll see, one of the things we want to do in development is to help end these civil wars.

States and Stages

Q: But does this mean that a person has to negotiate all the lower levels—say, levels 1 though 6—before the higher or spiritual stages can unfold?

KW: Not at all. Individuals can have a spiritual experience—a *peak experience* or an *altered state* of consciousness—at almost any stage of their growth. The basic levels, from the lowest to the highest, are potentials in every person's being. So you can tap into the higher dimensions under various conditions—moments of elation, of sexual passion, of stress, of dream-like reverie, of drug-induced states, and even during psychotic breaks.

But look what happens. Say a person is at Kohlberg's moral stage 3. And say they have an experience, an influx, of certain subtle-realm phenomena—perhaps an intense interior illumination. This can profoundly change a person's life and open them to new worlds, new dimensions, new modes of awareness.

And perhaps it can lead to an actual transformation or evolution or development in their consciousness. So if you give this person a moral-stage test, you might find that they have indeed transformed from moral stage 3 to . . . moral stage 4. There is nowhere else for them to go! Research has consistently shown that these stages cannot be bypassed, any more than you can go from an atom to a cell and bypass molecules. So a person at moral stage 3 who has a profound spiritual experience might be motivated to move to the next stage—in this case, to stage 4. They do not, under any circumstances, go from stage 3 to stage 7.

The genuinely spiritual or transpersonal stages of development (Kohlberg's stage 7 and beyond) depend for their development upon all of the previous developments in stages 6, 5, 4, 3, and so on. Each of those stages contributes something absolutely essential for the manifestation of stage 7. And although a person can have a peak experience of a higher dimension, the person's self still has to grow and develop and evolve in order to *permanently* accommodate to those higher or deeper dimensions, in order to turn an "altered state" into a "permanent trait."

Q: You have a quote from Aurobindo: "The spiritual evolution obeys the logic of a successive unfolding; it can take a new decisive main step only when the previous main step has been sufficiently conquered: even if certain minor stages can be swallowed up or leaped over by a rapid and brusque ascension, the consciousness has to turn back to assure itself that the ground passed over is securely annexed to the new condition; a greater or concentrated speed [of development, which is indeed possible] does not eliminate the steps themselves or the necessity of their successive surmounting."

KW: Yes. One of the great problems with the field of transpersonal psychology was that, in its beginning, it tended to focus on *peak experiences*. You had the ego, which was very bad, and you had anything that was not the ego, which was very good. In fact, the view was often that anything that is not the ego, is God. So you had: ego, booooooooo . . . not-ego, yayyyyyy.

And so you got this type of one-step transformation model: you go from the divisive and analytic and rational and nasty ego, straight to the expansive and liberated and cosmic God consciousness. Get rid of ego, you have God.

This naive notion of one-step transformation has now hooked up with a very flatland worldview, so that "cosmic consciousness" has come to mean simply that we go from the nasty Newtonian ego to the new-physics web-of-life one-with-Gaia self. We become one with flatland and we are enlightened and that saves the planet.

And, alas, it is nowhere near that simple. We don't go from an acorn to a forest in a quantum leap. There are stages in all growth, including human. These basic stages—I have listed nine of them, but that's just a summary—are based on a great deal of empirical, phenomenological, contemplative, and cross-cultural evidence. We are still refining these stages, and there are many questions that need to be answered. But this "one-step" transformation model now seems to be quite naive.

So people can have spiritual experiences and peak experiences and all sorts of altered states, but they still have to carry those experiences in their own structure. They still have to grow and develop to the point that they can actually accommodate the depth offered by the peak experiences. "States" still must be converted to "traits." You still have to go from acorn to oak if you are going to become one with the forest. So while "states" are important, "stages" are even more important.

Flatland Religion

Q: So a peak experience is kind of a "peek" experience; you get a glimpse of dimensions you might not be able to hold.

KW: Yes. And there's a related problem, which is actually more bothersome. *The ladder can develop way ahead of the self's willingness to climb it.* Technically, we say cognitive development is necessary but not sufficient for moral development.

This means, for example—and we all know cases like this—that a person can have access to level 5 rationality—they can be incredibly advanced intellectually—and still be at moral stage 1. Basically, a very bright Nazi. The ladder is much higher than the climber, who remains committed to the lower rungs. It's one thing to tap into a higher level; quite another to actually live there!

And the same thing can happen with spiritual experiences. People can temporarily access some very high rungs in the ladder or circle of awareness, but they refuse to *actually live* from those levels—they won't actually climb up there. Their center of gravity remains quite low, even debased.

And if they are to live up to their spiritual experiences, then they will have to grow and develop. They will have to start the developmental unfolding, the holarchical expansion, the actual inhabiting of the expanding spheres of consciousness. Their center of gravity has to shift—to transform—to these deeper or higher spheres of consciousness; it does no good to merely "idealize" them in theoretical chit-chat and talking religion.

So you can have a very powerful peak experience or satori. But then days, weeks, months later—where do you carry it? What happens to this experience? Where does it reside? Your actual self, your center of gravity, can only accommodate this experience according to its own structure, its own capacity, its own stage of growth. Spiritual experiences do not allow you to simply bypass the growth and development upon which enduring spiritual realization itself depends. Evolution can be accelerated, as Aurobindo said, but not fundamentally skipped over.

Q: There is such a resistance in "new paradigm" circles to this notion of stages.

KW: Yes, it's the same as the resistance to hierarchy or holarchy. Some of these objections are sincere and well-meaning, and we want to take these into account. But if you deny stages and holarchy, then you have to explain away the massive amounts of evidence that point to holarchical development, and that denial requires an aggressive ideology to explain why researchers keep finding these holarchies cross-culturally. I haven't seen any successful attempts to do this.

But some of the resistance is due to less sincere reasons. Many Americans don't like the idea of stages of anything, because we in America don't like the notion of degrees of depth. We are the living embodiment of flatland. The thought that somebody, somewhere, might be higher or deeper than me is simply intolerable.

So we prefer a "spirituality" that takes whatever level we are at and gives us a "one-step" process that will get us straight to God, instantly, like a microwave oven. We deny stages altogether and end up with a very flatland notion.

So various flatland paradigms are embraced, precisely because they do not demand actual transformation, just this "one-step" learning of the new paradigm, a sort of one-stop shopping. You just repeat that your being is one strand in the great web, and all is saved. And you aggressively *deny* there are any stages!

Q: I run into this antiholarchy prejudice all the time. It's very belligerent.

KW: The thing is, many of these "new paradigm" theorists have the same general goal: namely, the expansion of consciousness from the isolated and alienated individual to a type of global Kosmic consciousness, which includes the physiosphere and biosphere and noosphere all in one. So we can be very sympathetic with that overall goal. But these theorists are often unfamiliar with the numerous *interior transformations* that are necessary to go from an isolated bodyself to an all-inclusive Kosmic consciousness. They have a fine goal, but not much of a path. So we can agree with their goal, and help supply them with an actual path and its many important stages.

Freud and Buddha

Q: To return to the self's journey through this great spectrum of consciousness—we were talking about the fact that higher stages can be sabotaged by repressions at the lower stages—the internal civil wars.

KW: Yes, I think so. If the self represses or dissociates aspects of itself, it will have less potential left for further evolution and development. And sooner or later, this will drag development to a halt.

I don't mean to quantify this in such a simple way, but as a crude example, say the self at birth has 100 units of potential. And say that in its early growth it dissociates a small blob at moral stage 1—say it splits off 10 units of itself. It arrives at moral stage 2 with 90 units of its potential.

So the self is only 90 percent there, as it were. 10 percent of its awareness is stuck at moral stage 1, stuck in this little unconscious blob residing in the basement and using its 10 percent of awareness in an attempt to get the entire organism to act according to its archaic wishes and impulses and interpretations.

And so on, as growth and development continues. The point is that, by the time the self reaches adulthood, it might have lost 40 percent of its potential, as split-off or dissociated little selves, little blobs, little *hidden subjects*, and these little subjects tend to remain at the level of development that they had when they were split off.

So you have these little "barbarians" running around in the basement, impulsively demanding to be fed, to be catered to, to be the center of the universe, and they get very nasty if they aren't fed. They scream and yell and bite and claw, and since you don't even consciously know they are there, you *interpret* this interior commotion as depression, obsession, anxiety, or any number of neurotic symptoms that are completely baffling.

Q: So this would sabotage higher growth as well.

KW: Yes, the point is that these dissociated selves—these little hidden subjects that are clinging to lower worldviews—will take up a certain amount of your energy. Not only do they use energy themselves, your defenses against them use energy. And pretty soon, you run out of energy.

And yes, this will very likely sabotage higher or transpersonal development. Let's say it takes 65 units to get to the psychic or subtle level. If you only have 60 units left, you're not going to make it. This is why, in broad terms, we want to integrate Freud and Buddha, we want to integrate lower "depth psychology" with "height psychology."

And, in fact, we are at an extremely auspicious moment in human evolution, because, for the first time in history, we have access to both Freud and Buddha. The profound discoveries of the modern West—the whole notion of a psychodynamic unconscious, which is really found nowhere else—these discoveries can be integrated with the mystical or contemplative traditions, both East and West, for a more "full spectrum" approach.

Q: The point of uniting Freud and Buddha is that if you've got 40 units of your consciousness trapped in the basement, you're not going to make it to the higher levels, as a general rule.

KW: As a general rule. If you don't befriend Freud, it will be harder to get to Buddha.

So what we do with "depth" psychology—well, actually, that's misnamed. It's really shallow psychology, it's really dealing with the lowest and shallowest levels of the holarchy, *but for just that reason*, their narrow and narcissistic perspective can be so *crippling*.

But the point is, with "depth" psychology, we recontact these lower holons and expose them to consciousness, so that they can be released from their fixation and dissociation and rejoin the ongoing flow of consciousness evolution. They can get with the program, as it were, and cease this backward, reactionary, anti-evolutionary pull from the basement of your awareness. They can be reintegrated with your main self, so that your central self might now have 70 or 80 units of its potential available to it, and with that energy it can then continue its growth into the transpersonal.

And if that happens, and transpersonal growth is engaged with great intensity, then at some point you will climb not just up the ladder, but off it. As Zen would say, you're at the top of a hundred-foot pole, and yet you must take one more step. How do you step off a hundred-foot pole? You take that step, and where are you?

When you step off the ladder altogether, you are in free fall in Emptiness. Inside and outside, subject and object, lose all ultimate meaning. You are no longer "in here" looking at the world "out there." You are not looking at the Kosmos, you are the Kosmos. The universe of One Taste announces itself, bright and obvious, radiant and clear, with nothing outside, nothing inside, an unending gesture of great perfection, spontaneously accomplished. The very Divine sparkles in every sight and sound, and you are simply that. The sun shines not on you but within you, and galaxies are born and die, all within your heart. Time and space dance as shimmering images on the face of radiant Emptiness, and the entire universe loses its weight. You can swallow the Milky Way in a single gulp, and put Gaia in the palm of your hand and bless it, and it is all the most ordinary thing in the world, and so you think nothing of it.

10

On the Way to Global: Part 1

Q: We hear a lot about a "global perspective" or "global awareness"—think globally, act locally. Most of the "new paradigm" approaches emphasize that we are living in a global village, a planetary network, and we need a global and systems map to reflect that global territory.

KW: A global map is one thing. A mapmaker capable of living up to it, quite another.

A global perspective is not innate; the infant is not born with it; hominids did not possess it. A global perspective is a rare, elite, extraordinary perspective of great depth, and there are relatively few individuals who actually make it to that depth (greater depth, less span). So it is in understanding the evolution and emergence of global consciousness that we can actually begin to implement "new paradigms," if that is what is desired.

Q: You said that the new paradigm thinkers often have a goal of Kosmic consciousness, but not much of a path to it.

KW: Yes. There is little in the global or systems map about how this *interior development* in the mapmaker occurs. And yet that is by far the most important issue. So the global or systems map is actually of rather limited use—it's just a Right-Hand map—and yet the crucial issue is the Left-Hand development: how to get individuals to develop up to the point where they can actually inhabit a global awareness in the first place.

It is then from within and beyond this global perspective that genuinely spiritual or transpersonal states emerge, as Spirit begins to recognize its own global dimensions.

Q: That's what I want to talk about. We discussed this in abstract terms—ladder, climber, view. But I would like to look at concrete examples of this development on the way to global, evolution toward the global I. Let's climb the entire ladder! Starting at the start.

The Primary Matrix

KW: For the moment, let's call birth the start. The infant at birth is basically a sensorimotor organism, a holon containing within it cells, molecules, atoms—transcending and including those subholons.

But the infant doesn't possess language, or logic, or narrative capacity; it cannot grasp historical time, or orient itself in interior psychological space. It is basically identified with the sensoriphysical dimension, or stage 1 in figure 9-1. As Piaget put it, "The self is here material, so to speak."

Of course, the self isn't actually or merely physical, but it is still predominantly oriented to the lowest and most basic dimension of all, the material and sensorimotor. In fact, the self is largely *identified* with the sensorimotor world, so much so that it can't even distinguish between inside and outside. The physical self and the physical world are *fused*— that is, they are *not yet differentiated*. The infant can't tell the difference between inside and outside—chair and thumb are the same.

This early fusion state is often called the "primary matrix," because it is the fundamental matrix that will be differentiated in subsequent development. It is also referred to as primary autism, primary narcissism, oceanic, protoplasmic, adualistic, indissociated, and so on.

We saw that every fulcrum is a 1-2-3 process: the self first *identifies* with that rung, or is in fusion with that rung; then it *differentiates* from or transcends that rung; then *integrates* and includes it.

This primary matrix is simply phase 1 of fulcrum-1. The self is in *fusion* with the sensorimotor world, both internal and external.

Q: This primary fusion is beyond the duality of subject and object?

KW: No, it's beneath it. Many Romantics like to see this primary fusion state as some sort of prefiguration of cosmic consciousness, mystical unity consciousness, nonduality, and so on. But this primary fusion state doesn't transcend subject and object; it simply can't tell the difference between them in the first place. It's primary narcissism, where the physical world is swallowed by the autistic self—the infant is all mouth, the world is all food. It's a physical affair.

There is nothing particularly spiritual about this state. It cannot take the role of other; it is locked into its own egocentric orbit; it lacks inter-subjective love and compassion. Because it can't tell the difference between physical inside and physical outside, this fusion state is fairly "wide" but extremely *shallow*. There is nothing to impede it horizontally, but vertically it is stuck in the basement. And flatland theorists focus on this horizontal expanse—subject and object are one!—and thus they tend to miss the crucial factor—there is no vertical expanse at all, and thus this state is not more free, but less free, than subsequent developments. This is the shallowest and most cramped consciousness you can imagine!

And finally, this early fusion state cannot take the role of other. That is, it doesn't have the cognitive capacity to put itself in the shoes of others, and see the world through their eyes—it is stuck in only immediate impressions of the sensorimotor dimension, profoundly narcissistic. So it can't display anything resembling actual love—you can't truly love somebody until you can understand their perspective and perhaps even choose to put it above your own. So there is no compassion here, no genuine love, no tolerance and benevolence and altruism.

So in many ways, this fusion state is the complete antithesis of genuine spiritual awareness and compassion and love. Of course, we cannot rule out the fact that the infant has access to some types of spiritual states. As we said, altered states and peak experiences can occur at almost any stage of development. Nonetheless, even if the infant has a fluid access to some types of spiritual states, those states still must be converted into permanent traits if spirituality is to become a mature, stable, constant awareness, capable of taking the role of other and being reflected in genuine love and care. So once again, "states" might be important, but "stages" are even more important.

Birth Trauma

Q: What about the previous intrauterine state? Do you include that in your model?

KW: The evidence centering on the intrauterine state and the birth trauma is highly controversial. But I suspect some of it is legitimate, so I refer to these even earlier developments as fulcrum-0.

Like all fulcrums, it has that essential 1-2-3 structure: an initial fusion with the womb, then a painful process of differentiation (the actual birth trauma), then a period of consolidation and integration as a differentiated organism (post-uterine). At that point, the infant self has then begun fulcrum-1—it is now *fused* with the physical world in and around it.

Stan Grof has written extensively on these subphases of the birth process, which he calls the Basic Perinatal Matrices. Stan's research suggests that trauma at any of these subphases can result in a pathological complex. And conversely, under intense stress, or with certain types of meditation, or certain drugs, the self can regress to this fulcrum and relive its various subphases and traumas, which tends to alleviate the pathology. Stan's evidence is immensely suggestive, and if you are interested in this area, I recommend you start there.

The False Self

Q: So a trauma in the birth process could form a pathological complex that would affect subsequent development.

KW: Yes, but that is just one example of a much more general phenomenon, which is that a trauma at *any* of the fulcrums can form a pathological complex which "infects" all subsequent development. As we were saying, the self can take a bad step at any of the nine or so fulcrums, and the type of pathology that results depends upon the rung where the accident occurred.

Q: How so?

KW: As the self steps up to each new rung in expanding awareness, it faces that 1-2-3 process at each rung. And something can go wrong in any of those subphases—in the fusion subphase, the differentiation subphase, the integration subphase. The self can remain in *fusion*, or remain stuck at that stage—we have a *fixation*, a subphase 1 problem. Or the self can fail in the *differentiation* or subphase 2 of the fulcrum—it can fail to differentiate cleanly and clearly, and so it fails to establish a responsible boundary at that level. Or the self can fail in the *integration* or subphase 3 of the fulcrum—it doesn't integrate and include the previous level, but alienates and dissociates and represses it. It doesn't transcend and include, it dissociates and represses.

Once this accident occurs—once we get a "subphase malformation" at any level—then this pathology forms a *lesion in consciousness* that tends to infect and distort all subsequent development. Like a grain of sand caught in a developing pearl, the malformation "crinkles" all subsequent layers, tilts and twists and distorts them.

Q: The climber has lost an arm or a leg.

KW: Yes, there are now aspects of the self's being that it doesn't own or admit or acknowledge. It starts to hide from itself. In other words, the self begins lying to itself. A *false self system* begins to grow over the *actual self*, the self that is really there at any given moment, but is now denied or distorted or repressed. Repression, basically, is being untruthful about what is actually running around in your psyche.

And thus the *personal unconscious* begins its career. As we earlier put it, this unconscious is the locus of the self's lie. As we also put it, aspects of awareness are split off—"little blobs," little selves, little subjects, are forced into the subterranean dark. These little blobs remain at the level of development they had when they were split off and denied. They cease to grow. They remain in fusion with the level where they were repressed. They hide out in the basement, and the door to that basement is guarded by the lie.

So aspects of your potential, sealed off by the dissociation, begin eating up your energy and your awareness. They are a drain. They sabotage further growth and development. They are dead weight, the weight of a past age that should have been outgrown. But instead, protected and sheltered by the lie, they live on to terrorize.

Q: And therapy would address that lie, or untruthfulness.

KW: Interpretive therapies—Freudian to Jungian to Gestalt to cognitive—they attack the lie, yes. In all the ways that we already discussed (see chapter 7).

Q: So as we run through the stages of expanding awareness, we want to watch these fulcrums for anything that can go wrong, because that is what actually prevents the emergence of global awareness, correct?

KW: Yes, that's the central point.

Fulcrum-1: The Hatching of the Physical Self

Q: So we left off this developmental story with fulcrum-1.

KW: Yes, the self is in *fusion* with the sensorimotor world—the primary fusion state or primary narcissism. The self's identity is *physiocentric*, fused with the material dimension, with the physiosphere.

But somewhere around 4 months, the infant will begin to differentiate between physical sensations in its body and those in the environment. The infant bites a blanket and it does not hurt; bites its thumb and it does. There is a difference, it learns, between blanket and thumb. So it begins the *differentiation* phase of fulcrum-1, which is usually completed sometime in the first year, usually around 5–9 months, according to Margaret Mahler, a pioneer in this research.

She calls this the "hatching" phase—the physical self "hatches" out of this primary fusion matrix. (In other words, this hatching is phase 2 of fulcrum-1.) This hatching is the "real birth," so to speak, of the physical self.

Melanie Klein was particularly interested in this earliest of differentiations, as were Edith Jacobson, and René Spitz, not to mention Margaret Mahler. Interesting that women seem to have a particularly acute feel for these early developments, no?

Anyway, this hatching is the birth of the physical self. If the self *fails* in this differentiation—if it remains stuck or in fusion with the primary matrix—then it can't tell where its body stops and the chair begins. It is open to what is called *adualism*, which is one of the primary characteristics of *psychosis*. And that is why research consistently indicates that many of the really severe pathologies—psychosis, schizophrenia, severe affective disorders—have part of their etiology in problems with this early fulcrum, fulcrum-1. So we can start to see that a *type* of pathology is associated with the *level* at which the disruption occurs.

Q: Some of these are listed in figure 10-1 (page 201).

KW: Yes. With *psychosis*, there is severe reality distortion, marked especially by adualism, or the incapacity to establish even the physical boundaries of the self (fulcrum-1); there are often hallucinatory primary process images and thoughts; narcissistic delusions of reference; consciousness fails to seat in the physical body; thoughts of self and other are confused. There may also be an influx of subtle or transpersonal awareness, but this is fairly rare and is often badly distorted as well.

Fulcrum-2: The Birth of the Emotional Self

Q: But if all goes well with fulcrum-1?

KW: If this fulcrum is negotiated relatively well, then the infant will begin fulcrum-2, the emotional-phantasmic fulcrum. Because the infant has completed fulcrum-1, it has established the realistic boundaries of its *physical* self, but it still has not yet established the boundaries of its *emotional* self. So it can differentiate its physical self from the physical environment, but it still cannot differentiate its emotional self from the emotional environment. And this means that its emotional self is fused or identified with those around it, particularly the mother. (This is the initial fusion phase of fulcrum-2.)

And just as there was nothing "deep" or "profound" about the previous physical fusion state, there is nothing deep or profound about this

Basic Spheres of Consciousness		Corresponding Fulcrums	Characteristic Pathologies	Treatment Modalities
9	causal	F-9	causal pathology	formless mysticism
8	subtle	F-8	subtle pathology	deity mysticism
7	psychic	F-7	psychic disorders	nature mysticism
6	centauric (vision logic)	F-6	existential pathology	existential therapy
5	formal reflexive (formop)	F-5	identity neuroses	introspection
4	rule/role (conop)	F-4	script pathology	script analysis
3	rep-mind	F-3	psychoneuroses	uncovering techniques
2	phantasmic-emotional	F-2	narcissistic-borderline	structuring-building techniques
1	sensoriphysical	F-1	psychoses	physiological/pacification
0	undifferentiated or primary matrix	F-0	perinatal pathology	intense regressive therapies

FIGURE 10-1. *Spheres of consciousness correlated with fulcrums, pathologies, and treatments.*

emotional fusion state, even though it, too, sounds like a nice "holistic oneness with the world." But in fact, researchers are virtually unanimous in pointing out that this state is still extremely *egocentric* or *narcissistic*. As Mahler puts it, the self at this stage "treats the world like its oyster." Precisely because it cannot differentiate itself from the emotional and vital world around it, the infant self treats the world as an *extension of itself*—which is the technical meaning of "narcissism."

So this type of severe narcissism—which is normal, not pathological, at this stage—does not mean that the infant thinks selfishly about only itself, but on the contrary, it is incapable of thinking about itself. It is unable to differentiate itself from the world, the emotional world, and so it thinks that what it is feeling is what the world is feeling, that what it wants is what the world wants, that what it sees is what the world sees. It plays hide and seek in plain view; it thinks that if it can't see you, you can't see it; its own perspective is the only perspective in existence.

In other words, the self is here a purely ecological self, a biospheric self, a libidinal self, a natural-impulsive self. It is one with, in fusion with, the entire vital-emotional dimension of being, *both internal and external*. It is pushed and pulled by the currents of its vital life, and it does not differentiate itself from the ecological currents of existence. Its identity is *biocentric* or *ecocentric*, fused with the biosphere within and without.

And precisely because it is embedded in nature, in biology, in impulse, in the vital-emotional sphere, it cannot rise above that embeddedness and see that its perspective is not the only perspective in existence. *Biocentric* is extremely *egocentric*, as we will constantly see. It might have a certain horizontal expanse, but very little vertical depth, which is why it is so shallow and narcissistic (despite the use to which this emotional fusion has been put by Romantics in a search for any sort of "union"; I sympathize with their search, but I believe they are mistaken to look for it here [see chapter 16]).

Q: So the self at this stage has no sturdy emotional boundaries.

KW: That's right. Technically, we say self and object representations are still fused. This contributes to the general "magical" and narcissistic atmosphere that is so prevalent at this stage.

But somewhere around 15–24 months, the *emotional self* begins to differentiate itself from the *emotional environment*. Mahler actually calls this "the psychological birth of the infant." The infant is actually "born" as a separate emotional and feeling self at this stage. (The self has moved from the initial fusion phase of fulcrum-2 to the middle or differentiation phase.) The infant starts to wake up to the fact that it is a separate self existing in a separate world. It has hit the "terrible twos."

Q: Which is different from "hatching."

KW: Yes. Fulcrum-1 is hatching, or the birth of the physical self. Fulcrum-2 is the birth of the emotional self. With fulcrum-2, a truly separate-self sense awakens, with all the joy and all the terror that involves.

Q: Many theorists take this as the beginning of alienation, of really profound alienation. They have called it the basic fault, the basic default, the basic dualism, the split between subject and object, the beginning of fragmented awareness. . . .

KW: Yes, I know. An extraordinary amount has been read into this differentiation and the "loss" of the previous emotional fusion. It's supposed to be the ejection from a primal paradise, the beginning of massive alienation, the start of the human tragedy, the beginning of Paradise Lost. I think it also causes tooth decay, but I'm not sure.

The basic problem is that most of these theorists simply confuse *differentiation* with *dissociation*. Differentiation is a necessary and unavoidable part of all evolutionary growth and development, the counterpart to reaching higher integration, as when an acorn differentiates and integrates in order to become an oak. But these theorists look at any differentiation, not as prelude to higher integration, but as a brutal disruption of a prior and wonderful harmony, as if the oak were somehow a horrible violation of the acorn.

They then look back nostalgically to the days of wonderful acornness, prior to the differentiation, and wring their hands and gnash their teeth and moan the loss of paradise. They dramatically overidealize this primitive lack of differentiation. Just because the self is not aware of suffering does not mean it has a positive presence of spiritual bliss. *Lack* of awareness doesn't mean *presence* of paradise!

Q: But the Romantics assume otherwise about this early lack of differentiation. They read many positive virtues into it, so they must see the loss of this fusion as lamentable.

KW: Yes, they confuse fusion with freedom. But fusion is imprisonment; you are dominated by all that you have not transcended. But of course that transcendental growth is difficult and perilous and painful.

The manifest world is a brutal place, and as humans become aware of this, they suffer. The manifest world, the world of samsara, is an alienated and alienating place. And as the infant becomes vaguely aware of that, it suffers horribly. And yes, this is painful, but it's called waking up.

It's like frostbite disease. First there is no feeling at all; everything seems fine, you're in a paradise of no pain. You're diseased, you just don't know it. Then it thaws out, and feelings and emotions emerge, and it hurts like hell. These theorists confuse "hurts like hell" with the disease itself.

No, fulcrum-2 is simply starting to wake up to the disease of samsara. To the fact that, as a separate and sensitive emotional being, you are open to the slings and arrows of outrageous fortune. You are going to be put into a world of pain and suffering and nightmarish hell, and you have two, and only two, choices: retreat to the prior fusion, the prior frostbite, where there was no awareness of this alienation, or continue growth and transcendence until you can transcend this alienation in spiritual awakening.

But the retro-Romantic theorists simply eulogize the prior frostbitten state, and see that as a prefiguration of the Divine awakening, as being itself a type of unconscious Heaven. But the fusion state is not unconscious Heaven, it's unconscious Hell. With fulcrum-2, that hell becomes conscious, that's all. It's a big advance.

Q: Even though fulcrum-2 is a rather "unhappy" development.

KW: Bittersweet, yes. But the previous state is the state of numbness, not nonduality; ignorance, not bliss. My dog doesn't writhe in angst either, but liberation does not consist in reawakening dog consciousness. Or a "mature form" of dog consciousness.

No, when we awaken as a separate emotional self, with all the joy and all the terror that involves, we have actually *transcended* the previous fusion state. We have *awakened* to some degree. We have gained *more depth* and more consciousness, and that has its own intrinsic value, intrinsic worth. But, like all stages of growth, there is a price to be paid for every increase in consciousness. The dialectic of progress.

Q: So if everything goes relatively well at this fulcrum-2?

KW: Well, let me first say that if things go poorly at this fulcrum— that is, worse than the normal mess this fulcrum is anyway—then the self either remains in *fusion* at this emotionally narcissistic stage (the so-called narcissistic personality disorders), or the differentiation process begins but is *not resolved* and there is some sort of *dissociation* (the so-called borderline disorders). We find exactly this general classification and etiology in Kohut, Masterson, Kernberg, Mahler, Stone, and Gedo, to name a few.

In either case, there are no realistic *emotional boundaries* to the self. In the narcissistic and borderline syndromes, the individual therefore *lacks a sense of cohesive self*, and this is perhaps the central defining characteristic of these pathologies. The self either treats the world as an extension of itself (narcissistic), or is constantly invaded and tortured by the world (borderline). This level of pathology is called borderline because it is borderline between psychosis and neurosis. It's sometimes called "stably unstable." The growing self has taken a painful spill at the second big fork in the road.

Fulcrum-3: The Birth of the Conceptual Self

Q: But if all goes well at fulcrum-2?

KW: If all goes relatively well, then the self is no longer *exclusively* identified with the emotional level. It begins to transcend that level and identify with the mental or conceptual self, which is the beginning of fulcrum-3 and the representational mind.

The representational mind is similar to what Piaget called preoperational cognition. As I use it, the rep-mind consists of *images, symbols,* and *concepts.* You can see all of these listed on figure 5-3, for example.

Images begin to emerge around 7 months. A mental image looks more or less like the object it represents. If you close your eyes and picture a dog, it looks pretty much like a real dog. That's an *image.* A *symbol,* on the other hand, represents an object but does not look like the object at all, which is a much harder cognitive task. The symbol "Fido" represents my dog, but it doesn't look like my dog at all. Symbols emerge during the second year, usually with words like "ma" or "dada," and develop very rapidly. Symbols dominate awareness from 2 to 4 years, roughly.

At which point concepts begin to emerge. Where a simple symbol represents a single object, a *concept* represents an entire class of objects. The word "dog" represents all dogs, not just Fido. An even harder task. Concepts dominate awareness from 4 to 7 years. Of course, these are all basic units or holons of consciousness, so once they emerge in awareness, they will remain as basic capacities available to consciousness.

But it is when concepts emerge that a particularly *mental self*, a conceptual self, begins to emerge. When the self begins to identify with this conceptual mind, we have fulcrum-3. The self is now not just a bundle of sensations and impulses and emotions, it is also a set of symbols and concepts. It begins to enter the *linguistic* world, the noospheric world, and this, to put it mildly, changes everything. It has gone from the physiosphere of fulcrum-1 to the biosphere of fulcrum-2, and now it begins to especially enter the noosphere with fulcrum-3.

Every Neurosis Is an Ecological Crisis

Q: What would you say is the single most important thing about this new linguistic self?

KW: This new self exists in the noosphere, and the noosphere can repress the biosphere. Individually, this produces neurosis; collectively, ecological crisis.

In other words, the linguistic world is indeed a *new world*, a new worldspace. Here the self can think of the past and plan for the future (it is temporal and historical); it can begin to control its bodily functions; it can begin to picture things in its mind that are not actually present in its senses. Because it can anticipate the future, it can worry and suffer anxiety, and because it can think about the past, it can feel remorse and guilt and regret. All of these are part of its new worldspace, the linguistic world, the noosphere.

And precisely because it exists in this new and wider world, the conceptual mind can repress and dissociate its lower impulses. That is, precisely because the noosphere transcends the biosphere, it can not only transcend and include, it can repress and distort and deny. Not just differentiate, but dissociate. Both individually and at large. Individually, neurosis; at large, ecological crisis.

Q: For the moment, stick with the individual, or we'll get way off base.

KW: On an individual level, the result of the noosphere repressing the biosphere is called psychoneurosis, or simply neurosis. The mind can repress nature, both external nature (eco-crisis) and internal nature (libido).

Psychoneurosis—or just *neurosis*—in the technical sense means that a fairly stable, cohesive, mental self has emerged, and this mental-conceptual self (the ego) can repress or dissociate aspects of its bodily drives or impulses, and these repressed or distorted impulses—usually sexual or aggressive—therefore appear in disguised and painful forms known as neurotic symptoms.

In other words, every neurotic symptom is a miniature ecological crisis.

Q: So it's interesting that repression proper and the classical neuroses come into being with fulcrum-3.

KW: In a general sense, yes. You see, in the previous borderline conditions, repression proper is not so much in evidence—the self isn't strong enough to repress anything! The self can't repress its emotions, but rather, it is completely overwhelmed by them, lost in them, flooded by them. There's no "repressed unconscious" to dig up because there is no extensive repression in the first place, which is why these conditions are often referred to as "pre-neurotic."

So therapies aimed at the borderline conditions (fulcrum-2) are actually known as *structure building* therapies—they help the fragile self to differentiate and stabilize and build boundaries, as opposed to the *uncovering therapies* of the neurotic level (fulcrum-3), which aim at relaxing the repression barrier and recontacting the impulses and emotions and felt-sense that the stronger neurotic self has repressed. In fact, one of the aims of structure-building therapy is to get the borderline "up to" a capacity for repression!

Q: So neurosis is an improvement!

KW: Yes, and then you have to deal with *that*. The point is, as Vaillant demonstrated, the defense mechanisms themselves exist in a hierarchy of development. A typical fulcrum-1 defense mechanism is projective identification, where self and other are largely undifferentiated. Typical fulcrum-2 defense mechanisms include splitting and fusion (fusion of self and object representations and a splitting of all-good and all-bad objects). Repression proper is typical of fulcrum-3 defense mechanisms, and this is said to eventually give way to the "healthiest" defense of all, sublimation—which is just a psychoanalytically decontaminated word for transcendence.

Q: So defense mechanisms are holarchically arranged.

KW: In many ways, yes. Defense mechanisms, when operating naturally and normally, are like a psychological immune system. They help maintain the integrity and stability of the self boundary, and they toss out any invaders that threaten the self system.

But, as always, there can be too much of a good thing. Defense mechanisms can become an auto-immune disorder—the self starts attacking itself, eating itself up. The defending army turns into a repressive state police. The self starts defending against pain and terror by incarcerating its own citizens. It seals off its own potential. It closes its eyes. It starts to lie. No matter what the "level" of this lie—from splitting and fusion and projection to repression and reaction formation and displacement—the self hides from itself, lies to itself, becomes opaque to itself.

In place of the actual self, there grows up the false self. Beginning as early as fulcrum-1 (some would say fulcrum-0), the fledgling and grow-ing self can begin to distance itself from aspects of its own being, aspects that are too threatening, too painful, or too disruptive. It does so *using the defense mechanisms available to it at its own level of development.* The psychotic lie, the borderline lie, the neurotic lie, and so on. The "unconscious" in the most general sense is simply the locus of the run-ning lie—the layers of deception, layers of insincerity, hiding the actual self and its real potentials.

Q: So what happens to this false self?

KW: The false self—at whatever level—might simply remain in charge for a lifetime, as the individual limps through a life of internal insincerity. More often than not, however, the false self will at some point collapse under its own suffocating weight—there is a "break-down"—and the individual is then faced with several choices: rest and recover and then resume the same false-self trajectory; drug the dilemma out of awareness; behaviorally reinforce actions that avoid the problem; or take up an investigation into the life of the lie, usually with a therapist who will help you *interpret* your interior intentions more *truthfully.*

Q: The interpretive or Left-Hand therapies.

KW: Yes. In a *safe environment,* surrounded by empathy, congru-ence, and acceptance, the individual can begin to tell the truth about his or her interior without fear of retribution. And thus the false self—at whatever level—tends to lose the reason for its existence. The lie—the *resistance* to truthfulness—is *interpreted,* and the concealed pain and terror and anguish disclose themselves, and the false self slowly burns in the fire of truthful awareness. The truthful interiors are *shared* in an intersubjective circle of care and compassion, which releases them from their imprisonment in deception and allows them to join the ongoing growth of consciousness—the *beauty* of the actual self shines through, and the intrinsic joy of the new depth is its own reward.

Now we've only discussed the first three fulcrums and the pathologies that develop up to those points—psychosis, borderline, neurosis. But the same general phenomenon is operative throughout development, even into the higher and transpersonal domains. At whatever level of develop-ment, we can exist as the actual self in sincerity, or the false self in deception. And the different levels of the lie are the different levels of pathology.

Early Worldviews: Archaic, Magic, Mythic

Q: That takes us up through fulcrum-3—the first three major spheres or levels of consciousness growth, each of which has a different worldview.

KW: Yes. A worldview, as we were saying, is what the Kosmos looks like from a particular rung of consciousness. When you have only sensations and impulses, what does the Kosmos look like to you? We call that *archaic*. When you add images and symbols, what does the Kosmos look like then? *Magic*. When you add rules and roles, what does the Kosmos see? A *mythic* world. When formal operational emerges, what do you see? A *rational* world. And so on.

Q: Why don't you briefly summarize the early worldviews, and then we can move on to higher developments.

KW: "Archaic" is sort of a catch-all phrase. It loosely represents all the previous stages up to the hominid. Archaic is the general worldview of fulcrum-1. It's basically a sensorimotor worldview.

Q: And magic?

KW: As images and symbols begin to emerge, around the time of fulcrum-2, these early images and symbols are *not differentiated* clearly from the objects they represent. Thus, it seems that to manipulate the image is to actually change the object. If I make an image of you and stick a pin in the image, something bad will actually happen to you. The child lives in this world of magical displacement and condensation. Very "primary process." Very *magical*.

Likewise, because self and other are not well differentiated, the child populates its world with objects that have mental characteristics—the magical worldview is *animistic*. And I'm not talking about some sort of sophisticated panpsychic philosophy. It's very crude and very egocentric. The clouds move because they are following you, they want to see you. It rains because the sky wants to wash you off. It thunders because the sky is angry at you personally. Mind and world are not clearly differentiated, so their characteristics tend to get fused and confused, "magically." Inside and outside are *both* egocentric, narcissistic.

Q: What about mythic?

KW: As development moves into fulcrum-3, the child begins to understand that it cannot itself magically order the world around. It keeps hiding under the pillow, but people keep finding it! Something is not working here. Magic doesn't really work. The self can't really order the world around magically and omnipotently. But it thinks perhaps *somebody else can*, and so crashing onto the scene come a pantheon of gods and goddesses and demons and fairies and special forces, all of which can miraculously suspend the laws of nature for various, often trite and trivial, reasons. The child will ask its parents to turn the yucky spinach into candy. The child doesn't understand that the material world doesn't work like that.

But in the meantime the child develops a very complex *mythological worldview*, which is populated with all sorts of egocentric forces that are imagined to order the world around, and all of them are focused on the ego of the child. Whereas, in the previous magical phase, the infant thought that it itself could alter the world by the right word-magic, now it has to spend its time trying to appease the gods and demons and forces that can alter the world, often for the worse. Egocentric *power* gives way to egocentric *prayer* and ritual. There is a constant "bargaining" with these forces: if I eat all my dinner, the nice force will make my toothache go away.

This mythic worldview begins with the rep-mind and continues into the next major stage, the rule/role mind, and then dies down with the rational worldview, which realizes that if you want to change reality, you must work at it yourself: nobody is going to magically or mythically save you without a corresponding growth.

You can see these general correlations in figure 5-2. Worldviews are listed in the Lower Left, because they *collectively govern* individual perceptions within their horizon. (Whether magic or mythic possesses any genuinely spiritual aspects, we will discuss later. See chapter 11.)

Fulcrum-4: The Birth of the Role Self

Q: All right, so that brings us to fulcrum-4. The basic rung you have listed as the "rule/role" mind.

KW: Yes. This is roughly what Piaget called concrete operational cognition ("conop"), which emerges around age 6–7 on average, and dominates awareness until roughly age 11–14. "Concrete operational" sounds very dry and arid but is actually very rich and powerful. It involves the capacity to form mental *rules* and to take mental *roles*. And—this is crucial—the child finally learns to *take the role of other*.

There is a famous experiment, by Piaget and Inhelder, that first spotted this very clearly. I'll give a simplified version. If you take a ball colored red on one side and green on the other, and you place the ball between you and the child, and then ask the child two questions—"What color do you see?" and "What color do I see?"—preoperational children will answer both questions the same. That is, if the child is looking at the green side, he will correctly say he sees green, but he will also say *you* are seeing green. He doesn't know that you are seeing the red side. *He can't put himself in your shoes*, or see the world through your eyes. The child is still locked into his own perspective, which is still very egocentric, very preconventional, very selfcentric.

But the concrete operational child will correctly say, "I see green, you see red." The child at this stage can take the role of other. And this is a huge step *on the way to global*, on the way to being able to take a worldcentric perspective. The child is not yet fully there, but it is continuing to move in the right direction, because it is beginning to see that its view is not the only view in the world!

So its entire *moral stance* switches from a rather egocentric or *preconventional* stance to a *conventional* and often highly *conformist* stance— "my country right or wrong" and "law and order" stage. You can see this in figure 9-3.

Paradigm Shifts

Q: A change in view.

KW: It's an entire change in worldview—a paradigm shift, if you like—and as with the three previous rungs, or the three previous paradigm shifts, this involves a profound change in self-identity, in moral sense, and in self-needs, to mention a few. These changing views are all listed in figure 9-3.

Q: So each of the nine stages of consciousness evolution is actually a paradigm shift.

KW: In a broad sense, yes. Consequently, the typical adult in our culture has already undergone a half-dozen or so major paradigm shifts, worldview shifts—from archaic to magic to mythic to rational to existential, or thereabouts. You and I have *already* undergone these revolutions in consciousness, and although we might not remember any of the specifics, researchers on the scene report psychological earthquakes.

We tend to seal these earthquakes out of awareness. There are a lot of very funny stories about this. If you take children in the preoperational stage, and—right in front of their eyes—pour the water from a short glass into a tall glass, and ask them which glass has more water, they will always say the tall glass has more, even though they saw you pour the same amount from one glass to the other. They cannot "conserve volume." Certain "obvious" things that we see, they do not and *cannot* see—they live in a different worldspace. No matter how many times you pour the *same* amount of water back and forth between the two glasses, they will *insist* the tall glass has more. So much for the "pure" and "undistorted" perception of children.

If a few years later, after concrete operational awareness has emerged, you repeat this experiment, the kids will always say that both glasses have the same amount of water. They can hold volume in their mind and not be confused by its displacements. They have an internal *rule* that automatically does this (a concrete operational rule). And if you show them a videotape from the earlier period, where they were saying that the tall glass has more water, they will deny it's them! They think you've doctored the videotape. They simply cannot imagine somebody being so stupid as to think the tall glass has more water.

So they underwent this massive paradigm shift, and not a bit of it remains in awareness. The self will now *reinterpret* every single event of its previous life history from the perspective of the new worldview. It completely *rewrites its history* from within the new and higher paradigm.

So they—so all of us—will retroactively reread the earlier events in our life from this new perspective, and we tend to imagine that is the perspective we had from the start. When we think of ourselves at age 4 or 5, we think of the people around us at that time—our parents, our siblings, our friends—and we picture what they were thinking about us, or how they felt about certain things, or what was going through their minds, when in fact we could actually do none of that at the time! We could not take the role of other at that age. So we are automatically (and subconsciously) "retro-reading" our entire life from the perspective of a recently emerged worldview, and imagining all of this stuff was present from the start!

Needless to say, this considerably distorts what was actually occurring in the earlier periods. Memory is the last thing you can depend on to "report" childhood. And this leads to all sorts of problems. Romantics often imagine that childhood is a wonderful time where you see the world just like you do now, only in a marvelously "spontaneous" and "free" fashion. Archaic is nondual paradise, magic is holistically empowered wonderfulness, mythic is alive with spiritual powers, and it's all so marvelous and free. Whereas what is probably happening is that the Romantics, with access to the higher worldview of reflexive awareness, are simply reading all sorts of wonderful things back into a period which, if they could *actually* see it (on videotape, for example), they would deny any reality to at all!

Satanic Abuse and UFOs

Q: So can you recover childhood memories in any sense?

KW: The impressions of various childhood events are certainly present, sort of like bruises in the psyche. And these impressions retain the worldview of the level that was present when they were laid down—usually archaic or magical.

But when these impressions are recalled by adults, the impressions themselves are often interpreted in terms of the higher worldview now present. And then all sorts of present-day concerns can be injected back into these original impressions, and it vividly appears that these concerns were there from the start. It doesn't seem like you are reinterpreting these early impressions, because that is done subconsciously or preconsciously, and so you only see the conscious result of this extensive reworking.

In certain intense states of regression—with certain therapies, certain meditative practices, certain drugs, certain intense stresses—these original impressions can be accessed (precisely because the higher paradigm is temporarily decommissioned), but even then, a few seconds or a few minutes later, the higher worldview returns, and people begin extensive retro-reading of these impressions. And we have to be very careful about that.

Q: Satanic ritual child abuse?

KW: Well, that's one example. The FBI has found not one scrap of evidence of ritual child murder, even though thousands of people are claiming such. There ought to be corpses all over the backyards of this country. But these folks honestly and deeply believe this has happened to them. They do not feel that they are making this up. These impressions present themselves with vivid certainty. They will easily pass lie detector tests. The reworking has taken place subconsciously.

Samsara is a brutal place. Samsara, metaphorically, is a realm of ritual abuse. It is inherently a mechanism of terror. And people need to cope with this nightmare. One of the simplest ways is to imagine that this ritual abuse had a specific cause in your own personal history. So you search your childhood "memories," and eventually, with a little help from a friendly therapist, sure enough: there's mom with a butcher knife. The original impression is probably true enough: mom had a knife, she was carving the Thanksgiving turkey, and that impression is real. But it gets reworked, and now you're the turkey.

Q: Alien abduction? UFO abduction? These stories all have a very similar structure. The same events keep happening. There's the abduction, the medical experiments and anal probe and semen collection, the sending back to earth, often with a message for humanity. And it really alters these people's lives.

KW: I think the original impressions might go back to fulcrum-2 or fulcrum-1 or even fulcrum-0. But again, they get dramatically reworked. Maybe even some archetypal or Jungian material gets activated—Jung thought UFOs were actually projected archetypes. The UFO anal probe: where Freud meets Jung.

Many people are sincere in their beliefs about it. Perhaps even some higher or spiritual material gets injected into the impressions. But the impressions themselves retain a very *narcissistic* worldview. Imagine: humanity is about to enter a new phase, guided by a massive new alien intelligence. And of all the people in the entire world, you are chosen to carry this message. In fact, the aliens are collecting semen or ova from you because they are inseminating a new race, beginning a new race. And you are to be the father of this new race, the mother of this new race. The new saviors are coming, a new virgin birth is required.

You can't get much more narcissistic and egocentric than that. Some very deep fulcrum-2 (or earlier) material is being reactivated, in my opinion, and then injected with present-day adult "messages" about saving Gaia and healing the planet—which is all very nice, but it can't hide the primal scene in all of these fantasies: you are the center of the new world, the father or the mother of a new and higher race.

So it's an original and real enough impression, reworked and injected with adult material, so that it presents itself with a genuine and frightening vividness, and it retains the essential worldview of fulcrum-2 (or earlier)—namely, its intense narcissism—but then is reworked, often with the aid of a kindly and helpful therapist, into a powerful paradigm of world salvation, courtesy of you.

Q: No spiritual components at all?

KW: We haven't talked much about any of the higher stages, but it's always possible that some genuinely transpersonal or spiritual dimensions are temporarily "peek-experienced" and then translated downward into terms that will both satisfy the fulcrum-2 fixation and fit the "world-saving" paradigm fabricated by the client, often in collusion with the therapist. All of which presents itself as *vividly real* and undeniable. As we said, these individuals will, and often do, pass a lie detector test, because they are sincere in their beliefs, and their therapists are equally sincere, and neither has spotted the lie, the deep reworking that converts impressions into realities.

The therapists investigating these phenomena had a real opportunity to make pioneering observations on new forms of hysterical syndromes emerging as a sign of our troubled times, but by and large they lost that opportunity by allowing the vividness of the impressions to persuade them that they were dealing with ontological realities. They converted phenomenology into ontology. At the very worst, they were propelled by their own deep narcissism: I am therapist to the new race. At the very least, they became facilitators in the mass hysteria, and this has understandably thrown the whole profession into turmoil and bitter self-recrimination.

I suspect ritual satanic child abuse and UFO abduction are both powerful examples of what happens to spiritual realities in a culture that denies spiritual realities—casualties on the way to global, souls washed ashore on an island of cultural insincerity.

11

On the Way to Global: Part 2

Q: We were discussing the interior transformations that occur "on the way to global," and all of the problems that can prevent the emergence of this global awareness.

KW: Yes, and we had reached the point where there is a paradigm shift from preconventional to conventional modes of awareness—from fulcrum-3 to fulcrum-4, which is especially evidenced in the capacity to take the role of other. And in this shift we see a *continuing decrease in egocentrism*. In fact, the overall direction of development in humans—the telos of human development—is toward less and less egocentric states.

But this is true in general. The archbattle in the universe is always: evolution versus egocentrism. The evolutionary drive to produce greater depth is synonymous with the drive to overcome egocentrism, to find wider and deeper wholes, to unfold greater and greater unions. A molecule overcomes the egocentrism of an atom. A cell overcomes the egocentrism of a molecule. And nowhere is this trend more obvious than in human development itself.

Evolution versus Egocentrism

Q: So evolution is a continual decline of egocentrism.

KW: Yes, a continual *decentering*. Howard Gardner gives a perfect summary of the research in this area, and I want to read a short quote from him, because it pretty much says it all.

He begins by pointing out that development in general is marked by "the decline of egocentrism." He reports: "The young child is totally egocentric—meaning not that he thinks selfishly only about himself, but to the contrary, that he is incapable of thinking about himself. The egocentric child is unable to differentiate himself from the rest of the world; he has not separated himself out from others or from objects. Thus he feels that others share his pain or his pleasure, that his mumblings will inevitably be understood, that his perspective is shared by all persons, that even animals and plants partake of his consciousness. In playing hide-and-seek he will 'hide' in broad view of other persons, because his egocentrism prevents him from recognizing that others are aware of his location. The whole course of human development can be viewed as a *continuing decline in egocentrism. . . .*"

Q: So narcissism or egocentrism is *greatest* at fulcrum-1 and then steadily declines?

KW: Yes, exactly. Because differentiation is at its least, narcissism is at its worst!

This selfcentrism lessens somewhat as the infant's identity switches from physiocentric to biocentric—from fulcrum-1 to fulcrum-2. The child does not treat the physical world as an extension of itself, because physical self and physical world are now differentiated. But the emotional self and emotional world are not yet differentiated, and so the entire emotional world is an extension of the self: emotional narcissism is at its peak. The biocentric or ecological self of fulcrum-2 is thus still profoundly egocentric. What it's feeling, the world is feeling.

This narcissism is lessened, or declines once again, with the emergence of the conceptual self (fulcrum-3). The self is now a conceptual ego, but that ego still cannot yet take the role of other, so the early ego is still largely narcissistic, preconventional, egocentric.

So I sometimes summarize this declining narcissism as going from physiocentric to biocentric to egocentric, with the understanding that all three are egocentric in the general sense, but less and less so. And the whole egocentric perspective undergoes yet another radical shift with the emergence of the capacity to *take the role of other*. At which point *egocentric* shifts to *sociocentric*.

Fulcrum-4 (Continued): Life's Social Scripts

Q: In other words, fulcrum-4.

KW: Yes. At this stage, what becomes crucially important for me is not how I *fit with my biological impulses*, but how I *fit with my social roles*, my group, my peer group, or—a bit wider—how I fit with my country, my state, my people. I am now taking the role of other, and how I fit with the other is crucially important. I have *decentered* once again, differentiated once again, transcended once again—my ego is not the only ego in the universe.

So this sociocentric stance is a major transformation—or paradigm shift—from the previous and especially egocentric stances of the first three fulcrums. But notice: with fulcrum-4, care and concern are expanded from me to the group—but no further! If you are a member of the group—a member of my tribe, my mythology, my ideology—then you are "saved" as well. But if you belong to a different culture, a different group, a different mythology, a different god, then you are damned.

So this sociocentric or conventional stance tends to be very *ethnocentric*. Care and concern are expanded from me to my group, and there it stops.

So I also call this conventional or sociocentric stance by the term *mythic-membership*. The worldview of fulcrum-4 is still mythological, and so care and concern are extended to believers in the same mythology, the same ideology, the same race, the same creed, the same culture—but no further. If you are a member of the myth, you are my brother, my sister. If not, you go to hell.

In other words, I can decenter from my ego to my group, but I cannot yet decenter my group. My group is the only group in the universe. I cannot yet move from sociocentric and ethnocentric to a truly *worldcentric* or universal or global stance—a decentered, universal, pluralistic stance. But I am getting there, slowly! I am on the way to global, with each stage in this journey marked by a profound decentering, a lessening of egocentrism, a lessening of narcissism, a transcendence of the shallower and a disclosure of the deeper. Decentering, transcendence, decreasing egocentrism—so many words for the same thing, the same telos of evolution.

And, in fact, the postconventional or global or worldcentric stance is the next fulcrum, fulcrum-5.

Q: Okay, so let's finish with fulcrum-4 first. Identity switches from egocentric to sociocentric.

KW: Yes. The self is no longer relating only or primarily to its body and its immediate impulses, but is also ushered into a world of *roles* and *rules*. The self will have all sorts of *scripts*, or learned roles and rules, which it will have to play out.

Most of these scripts are useful and absolutely necessary—they are the means whereby you pull yourself out of yourself and into the circle of intersubjective culture, the circle of care and concern and relatedness and responsibility, where you begin to see in others your own expanded self, and extend care to each. You see the world through the eyes of the other, and thus find a wider consciousness that shines beyond the confines of the me and the mine.

But some of these scripts are distorted or cruel or maladaptive, and if something goes wrong with these scripts, we call this "script pathology." The person has all these false and distorted social masks and myths— "I'm a rotten person, I'm no good, I can never do anything right"—all these cruel scripts that are self-defeating and injurious.

That are, in short, lies. These false scripts are the form of the lie at this level, and the false self lives by these social lies. It is not just out of touch with its emotions; it is out of touch with the self it could be in the cultural world—out of touch with all the positive roles it could assume if it didn't keep telling itself that it can't.

Q: Which is what cognitive therapists tend to work with.

KW: Yes, and family therapy, and transactional analysis, and narrative therapy, to mention a few. It's not so much working back into the past and earlier fulcrums and trying to dig up and uncover some buried emotion or impulse, although that can definitely happen. It's more a case of directly attacking these false and distorted rules and scripts and games. These scripts are simply not true, they are not based on present evidence—they are lies, they are myths. They are anchored in a mythic disposition, which will not expose itself to rational evidence.

Aron Beck, for example, a pioneer in cognitive therapy, has found that in most cases of depression, people have a series of false scripts or beliefs, and they keep repeating these myths as if they were true. When we are depressed, we *talk* to ourselves in *untruthful* ways. "If one person doesn't like me, it means nobody will like me. If I fail at this particular task, it means I will fail at everything. If I don't get this job, my life is over. If she doesn't love me, nobody else will." And so on.

Now perhaps these false scripts got started at an earlier fulcrum, perhaps fulcrum-3 or fulcrum-2 or earlier. And a more psychoanalytically oriented therapist (or an "uncovering therapist") might try to dig back to these earlier traumas and find out why the person is generating these myths (and even magical beliefs or archaic impulses).

But the cognitive therapist tends to simply attack the myths head on. The person will be asked to monitor their interior dialogue and look for these myths, and then expose them to reason and evidence. "Okay, if I don't get this job, I guess it doesn't really mean my life is over."

Q: Most typical therapy seems to work at this level.

KW: Pretty much. Most typical therapy—your general interpretive psychotherapist—will use an amalgam of fulcrum-3 and fulcrum-4 techniques. Most therapy is simply talking about your problems, and the therapist will be on the lookout for any distorting scripts that tell you that you are a rotten person, that you're no good, that you're a failure, and so on. A false self, built on myths and deceptions, has taken charge of your life. And the therapist helps you to uproot these false scripts and replace them with a more realistic interpretation of yourself, a more *truthful interpretation* of your interior, so that the false self can give way to the actual self.

These therapists might not use terms like "scripts" and "myths" and "narrative analysis" and so on, but that is generally what is involved on the fulcrum-4 side, the script pathology side. Myths cause symptoms; expose the myths to evidence, and the symptoms go away. The idea is, *think* differently, and you will start to *feel* differently.

But if it looks like there are some strong feelings or emotions or impulses that the person *cannot* deal with or acknowledge, then the therapist often tends to switch to an "uncovering mode." What are your *feelings* about this? What is your *felt-sense*? And the therapist might notice that there are certain feelings and impulses that you are not comfortable with—you have certain "buried emotions," and therapy then tends to work at uncovering these repressed emotions, by whatever name.

So typical therapy is usually an amalgam of fulcrum-4 script analysis and fulcrum-3 uncovering analysis, although the different therapists will bring a wide variety of tools and techniques to the process.

(Fulcrum-1 pathologies are so severe they are usually handled by a medical psychiatrist, who prescribes medication. And fulcrum-2 is usually the province of therapists who specialize in structure-building techniques. These techniques have been pioneered by Kernberg, Kohut, Masterson, and Blanck and Blanck—often with reference to Margaret Mahler's groundbreaking research, which we briefly discussed earlier. Certain intense regressive therapies—e.g., Grof's holotropic breathwork and Janov's primal therapy—claim to deal with fulcrum-0, although these claims are highly controversial.)

Fulcrum-5: The Worldcentric or Mature Ego

Q: Which brings us to fulcrum-5.

KW: Around the age of 11–15 years in our culture, the capacity for formal operational awareness emerges (this is "formop" on figure 5-2). Where concrete operational awareness can operate on the concrete world, formal operational awareness can operate on thought itself. It's not just thinking about the world, it's thinking about thinking. This is not nearly as dry and abstract as it sounds!

There's also a classical experiment that Piaget used to spot this extremely important emergence or paradigm shift or worldview shift. In simplified version: the person is given three glasses of clear liquid and told that they can be mixed in a way that will produce a yellow color. The person is then asked to produce the yellow color.

Concrete operational children will simply start mixing the liquids together haphazardly. They will keep doing this until they stumble on the right combination or give up. In other words, as the name implies, they perform *concrete operations*—they have to actually do it in a concrete way.

Formal operational adolescents will first form a general picture of the fact that you have to try glass A with glass B, then A with C, then B with C, and so on. If you ask them about it, they will say something like, "Well, I need to try all the various combinations one at a time." In other words, they have a formal operation in their mind, a scheme that lets them know that you have to try *all the possible* combinations.

Q: That still sounds pretty dry and abstract to me.

KW: It's really quite the opposite. It means the person can begin to imagine different possible worlds. "What if" and "as if" can be grasped for the first time, and this ushers the person into the wild world of the true dreamer. All sorts of idealistic possibilities open up, and the person's awareness can dream of things that are not yet, and picture future worlds of ideal possibilities, and work to change the world according to those dreams. You can imagine what yet might be! Adolescence is such a wild time, not just because of sexual blossoming, but because *possible worlds* open up to the mind's eye—it's the "age of reason and revolution."

Likewise, thinking about thought means true introspection becomes possible. The interior world, for the first time, opens up before the mind's eye; psychological space becomes a new and exciting terrain.

Inward visions dance in the head, and for the first time they are not coming from external nature, nor from a mythic god, nor from a conventional other, but, in some strange and miraculous way, they come from a voice within.

And this means one other very important thing. Because you can think about thinking, you can start to *judge* the roles and the rules which, at the previous stage, you simply swallowed unreflexively. Your moral stance moves from conventional to *postconventional*. (See figure 9-3.) You can *criticize* your own conventional society. Because you can "think about thought," you can "norm the norms." You might end up agreeing with the norms, or you might disagree with them. But the point is, you can scrutinize many of them. You are no longer merely *identified* with them, and so you have some critical distance from them. To some degree, you have transcended them.

This, of course, is the 1-2-3 process as it moves from fulcrum-4 to fulcrum-5. You start out, at fulcrum-4, in *fusion* with the conventional roles and rules—you are *identified* with them, merged with them (and thus utterly at their mercy, a true conformist). Then you begin to *differentiate* or *transcend* them, gain some freedom from them, and move to the next higher stage (fulcrum-5), whereupon you will still have to *integrate* these social roles—you can still be a father without being lost in that role. But you have in general moved away from, or differentiated from, an exclusive identity with your sociocentric roles, and you particularly begin to scrutinize the rightness or appropriateness of your sociocentric and ethnocentric perspectives, which previously you would not—and could not—even question.

In short, you have gone from *sociocentric* to *worldcentric*. Another decline in narcissism. Another decentering, another transcendence. You want to know what is right and fair, not just for you and your people, but for all peoples. You take a postconventional or global or worldcentric stance. (And, just as important, you are getting very close to a genuinely spiritual or transpersonal opening.)

So, in this transformation from sociocentric to worldcentric, the self decenters once again: my group is not the only group in the universe, my tribe is not the only tribe, my god is not the only god, my ideology is not the only ideology. I went from egocentric to ethnocentric by decentering my ego into the group; now I go from ethnocentric to worldcentric by decentering my group into the world.

This is a very difficult transformation! But when it succeeds (which is fairly rare: greater depth, less span), then we have the first truly universal or global or worldcentric stance.

For the very first time in all of consciousness development and evolution, we have a worldcentric and global perspective. What a long journey!—what a rocky road!—this precious path to global.

And just as important, all further and higher developments will have this worldcentric platform as their base. It is an irreversible shift. Once you see the world in global perspectives, you cannot prevent yourself from doing so. You can never go back.

And thus Spirit has, for the first time in evolution, looked through your eyes and seen a global world, a world that is decentered from the me and the mine, a world that demands care and concern and compassion and conviction—a Spirit that is unfolding its own intrinsic value and worth, but a Spirit that announces itself only through the voice of those who have the courage to stand in the worldcentric space and defend it against lesser and shallower engagements.

Diversity and Multiculturalism

Q: Which relates directly to the moral stance. I mean, that's why it's called *post*conventional, right? Where conventional morality is sociocentric, postconventional is worldcentric, based on principles of universal pluralism, or global tolerance and fairness.

KW: Yes, that's right.

Q: Is this the same as multiculturalism?

KW: Well, we have to be very careful here. Multiculturalism does indeed emphasize cultural diversity and universal tolerance. But this fulcrum-5 stance is a very rare and very elite and very difficult accomplishment. Look at all the ground we have covered in order to get to this worldcentric stance!

Now you yourself might indeed have evolved from egocentric to ethnocentric to worldcentric perspectives, and so you will easily understand that all individuals are to be accorded equal consideration and equal opportunity, regardless of race, sex, or creed. From this stance of universal pluralism, you are genuinely multicultural and postconventional. The problem is, most individuals that you treat with universal coverage do not share your universalism. They are still egocentric or ethnocentric to the core. So you are extending universal consideration to individuals who will absolutely not extend the same courtesy to you.

So typical multiculturalists are thrown into a series of very bizarre contradictions. To begin with, they claim to be non-elitist or anti-elitist. But the capacity for postconventional and worldcentric pluralism is a very rare, very elite accomplishment. One survey found that only 10 percent of the American population actually reach this highly developed stage. So multiculturalism is a very elite stance that then claims it is not elitist. In other words, it starts to lie about its own identity, and this will lead it down some very murky roads.

Q: For instance?

KW: Multiculturalism does embrace the very noble drive to treat individuals equally and fairly, from a decentered and worldcentric perspective—everybody is equal in that sense—but it then confuses that high stance with the fact that *getting to that high stance* is a very rare accomplishment. It *ignores* the *getting there*, the developmental process that allowed it to embrace universal pluralism in the first place. So it then extends the *results* of that development to individuals who have *not* gotten to that stance themselves, and who are therefore perfectly willing to take your nice universal pluralistic stance and wipe their shoes all over it.

The multicults therefore naturally but confusedly say that we have to treat all individuals and all cultural movements as being completely equal, since no stance is better than another. They then cannot explain why Nazis and the Ku Klux Klan should be shunned. If we are really multicultural and all for diversity, how can we exclude the Nazis? Isn't everybody equal?

The answer, of course, is that no, not every stance is equal. Worldcentric is *better* than ethnocentric, which is *better* than egocentric, because each has more depth. The Nazis and the KKK are ethnocentric movements based on a particular mythology of race supremacy, and from a worldcentric perspective we judge them to be *inferior* stances.

But the typical multiculturalist cannot allow this *judgment*, because they confusedly deny distinctions between moral stances altogether—all stances are equal, no judgments allowed! (This is the typical "anti-hierarchy" stance of the extreme postmodernists.)

And so what happens, of course, is that they simply tend to become completely intolerant of those who disagree with them. They know that they have a noble stance, which in part they certainly do, but because they don't understand how they got there, they simply try to force their view down everybody's throat. Everybody is equal! No moral stance is better than another! No hierarchies here! And so off we go with vicious intolerance in the name of tolerance, with censorship in the name of compassion, with we-know-best thought police and mindless political correctness—with a bunch of elitists trying to outlaw everybody else's elitisms. It would be hilarious if it weren't so fundamentally wretched.

Q: So is this related to the pathology of this stage?

KW: This stage and the next, yes. Once you start to go worldcentric, once you begin scrutinizing your culture, and perhaps distancing yourself from its sociocentric or ethnocentric prejudice, and you strike out on your own—once you do that, then *who*, exactly, *are you*? Without all the old and comfortable roles, *who are you*? How can you fashion your own identity? What do you want from life? What do you want to be? Who are you, anyway? Erikson called this an "identity crisis," and it is perhaps the central "un-ease" or "dis-ease" of this fulcrum.

And the multicults are in a massive identity crisis. Since their official stance is that elitism of any sort is bad, but since their actual self is in fact an elite self, then they must lie about their actual self—they must conceal, distort, deceive.

So they go from saying everybody should be judged fairly, in a non-ethnocentric way, to saying that everybody should *not be judged at all*, that all moral stances are equivalent. Except *their* stance, of course, which is superior in a world where nothing is supposed to be superior at all (oops). So they have an elite stance that denies its own elitism—they are *lying* about their actual identity. They have a false self system. And that is an identity crisis.

Q: It's very spooky. It's Orwell's newspeak and thought police. But it seems to be fairly pervasive. The universities have all but been hijacked by it.

KW: Yes, American universities today seem to specialize in it. All this is actually doing is contributing to the retribalization of America, by encouraging every egocentric and ethnocentric fragmentation and grievance politics, the politics of narcissism. All stances are equal means every preconventional and ethnocentric shallowness is given encouragement. The country is facing its own identity crisis, we might say, but I suppose that's another discussion.

Fulcrum-6: The Bodymind Integration of the Centaur

Q: Which brings us to the last major "orthodox" stage, or the highest stage most conventional researchers tend to recognize.

KW: Yes, fulcrum-6. The basic structure at this stage is vision-logic, which you can see on several figures, including 5-2 and 10-1. Vision-logic or network-logic is a type of synthesizing and integrating aware-ness. Formal operational awareness is synthesizing and integrating in many important and impressive ways, but it still tends to possess a kind of dichotomizing logic, a logic of either/or, rather like Aristotelian logic.

But vision-logic adds up the parts and sees networks of interactions. When employed in a merely objectifying or Right-Hand fashion, it pro-duces objective systems theory in general. But when it is the basis of actual interior transformation—which is not covered by systems theory! and which is very rare!—then it supports an integrated personality. When the self's center of gravity identifies with vision-logic, when the person lives from that level, then we tend to get a very highly integrated personality, a self that can actually inhabit a global perspective, and not merely talk about it.

So the highly integrative capacity of vision-logic supports an equally integrated self. Which is why I call the self of this stage the *centaur*, representing an integration of the mind and the body, the noosphere and the biosphere, in a relatively autonomous self—which doesn't mean isolated self or atomistic self or egocentric self, but rather a self inte-grated in its networks of responsibility and service.

Q: You have often used John Broughton's research on this particular stage, although he's not very well known.

KW: Well, several researchers have looked at this stage very care-fully—Loevinger, Selman, Habermas, Erikson, Graves, and Maslow, for example. But I have always liked the summary of Broughton's research: at this stage, "mind and body are both experiences of an integrated self."

That says it all in a very succinct fashion. First of all, the self at this stage is *aware of* both the mind and the body *as experiences*. That is, the *observing self* is beginning to *transcend* both the mind and the body and thus can be aware of them as objects in awareness, as experiences. It is not just the mind looking at the world; it is the observing self look-ing at both the mind and the world. This is a very powerful transcen-dence, which we will see intensify in the higher stages.

And second, precisely because the observing self is beginning to tran-scend the mind and the body, it can for just that reason begin to *integrate* the mind and body. Thus, "centaur."

So in this fulcrum, we have the same 1-2-3 process that we see in every other fulcrum, namely, initial fusion, differentiation, and integra-tion. In this case, there is the initial identification with the formal mind (of fulcrum-5). The observing self then begins to differentiate from the mind and to see it as an object. Since it is no longer exclusively identified with the mind, it can integrate the mind with the other components in awareness, with the body and its impulses. Hence, centaur—mind and body are both experiences of an integrated self.

Aperspectival Madness

Q: You also call the centaur the existential level.

KW: Well, at this stage you are really, as it were, on your own, at least at this point in evolution. You no longer have blind faith in the conventional roles and rules of society. You are no longer ethnocentric and sociocentric. You have moved deeply into a worldcentric space, where . . .

Q: This stage is also worldcentric?

KW: All stages at and beyond formal operational (fulcrum-5) are worldcentric or global—they all have a foundation of postconventional and universal perspectivism. The higher or deeper stages simply disclose more and more of this worldcentric freedom as it moves into deeper and genuinely spiritual domains.

Which is a bit ahead of the story. At the centaur level, the existential level, you are no longer egocentric or ethnocentric. You have moved deeply into a worldcentric space, where, as the multicults demonstrate, you can slip and take a very bad spill in this new freedom.

Q: You call this new freedom "aperspectival."

KW: Jean Gebser's term, yes. Vision-logic adds up all the different perspectives, and therefore it doesn't automatically privilege any one perspective over the others—it is aperspectival. But as you begin to take all the different perspectives into account, it gets very dizzifying, very aperspectival, very disorienting.

And you can get very lost in this new aperspectival awareness of vision-logic, because all perspectives start to become relative and interdependent; there is nothing absolutely foundational; no final place to rest your head and say, I've got it!

But the fact that all perspectives are *relative* does *not* mean that all perspectives are equal. That all perspectives are relative does not prevent some from being relatively better than others all the time! Worldcentric is better than ethnocentric is better than egocentric, because each has more depth than its shallower predecessors.

But forgetting that, and focusing merely on the relativity of perspectives, throws you into aperspectival madness, a dizzifying paralysis of will and judgment. "It's all relative, so there is no better and worse, and no stance is better than another." Overlooking the fact that that stance itself claims to be *better* than the alternatives—the standard performative contradiction. The multicults often rise to this level of vision-logic, with a very noble intent, but often succumb to aperspectival madness, which they sell to nice, unsuspecting students.

The aperspectival space of vision-logic simply means that Spirit is looking at the world through infinitely wondrous perspectives; it does not mean it has gone blind in the process. This is simply a further decentering, a further transcendence, another spiral in the evolution beyond egocentrism.

On the Brink of the Transpersonal

Q: So that's part of the good news of this existential or centauric stage.

KW: Yes. One of the characteristics of the *actual self* of this stage (the centaur) is precisely that it no longer buys all the conventional and numbing consolations—as Kierkegaard put it, the self can no longer tranquilize itself with the trivial. The emergence of this more authentic or existential self is the primary task of fulcrum-6.

The finite self is going to die—magic will not save it, mythic gods will not save it, rational science will not save it—and facing that cutting fact is part of becoming authentic. This was one of Heidegger's constant points. Coming to terms with one's mortality and one's finitude—this is part of finding one's own authentic being-in-the-world (authentic agency-in-communion).

The existentialists have beautifully analyzed this authentic self, the actual centauric self—its characteristics, its mode of being, its stance in the world—and most important, they have analyzed the common lies and bad faith that sabotage this authenticity. We lie about our mortality and finitude by constructing immortality symbols—vain attempts to beat time and exist everlastingly in some mythic heaven, some rational project, some great artwork, through which we project our incapacity to face death. We lie about the responsibility for our own choices, preferring to see ourselves as passive victims of some outside force. We lie about the richness of the present by projecting ourselves backward in guilt and forward in anxiety. We lie about our fundamental responsibility by hiding in the herd mentality, getting lost in the Other. In place of the authentic or actual self, we live as the inauthentic self, the false self, fashioning its projects of deception to hide itself from the shocking truth of existence.

I fully agree with all of that analysis, as far as it goes. Because, from my own point of view, not only is this type of existential authenticity important for its own sake, it is a prerequisite for entering the transpersonal not burdened with myths, or magical expectations, or egocentric and ethnocentric exaltations.

Q: But there is such a grim atmosphere in these existential writers.

KW: Yes, this is classically the home of existential dread, despair, angst, fear and trembling, sickness unto death—precisely because you have lost all the comforting consolations!

All of which is true enough, but because the existentialists recognize no sphere of consciousness higher than this, they are stuck with the existential worldview, which limits their perceptions to within its horizon.

So they make it something of a point of honor to embrace drab existential nightmares with dreadful seriousness. And if you claim there are any modes of awareness that go beyond existential angst, then you *must* be lapsing into death-denial, immortality projects, inauthenticity, bad faith. Any claim of a higher horizon is met with icy stares, and the heinous charge of "inauthentic!" comes to rest upon your head. If you *smile*, you're probably being inauthentic, because you have broken the sacred circle of the unendingly dreary.

Q: Stuck in the centaur, identified with the centaur and its existential worldview—that's the fusion phase of fulcrum-6.

KW: Yes. And that existential embeddedness becomes your point of reference for all reality. The more angst you can display, the more you can gnash your teeth as an example of cosmic insanity, then the more authentic you are. It might also help to drive a few nails into your forehead, as a sort of reminder. But in any event, never, never, never let them see you smile, or that will divulge your inauthenticity.

The whole point of the existential level is that you are not yet in the transpersonal, but you are no longer totally anchored in the personal—the whole personal domain has started to lose its flavor, has started to become profoundly meaningless. And so of course there is not much reason to smile. What good is the personal anyway—it's just going to die. Why even inhabit it?

This concern with *meaning*, and with its pervasive lack, is perhaps the central feature of fulcrum-6 pathologies, and with existential therapy.

But the interesting point is that the centaur, by all orthodox standards, ought to be happy and full and joyous. After all, it's an integrated and autonomous self, as you can see in figure 9-3. Why, by all standards, this self ought to be smiling all the time. But more often than not, it is not smiling. It is profoundly unhappy. It is integrated, and autonomous, and miserable.

It has tasted everything that the personal realm can offer, and it's not enough. The world has started to go flat in its appeal. No experience tastes good anymore. Nothing satisfies anymore. Nothing is worth pursuing anymore. Not because one has failed to get these rewards, but precisely because one has achieved them royally, tasted it all, and found it all lacking.

And so naturally this soul does not smile very much. This is a soul for whom all consolations have gone sour. The world has gone flat at exactly the moment of its greatest triumph. The magnificent banquet has come and gone; the skull grins silently over the whole affair. The feast is ephemeral, even in its grandest glories. The things on which I once could hang so much meaning and so much desire and so much fervent hope, all have melted into air, evaporated at some strange point during the long and lonely night. To whom can I sing songs of joy and exaltation? Who will hear my calls for help sent silently into that dark and hellish night? Where will I find the fortitude to withstand the swords and spears that daily pierce my side? And why even should I try? It all comes to dust, yes?, and where am I then? Fight or surrender, it matters not the least, for still my life goals bleed quietly to death, in a hemorrhage of despair.

This is a soul for whom all desires have become thin and pale and anemic. This is a soul who, in facing existence squarely, is thoroughly sick of it. This is a soul for whom the personal has gone totally flat. This is, in other words, a soul on the brink of the transpersonal.

12

Realms of the Superconscious: Part 1

Q: We can now move into the transpersonal stages, the superconscious domains. We left off development at the centaur. You described this as the observing self becoming aware of both mind and body, and thus beginning to transcend them.

KW: Yes, even orthodox research confirms this, and we gave several examples, from Broughton to Loevinger. By the time of the centaur, the observing self can witness or experience both the mind and the body, in a general sense, which means it is indeed beginning to transcend them in some important ways. As consciousness evolution continues, it discloses more and more depth—or height—to this observing self. What is this observing self? How deep, or how high, does it actually go?

And the answer given by the world's great mystics and sages is that this observing self goes straight to God, straight to Spirit, straight to the very Divine. In the ultimate depths of your own awareness, you intersect infinity.

This observing self is usually called the Self with a capital *S*, or the Witness, or pure Presence, or pure awareness, or consciousness as such, and this Self as transparent Witness is a direct ray of the living Divine. The ultimate I is Christ, is Buddha, is Emptiness itself: such is the startling testimony of the world's great mystics and sages.

Where the Mind Leaves Off

Q: So is this Witness an emergent?

KW: Not exactly, because pure consciousness is not an emergent.

This Self or Witness was present from the start as the basic form of awareness at whatever stage of growth a holon happened to be—it was present as prehension, as sensation, as impulse, as emotion, as symbols, as reason—but it becomes increasingly obvious as growth and transcendence matures. In other words, this Witness, this consciousness as such, is simply the depth of any holon, the interior of any holon. As we said, depth is consciousness, and depth goes all the way down. But as depth increases, consciousness shines forth more noticeably.

In humans, by the time of the centaur, this observing Witness has shed its lesser identification with both the body and the mind—it has transcended and included them—and so now it can simply witness them, which is why "both mind and body are experiences of an integrated self."

Q: It is beginning to transcend them.

KW: Yes. There is nothing occult or spooky about any of this. We have already seen identity shift from matter to body to mind, each of which involved a decentering or a dis-identifying with the lesser dimension. And by the time of the centaur, consciousness is simply continuing this process and starting to *dis-identify with the mind itself*, which is precisely why it can witness the mind, see the mind, experience the mind. The mind is no longer merely a subject; it is starting to become an object. An object of . . . the observing Self, the Witness.

And so the mystical, contemplative, and yogic traditions pick up where the mind leaves off. They pick up with the observing Self as it begins to transcend the mind, as it begins to go transmental or supramental or overmental. Or transrational, transegoic, transpersonal.

The contemplative traditions are based on a series of experiments in awareness: what if you pursue this Witness to its source? What if you inquire within, pushing deeper and deeper into the source of awareness itself? What if you push beyond or behind the mind, into a depth of consciousness that is not confined to the ego or the individual self? What do you find? As a repeatable, reproducible experiment in awareness, what do you find?

"There is a subtle essence that pervades all reality," begins one of the most famous answers to that question. "It is the reality of all that is, and the foundation of all that is. That essence is all. That essence is the real. And thou, thou art that."

In other words, this observing Self eventually discloses its own source, which is Spirit itself, Emptiness itself. And that is why the mystics maintain that this observing Self is a ray of the Sun that is the radiant Abyss and ultimate Ground upon which the entire manifest Kosmos depends. Your very Self intersects the Self of the Kosmos at large—a supreme identity that outshines the entire manifest world, a supreme identity that undoes the knot of the separate self and buries it in splendor.

So from matter to body to mind to Spirit. In each case consciousness or the observing Self sheds an exclusive identity with a lesser and shallower dimension, and opens up to deeper and higher and wider occasions, until it opens up to its own ultimate ground in Spirit itself.

And the stages of transpersonal growth and development are basically the stages of following this observing Self to its ultimate abode, which is pure Spirit or pure Emptiness, the ground, path, and fruition of the entire display.

The Transpersonal Stages

Q: So these stages . . . there are, what, several stages in this transpersonal growth?

KW: Yes, that's right, but again, in a very fluid and flowing way. In looking at these higher stages or waves of consciousness, we have a rather small pool of daring men and women—both yesterday and today—who have bucked the system, fought the average and normal, and struck out toward the new and higher spheres of awareness. In this quest, they joined with a small group or sangha of like-spirited souls, and developed *practices* or *injunctions* or *paradigms* that would disclose these higher worldspaces—injunctions or paradigms or interior *experiments* that would allow others to reproduce their results and therefore check and validate (or reject) their findings. And they left us their maps of this interior journey, with the crucial proviso that simply memorizing the map will not do, any more than studying a map of the Bahamas will replace actually going there.

So we take all these various maps and paths left by the great contemplative traditions, East and West, North and South, and we compare and contrast them (which demands that we *practice* many of them as well! This is a Left-Hand endeavor for *participant* observers, not merely a Right-Hand representation for academic study). Some paths are more complete than others; some specialize in a particular level; some leave out certain levels; some divide particular levels into literally dozens of sublevels.

From this cross-cultural comparison, grounded in practice, we attempt to create a "master template" that gives a fairly comprehensive and composite map of the various higher levels of consciousness that are available to men and women. These are higher *basic levels* present as *potentials* in all of us, but awaiting actual manifestation and growth and development.

Q: So how complicated do these higher maps get?

KW: Well, some traditions are so sophisticated they have literally hundreds of minute divisions of the various stages and components of consciousness development. But, based on the state of present research, it is fairly safe to say that there are *at least four major stages* of transpersonal development or evolution.

These four stages I call the *psychic*, the *subtle*, the *causal*, and the *nondual* (you can see these in figures 9-1 and 10-1; the nondual is the paper on which the diagram is drawn, which I'll explain in a moment). These are basic levels or spheres of consciousness, and so of course each of them has a different worldview, which I call, respectively, *nature mysticism*, *deity mysticism*, *formless mysticism*, and *nondual mysticism*.

Q: Now in what sense are these actually *stages*?

KW: The basic levels themselves are fairly discrete, identifiable structures. Their worldviews are very specific, and they differ from each other in important and easily identifiable ways—each has a different architecture with different cognitions, which support a different self-sense, different moral stances, different self-needs, and so on.

But, as always, the "ladder" is not where the real action is. The real action is the climber of the ladder—the self-system—and the fulcrums that are generated with this climb. And the self, as we said, can be all over the place. It can have a peak experience of a higher level, only to fall back into its actual and present self-stage. Conversely, a taste of the higher levels can so disrupt the self that it *regresses* to earlier fulcrums, fulcrums at which there is still some sort of fixation or repression or unfinished business. As egoic translation starts to wind down, these earlier "stick-points" jump out.

Q: So the actual growth of the self in the transpersonal stages is not linear in any sort of rigid sense.

KW: No, it's not. The fact that the higher realms are ladder-like—which means concentric spheres or nested holarchy—doesn't mean that growth through them is ladder-like. There are all sorts of ups and downs and spirals.

Q: Not to mention altered states.

KW: Yes, as we talked about earlier, the self at virtually any stage of development can have various types of peak experiences or altered states, including peak experiences of the transpersonal realms. For example, a self at the magic, mythic, rational, or existential levels can have a peak experience of the psychic, subtle, causal, or nondual realms, and in each case you would get a different type of "spiritual experience" [see *Integral Psychology*]. But, as we were also saying, these temporary states still need to be converted into enduring traits if development into these realms is to become permanent. And so even though altered states and nonordinary states get most of the attention—they're pretty exciting, after all—still, it comes back to actual development and evolution.

Q: Back to actual development through the higher levels, and not just their "peek" experience.

KW: Yes. As the self unfolds—slops and blobs—on up the spiral, the self's center of gravity will tend to organize itself around a predominant higher basic level. It will tend to *identify* its center of gravity with this level; this will be its "home base"—its major fulcrum—around which it will organize most of its perceptions, its moral responses, its motivations, its drives, and so on. Thus, its center of gravity tends to shift through these higher basic spheres of consciousness with an averagely identifiable sequence.

Q: The traditions themselves usually give various stages.

KW: Yes, the traditions themselves know this. They all have their stages of growth and development; they know the characteristics of each stage; they can spot progress and they can spot regression. And, as Aurobindo and Plotinus and Da Avabhasa have pointed out, although one can indeed speed up development through these stages, they cannot fundamentally be bypassed. You can peak-experience ahead, jump ahead, but you will have to make up the ground later, integrate and consolidate it later. Otherwise you get too "top-heavy," so to speak—you are floating upward and upward, with no grounding and no connection to the lower structures, to the mind and body and earth and senses.

Fulcrum-7: The Psychic

Q: So the first of these transpersonal stages, the psychic.

KW: As I use it, the psychic level simply means the great transition stage from ordinary, gross-oriented reality—sensorimotor and rational and existential—into the properly transpersonal domains. Paranormal events sometimes increase in frequency at the psychic level, but that is not what defines this level. The defining characteristic, the deep structure, of this psychic level is an awareness that is no longer confined exclusively to the individual ego or centaur.

Q: A few examples, perhaps.

KW: At the psychic level, a person might temporarily dissolve the separate-self sense (the ego or centaur) and find an identity with the entire gross or sensorimotor world—so-called *nature mysticism*. You're on a nice nature walk, relaxed and expansive in your awareness, and you look at a beautiful mountain, and wham!—suddenly there is no looker, just the mountain—and you are the mountain. You are not in here looking at the mountain out there. There is just the mountain, and it seems to see itself, or you seem to be seeing it from within. The mountain is closer to you than your own skin.

By any other terms, there is no separation between subject and object, between you and the entire natural world "out there." Inside and outside—they don't have any meaning anymore. You can still tell perfectly well where your body stops and the environment begins—this is *not* psychotic adualism or a "resurrection in mature form" of psychotic adualism. It is your own higher Self at this stage—fulcrum-7—which can be called the Eco-Noetic Self; some call it the Over-Soul or the World Soul. This is the fusion phase of fulcrum-7. You are a "nature mystic."

Q: But this seems like such an abrupt switch—from the individual centaur to an identity with all of nature, as it were. I don't see the smooth evolutionary progression here.

KW: Actually, it's not much of a jump at all. I think people get confused because we say identity moves from the "individual" bodymind to the "whole world," which does indeed look rather abrupt.

But that's not what happens. Look at what is actually involved. At the worldcentric centaur, one's awareness has *already* moved from an identity with the material dimension (fulcrum-1) to an identity with the biological dimension (fulcrum-2) to an identity with a mental self (fulcrum-3). That early mental self, like the previous two fulcrums, is very egocentric and narcissistic.

But with fulcrum-4, identity switches from egocentric to sociocentric. Here your awareness *already* transcends its merely *individual* aspects. Your very awareness, your very *identity*, is based upon cultural roles and collective identities and shared values. It is no longer a *body* identity, it is a *role* identity.

Thus, when you say, I am a father, I am a mother, I am a husband, I am a wife, I work at this job, I value this goal—those are already transbody identities. Those already move beyond the individual body and its sensations, and into a circle of intersubjective roles and values and goals. Most of the items that you call your "self" are not egocentric at all, but cultural and sociocentric. When you feel your "self," you are actually feeling a circle of intersubjective events, and you exist in that cultural circle, you do not exist merely inside your skin. You have decentered, transcended, a merely body-bound identity. You can't even think who you are without existing in this cultural circle, and that circle already goes way beyond your skin boundary!

With rationality and fulcrum-5, your identity decenters or expands once again, this time transcending any merely ethnocentric or sociocentric identity, and finding instead a postconventional or worldcentric identity. You actually identify yourself from a global perspective. You can no longer exist as, or identify yourself as, an ethnocentric being. It *pains* you to be merely ethnocentric. You are *embarrassed* by ethnocentric talk. You have again decentered, transcended. Your *actual identity* floats through, and exists by virtue of, a worldcentric or global awareness, an identity in the circle of *all* human beings.

It's only a small step further to actually experience your central identity, not just with all human beings, but all living beings. The global or worldcentric awareness simply steps up another notch, escapes its anthropocentric prejudice, and announces itself as all sentient beings. You experience the World Soul.

Worldcentric to World Soul is thus a fairly modest step, considering what has already happened in the expansion of conscious identity. It's a simple and natural continuation of the evolutionary process of transcend and include, unfold and enfold. Each emergence is a decentering, a transcendence, that finds more of the "external world" to actually be "internal," or part of its very being.

Molecules awoke one morning to find that atoms were inside them, enfolded in their very being. And cells awoke one morning to find that molecules were actually inside them, as part of their very being. And you might awake one morning and find that nature is a part of you, literally internal to your being. You are not a part of nature, nature is a part of you. And for just that reason, you treat nature as you would treat your lungs or your kidneys. A spontaneous environmental ethics surges forth from your heart, and you will never again look at a river, a leaf, a deer, a robin, in the same way.

This sounds very weird and far out—until you have that experience. You might ask the Apollo astronauts about it.

Q: So it really is a rather natural progression.

KW: Very much so. As I said, this looks like a radical rupture— centaur to world—because we tend to think of the individual centaur as being a single *body-bound* awareness. But the *only* stage where awareness is actually and merely body-bound is fulcrum-2. *Every* stage past that is *already* quite beyond a mere bodily identity!

And nothing but trouble has come from trying to define this transpersonal awareness as a "single-step" transformation from the "skin-encapsulated ego" to the nice World Soul. That is not a single-step process—that is at least a seven-step process! There are at least seven fulcrums, seven massive paradigm shifts, involved in getting you to a realization of this World Soul!

Deep Ecology and Ecofeminism

Q: Deep ecology, ecopsychology, and ecofeminism often emphasize this deeper Self, this Eco-Noetic Self.

KW: Yes, and in that particular regard I am a big fan of their work. They have an important message for the modern world: to find that deep Self that embraces all of nature, and thus to treat nature with the same reverence you would extend to your own being.

But here is where I believe they often get into a great deal of trouble: they take this experience of the Eco-Noetic Self, the World Soul, and they reduce it to the Lower-Right quadrant, to "we're all strands in the great web"—empirical holism, Right-Hand holism, functional fit—which actually guts the interior dimensions. These theorists reduce the Kosmos to a *monological map* of the eco-social system—which they usually call Gaia—a flatland map that ignores the six or seven profound *interior transformations* that got them to the point that they could even conceive of a global system in the first place.

Consequently, this otherwise true and noble intuition of the Eco-Noetic Self gets collapsed into "we're all strands in the great web." But that is exactly *not* the experience of the Eco-Noetic Self. In the nature-mystic experience, you are *not* a strand in the web. You are the entire web. You are doing something no mere strand ever does—you are escaping your "strandness," *transcending* it, and becoming one with the entire display. To be aware of the whole system shows precisely that you are *not* merely a strand, which is supposed to be your official stance.

So, "explaining" this experience in systems or "web-of-life" terms is a very poor way to *interpret* it. Ecomasculinists often prefer systems theory terms; ecofeminists generally believe that systems theory is too masculine and abstract, and prefer instead eco-sentimentalism and relationship terms: both are equally grounded in the monochrome world of simple location, the empirical or Right-Hand world.

But once you've committed that flatland reductionism, you start to think that the way to transform the world is to simply get everybody to agree with your monological map, forgetting the six or seven interior stages the mapmaker actually had to go through in order to *get* to this point where you *can* agree in the first place.

Q: Similar to the multicults.

KW: Yes, like the multicults, you forget all the stages of transcendence that got you to this noble point, and so not only do you bizarrely condemn transcendence itself (the actual path!), you simply collapse all those stages into an incredibly simplistic "one-step" transformation: agree with my holistic Gaia map, and you will be saved. And so like many of the multicults, these folks often become rather belligerent and intolerant, claiming that all the strands in the web are equally important, but despising the strands that disagree with them.

So instead, we need to take into account the *interior* dimensions—we have to take into account the Left Hand and not just the Right Hand. We have to take into account linguistic and cultural backgrounds, methods of interpretation, the many stages of consciousness evolution, the intricate stages of moral development and decentering, the validity claims of truthfulness and sincerity and justness, holarchical degrees of depth, the hierarchy of expanding self-identity and methods of transcendence—all of those are Left-Hand dimensions, and none of those items is found on the monological and Right-Hand Gaia map!

And for just that reason, you won't find a decent discussion of the interior stages of development in any books on deep ecology, ecofeminism, or ecophilosophy. But without those factors you'll never make it to the New World, because you won't know how to get people into the boat and on their way. You have, as we said, a fine goal with no real path.

Q: So the experience of the Eco-Noetic Self might be very genuine, but it is unpacked or interpreted in an inadequate fashion.

KW: I think so. And we want to rescue this profound intuition of the Eco-Noetic Self and its Community of all beings by giving it perhaps a more adequate interpretation, based on all four quadrants of manifestation, and not based on reducing all quadrants to the Lower Right or "Gaia." Pushing that reductionistic "new paradigm" map as the central aspect of transformation simply diverts attention away from the Left-Hand dimensions where the real transformation is occurring. As such, more often than not these approaches inadvertently sabotage and derail actual transcendence and transformation, and simply encourage the various fragments to retribalize at their own level of adaptation, no matter how shallow. Any egocentric person can sell a Gaia-centric map.

Q: So the point would be, remember the Left-Hand path!

KW: Yes, very much so. We don't want to get caught in a holistic map of flatland. As we saw, that holistic flatland map *is* the fundamental Enlightenment paradigm. That *is* subtle reductionism. That collapses the Left into the Right. That reduces all "I's" and "we's" to interwoven "its"; collapses all interior depths into exterior span; collapses all values into functional fit; reduces all translogical and all dialogical to monological. That is the great holistic web of interwoven its.

Perhaps these theorists have a genuine intuition of the Eco-Noetic Self—I believe some of them do. But they tend to collapse it into flatland and monological Right-Hand terms, which does not promote global transformation but rather encourages retribalization and regressive fragmentation in consciousness. And so these often turn out to be very *preconventional* approaches that covertly encourage *egocentric* consciousness, which their maps do not let them spot because their maps contain none of this.

The Enneagram and the Basic Skeleton

Q: I want to come back to all of that when we discuss flatland and the religion of Gaia (see Part Three). But we were talking about the Eco-Noetic Self, and you said it is one of the forms of this psychic level of consciousness development. What are some others?

KW: What all of the psychic-level developments have in common is that they have one foot in the gross, ordinary, personal realm and one foot in the transpersonal realm. And so, however different these various psychic phenomena seem, they do share a specific deep structure, which involves the beginning transcendence of gross-oriented reality, the transcendence of the ordinary body and mind and culture.

Some of these transcendental phenomena include preliminary meditative states; shamanic visions and voyages; arousal of kundalini energy (and disclosure of the whole psychic anatomy of subtle channels, energies, and essences); overwhelming feelings of the numinous; spontaneous spiritual awakenings; reliving of deep past traumas, even the birth trauma; identification with aspects of nature—plant identification, animal identification—up to an identification with all of nature (cosmic consciousness, nature mysticism, and the World Soul).

Q: How do you know those phenomena actually exist?

KW: As the observing Self begins to transcend the centaur, deeper or higher dimensions of consciousness come into being, and a new world-view or worldspace comes into focus. All of the items on that list are objects that can be directly perceived in this new *psychic worldspace*. Those items are as real in the psychic worldspace as rocks are in the sensorimotor worldspace and concepts are in the mental worldspace.

If cognition awakens or develops to this psychic level, you simply perceive these new objects, as simply as you perceive rocks in the sensory world or images in the mental world. They are simply given to awareness, they simply present themselves, and you don't have to spend a lot of time trying to figure out if they're real or not.

Of course, if you haven't awakened psychic cognition, then you will see none of this, just as a rock cannot see mental images. And you will probably have unpleasant things to say about people who do see them.

Q: So the psychic level is simply a broad space, a worldspace, within which a vast array of different phenomena can occur.

KW: Yes, which is true of any worldspace. These basic spheres of consciousness that I am outlining, from the lowest to the highest, are really just the skeleton of a very rich and complex reality. And there is much important work to be done in fleshing out this skeleton—in the lower as well as higher domains.

Take, for example, the work of Howard Gardner on multiple intelligences—the idea that development involves not one capacity but many relatively independent capacities (from musical to artistic to mathematical to athletic, and so on), which I think is quite right. We can plot the depth of those developmental capacities as well. They will fall within the same basic levels of consciousness development, but they are nonetheless relatively separate talents that unfold with their own logics, as it were. None of that is denied; in fact, I very much support those approaches. In my view, there are numerous different developmental lines or streams (e.g., cognitive, moral, aesthetic, interpersonal, needs, etc.) that move relatively independently through the basic levels or waves (body to mind to soul to spirit), giving us a very rich, multidimensional tapestry of waves and streams of consciousness unfolding.

Q: Also, the basic levels or waves themselves continue to develop, right?

KW: Yes, that's right. If you look at figure 9-1 (page 179), you'll see that each of the basic levels continues outward in a curved line of ongoing development. So just because sensorimotor cognition, for example, is listed as level 1 does not mean that its development simply stops with level 2. On the contrary, as the sensorimotor dimension is taken up and enfolded in higher development, some extremely advanced sensorimotor skills can emerge. That there is a "psychic side of sports," for example, is now widely acknowledged. As Michael Murphy has documented, many great athletes and dancers enter some very profound psychic spaces, and this translates into almost unbelievable performances.

Q: How do different personality types fit in the spectrum of consciousness?

KW: Most typologies are types of character formations that can and do occur on all of the levels (except usually the end limits). The simplest and best known is probably introverted and extroverted. These are not *levels* of consciousness, they are *types* that occur on *every* level. So you can be at level 4, for example, and be an introvert or an extrovert.

Q: How about the Enneagram?

KW: The same. The Enneagram divides personality into nine basic types. These nine types are *not* levels of consciousness. They are personality types that exist on all levels of consciousness. So what you have are nine types on each of the nine or so major levels of consciousness—and you can start to see what a truly multidimensional and full-spectrum model looks like.

As the personality begins to grow and develop, during the first three fulcrums, it tends to settle into one of these nine Enneagram types, depending largely on the self's major defense mechanism as well as its major innate strength. These types persist and dominate consciousness until roughly fulcrum-7, or the beginning of the transpersonal domain, where they begin to transform into their correlative wisdom or essence.

Q: Which means what, exactly?

KW: The idea is based on the central tantric notion, found from Sufism to Buddhism, that if you enter a lower state or even a defiled state with clear awareness, then that state will transform into its corresponding wisdom. So if you enter passion with awareness, you will find compassion. If you enter anger with awareness, you will find clarity. And so on. The traditions give various accounts of these transformations, but you can see the general point, which I think is quite valid. And with higher development, the Enneagram types likewise begin to unfold their corresponding essence or wisdom.

The Enneagram does not cover subtle dimensions very well, and it does not cover the causal at all. But it does incorporate these beginning transpersonal wisdoms, and so it can be a very powerful tool in the right hands. The Enneagram itself was largely created by Oscar Ichazo. Helen

Palmer has done much work with it, and Don Riso has recently begun to use the different Enneagram types in conjunction with the spectrum of consciousness, which I would certainly support. Hameed Ali's "Diamond Approach" has its roots in the Enneagram and Sufism, but adds its own distinctive and useful tools and perspectives.

Right now the Enneagram is being popularized in America and used as a new psychological parlor game—"Want to find your Self? Take a number!"—which is a lot of fun. But it also has higher uses.

Q: So at their best, types and levels cover horizontal and vertical—both important.

KW: Yes. On the higher levels themselves, I might give the example of Roger Walsh's treatment of shamanism. Walsh accepts the basic levels of psychic/subtle, causal, and nondual, and he uses that as a type of vertical scale. He then adds a very sophisticated horizontal scale that analyzes a dozen variables on each of those levels, from ease of control to arousal to emotional affect to the ability to concentrate. He thus arrives at a multidimensional grid for the analysis of transpersonal states, and this grid has enormously advanced our knowledge of the field.

So those are all examples of how to flesh out this basic skeleton that I am presenting. And the fact that we are focusing on the evolution of just this skeleton does not mean these other aspects aren't equally important.

Fulcrum-8: The Subtle

Q: So as this general evolution continues from psychic to subtle . . . ?

KW: "Subtle" simply means processes that are subtler than gross, ordinary, waking consciousness. These include interior luminosities and sounds, archetypal forms and patterns, extremely subtle bliss currents and cognitions (shabd, nada), expansive affective states of love and compassion, as well as subtler *pathological* states of what can only be called Kosmic terror, Kosmic evil, Kosmic horror. As always, because of the dialectic of progress, this subtle development is most definitely not just a day at the beach.

But this overall type of mysticism we call *deity mysticism*, because it involves your own Archetypal Form, a union with God or Goddess, a union with saguna Brahman, a state of savikalpa samadhi, and so on. This union or fusion with Deity—union with God, by whatever name—is the beginning or fusion phase of fulcrum-8.

This is not just nature mysticism, not just a union with the gross or natural world—what the Buddhists call the Nirmanakaya—but a deeper union with the subtler dimensions of the Sambhogakaya, the interior bliss body or transformational body, which transcends and includes the gross or natural domain, but is not confined to it—nature mysticism gives way to deity mysticism.

Q: Are any of these higher levels fully present in human beings prior to their emergence? Are they lying around waiting to emerge?

KW: Fully formed, no. The *deep structures* of these higher levels are present as *potentials* in all human beings, as far as we can tell. But as these deep potentials unfold, their actual *surface structures* are created and molded *by all four quadrants*. That is, the surface structures are created and molded by intentional, behavioral, cultural, and social patterns.

The classic example is that a person has an experience of intense interior illumination, a subtle-level illumination (perhaps in a near-death experience). A Christian might see it as Christ or an angel or a saint, a Buddhist might see it as the Sambhogakaya or bliss body of Buddha, a Jungian might see it as an archetypal experience of the Self, and so on. As we said, *all depth must be interpreted*, and these interpretations are not possible without a whole set of *background contexts* which provide many of the tools with which the interpretation will proceed. One's own individual background, one's cultural background, and one's social institutions will all have a hand in interpreting this depth-experience. This is *unavoidable*.

So these higher structures are not like fully formed little treasure chests buried in your psyche, waiting to pop to the surface. The deep structures are given, but the surface structures are not, and the experience itself involves an interpretive component, which cannot proceed without various backgrounds—and those backgrounds do not exist merely in your psyche!

But if we reject that pregiven extreme, it doesn't mean we have to fall into the opposite error of extreme constructivism. The basic reality of this subtle experience of interior illumination is not simply or arbitrarily constructed by culture, because these experiences occur cross-culturally, and further, in many cases the cultural background officially denies or prohibits these experiences, and yet they still happen all the time anyway.

So just because these experiences have an interpretive component does not mean they are merely cultural creations. When you watch the sun set, you will bring interpretations to that experience as well—

perhaps romantic, perhaps rational, each with a cultural coloring, but that doesn't mean that the sun ceases to exist if your culture disappears!

No, these are ontologically real events. They actually exist. They have real referents. But these referents do not exist in the sensorimotor world-space, they do not exist in the rational worldspace, they do not exist in the existential worldspace. So you can find evidence for them in none of those worldspaces. Rather, they *exist* in the subtle worldspace, and evidence for them can be plentifully found *there*.

Jung and the Archetypes

Q: Now you mentioned this subtle level as being an archetypal level, but I know that by "archetype" you don't mean Jungian archetype.

KW: That's right. This is a very complex topic, and I don't think we have time to do it justice. But I might say that, for the most part, the Jungian archetypes are basic, collectively inherited images or forms lying in the magic and mythic dimensions of human awareness, and generally speaking these should not be confused with the developments in the psychic and subtle domains.

Q: The Jungian archetype is . . . ?

KW: The typical Jungian archetype is a basic, inherited image or form in the psyche. These basic or primordial images represent very common, very typical experiences that humans everywhere are exposed to: the experience of birth, of the mother, the father, the shadow, the wise old man, the trickster, the ego, the animus and anima (masculine and feminine), and so on.

Millions upon millions of past encounters with these *typical situations* have, so to speak, ingrained these basic images into the collective psyche of the human race. You find these basic and primordial images worldwide, and you find an especially rich fund of them in the world's great myths.

Since the rudimentary forms of these mythic images come embedded in the individual psyche, then when you have an encounter with, say, your own mother, you are not just encountering your particular mother. You also have this archetype or basic image of millions of years of mothering stamped into your psyche. So you are not just interacting with your mother, you are interacting with the world Mother, with the Great Mother, and this archetypal image can therefore have an impact on you that is way out of proportion to anything your actual mother may or may not do to you.

So in classical Jungian analysis, you have to analyze and *interpret*, not just your own individual unconscious—the specific events that happened to you in your own life, with your own mother and father, your own shadow, and so on—you also need to analyze and interpret this collective level of archetypal material.

Perhaps, for example, you have activated the Devouring Mother archetype; maybe it has nothing to do with your actual mother; maybe she is for the most part loving and attentive; and yet you are horrified of being engulfed in relationships, devoured by emotional closeness, torn apart by personal intimacy. Maybe you are in the grip, not of your actual mother, but of an archetype. And this might especially show up in dreams: maybe a big black spider is trying to eat you.

So one of the things you might want to do, as you analyze this collective archetypal level, is study the world's great mythologies, because they are repositories of the earlier and typical (and therefore archetypal) encounters, including the mothering one in general. In other words, this will give you a *background* against which to *interpret* these primordial images, and so you will be able to more sincerely and truthfully approach these images and interpret them more clearly in yourself. You will be able to *differentiate* from their choking grip on your awareness, and then *integrate* them more carefully in your life. And there is much truth to all of that, I think.

Q: So Jungian archetypes tend to be repositories of basic, collective, typical encounters of the human race in general.

KW: For the most part. And as far as it goes, I am in substantial agreement with those Jungian archetypes. I am in almost complete accord with most of that Jungian perspective, and in that specific regard I consider myself a Jungian.

But the crucial point is that *collective* is not necessarily *transpersonal*. Most of the Jungian archetypes, as I said, are simply archaic images lying in the *magic* and *mythic* structures. They exert a pull on awareness from the level of fulcrums 2, 3, and 4. There is little transrational or transpersonal about them. It is important to come to terms with these "archetypes," to differentiate them and integrate them (transcend and include), but they are not themselves the source of a transpersonal or genuinely spiritual awareness. In fact, for the most part they are regressive pulls in awareness, lead weights around higher development—precisely what has to be overcome, not simply embraced.

The point is, just because something is collective does not mean it is transpersonal. There are collective prepersonal structures (magic and mythic), collective personal structures (rational and existential), and collective transpersonal structures (psychic and subtle). Collective simply means that the structure is universally present, like the capacity for sensation, perception, impulse, emotion, and so on. This is not necessarily *transpersonal*; it is simply *collective* or common. We all collectively inherit ten toes, but if I experience my toes, I am not having a transpersonal experience.

Q: But what about the enormously popular books like Jean Bolen's *Goddesses in Everywoman* and *Gods in Everyman*? They are definitely based on mythological motifs or archetypes, and those are spiritual, aren't they?

KW: Depends on what you mean by "spiritual." If you mean "transpersonal," no, I don't think those books are particularly transpersonal. I like those books, incidentally, but there is little in them that is actually transpersonal or genuinely spiritual. In those books, there is a wonderful presentation of all the "archetypal" gods and goddesses that are collectively inherited by men and women, from the steadiness and patience of Hestia to the sexuality and sensuality of Aphrodite to the strength and independence of Artemis. But those gods and goddesses are not transpersonal modes of awareness, or genuinely mystical luminosities, but simply a collection of typical and everyday self-images and self-roles available to men and women. They are simply self-concepts (fulcrum-3) and self-roles (fulcrum-4) that represent common and typical potentials available to men and women pretty much everywhere.

And those *mythic roles* are very useful in this sense: Perhaps, as a woman, you are not aware of your own capacity for strength and independence. Perhaps you need to be more in touch with the Artemis in you. By reading the various Artemis myths and stories, you can more easily access this archetypal level in your own psyche, and thus bring forth that potential in your own life. This is terrific.

But this is not transpersonal. This is just a mythic-membership role, a persona, a type of ego relation. It is not trans-egoic. Collective typical is not transpersonal. Part of the spiritual anemia in this country is that something as prosaic as getting in touch with the strong Artemis ego in you is called transpersonal or spiritual. It's rather sad, actually.

Q: So are any of the Jungian archetypes transpersonal or transrational?

KW: Most Jungian archetypes, the mythic archetypes, are prepersonal or at least prerational (magical and mythic). A few Jungian archetypes are personal (ego, persona), and a few are vaguely transpersonal (wise old man, the Self, mandala). But those "transpersonal" archetypes are rather anemic compared to what we know about the transpersonal domains.

Take, as only one example, the eighteen stages of actual transpersonal growth outlined in the Mahamudra tradition of Tibetan Buddhism. These are extraordinarily detailed descriptions of the stages of evolution of higher and transpersonal awareness. And *none* of those stages appear in any of the world's classical myths. You will not find those stages in Zeus or Hector or Little Red Riding Hood.

The reason is, those eighteen stages of contemplative unfolding actually describe very rare, nontypical, nonordinary, transpersonal growth through the psychic and subtle and causal domains—they do not describe, nor do they spring from, typical and common and everyday experiences, and so they are not found in the archaic and magic and mythic structures, and therefore they show up in none of the world's typical mythologies. Hera and Demeter and Goldilocks, and Artemis and Persephone and Hansel and Gretel, never attempted these stages! And therefore you rarely find these higher stages in Robert Bly, James Hillman, Edward Edinger, Marie-Louise von Franz, Walter Odajnyk, or any of the great Jungian theorists.

Q: This has caused a great deal of confusion in religious studies, because for a long time Jung was the only game in town. If you were interested in both psychology and spirituality, then you were a Jungian.

KW: Pretty much. The Jungian mythic archetypes are real enough, and they are very important, as I said. But Jung consistently failed to carefully differentiate the archetypes into their prepersonal, personal, and transpersonal components, and since all three of those are collectively inherited, then there is a constant confusing of *collective* (and "archetypal") with *transpersonal* and spiritual and mystical.

And so consciousness is simply divided into two great domains: *personal* and *collective*. And the tendency is then to take *anything* collective and call it spiritual, mystical, transpersonal, whereas much of it is simply prepersonal, prerational, preconventional, and even regressive.

So we have some very popular theorists who, tired of the burdens of postconventional and worldcentric rational perspectivism, recommend a regressive slide into egocentric, vital-impulsive, polymorphous, phantasmic-emotional revival—in other words, they recommend the fulcrum-2 self. They call this fulcrum-2 self the "soul." They would like us to live from this level. But that, in my opinion, is looking for Spirit in precisely those approaches that do not transcend the ego but merely prevent its emergence in the first place.

Q: So the "real" archetypes are, what?

KW: From the Neoplatonic traditions in the West, to the Vedanta and Mahayana and Trikaya traditions in the East, the real archetypes are subtle seed-forms upon which all of manifestation depends. In deep states of contemplative awareness, one begins to understand that the entire Kosmos emerges straight out of Emptiness, out of primordial Purity, out of nirguna Brahman, out of the Dharmakaya, out of unqualifiable Godhead, radiant Ein Sof, and the first *Forms* that emerge out of this Emptiness are the basic Forms upon which all lesser forms depend for their being.

These Forms are the actual archetypes, a term which means "original pattern" or "primary mold." There is a Light of which all lesser lights are pale shadows, there is a Bliss of which all lesser joys are anemic copies, there is a Consciousness of which all lesser cognitions are mere reflections, there is a primordial Sound of which all lesser sounds are thin echoes. Those are the real archetypes.

When we find those types of statements in Plotinus or Asanga or Garab Dorje or Abhinavigupta or Shankara, they are not simply theoretical hunches or metaphysical postulates. They are direct experiential disclosures issuing directly from the subtle dimension of reality, *interpreted* according to the *backgrounds* of those individuals, but *issuing* from this profound ontological reality, this subtle worldspace.

And if you want to know what these men and women are actually talking about, then you must take up the contemplative practice or injunction or paradigm, and perform the experiment yourself. These archetypes, the true archetypes, are a meditative experience, and it is very hard to understand these archetypes without performing the experiment. They are not images existing in the mythic worldspace, they are not philosophical concepts existing in the rational worldspace; they are meditative phenomena existing in the subtle worldspace.

So this experiment will disclose these archetypal data, and then you can help interpret what they mean. And by far the most commonly accepted interpretation is, you are looking at the basic forms and foundations of the entire manifest world. You are looking directly into the Face of the Divine. As Emerson said, bid the intruders take the shoes off their feet, for here is the God within.

13

Realms of the Superconscious: Part 2

Q: You said that with the archetypes, you are looking into the Face of the Divine, the first Forms of the Divine. Most modern researchers reject all of that as "mere metaphysics" at best, none of which can be verified.

KW: Well, you yourself should perform this experiment and look at the data yourself. Then you can help interpret it. If you don't perform the experiment—the meditative injunction, the exemplar, the paradigm—then you don't have the data from which to make a good interpretation.

If you take somebody from the magic or mythic worldview, and you try to explain to them that the sum of the squares of the right sides of a right triangle is equal to the square of the hypotenuse, you won't get very far. What you are doing cannot be seen in those worlds. And yet you are correct. You are performing an experiment in the rational worldspace, and your mathematical results can be checked by all those who perform the same experiment. It's very public, very reproducible, very fallibilist, very communal knowledge *in the rational worldspace*: its results exist and can be readily checked by all who enter the rational worldspace and try the experiment.

Just so with any of the other interior experiments in awareness disclosing yet higher realms, of which meditation is one of the oldest, most tested, and most reproduced. So if you're skeptical, that's a healthy attitude, and we invite you to find out for yourself, and perform this interior experiment with us, and get the data, and help us interpret it. But if you won't perform the experiment, please don't ridicule those who do.

And by far the most common interpretation of those who have seen this data is: you are face to face with the Divine.

Fulcrum-9: The Causal

Q: You mentioned that these subtle or archetypal Forms issue directly from Emptiness, from the causal, which is the next stage, fulcrum-9.

KW: When, as a specific type of meditation, you pursue the observing Self, the Witness, to its very *source* in pure Emptiness, then no objects arise in consciousness at all. This is a discrete, identifiable state of awareness—namely, *unmanifest absorption* or *cessation*, variously known as nirvikalpa samadhi, jnana samadhi, ayin, vergezzen, nirodh, classical nirvana, the cloud of unknowing.

This is the causal state, a discrete state, which is often likened to the state of deep dreamless sleep, except that this state is not a mere blank but rather an utter fullness, and it is experienced as such—as infinitely drenched in the fullness of Being, so full that no manifestation can even begin to contain it. Because it can never be seen as an object, this pure Self is pure Emptiness.

Q: That's all very abstract. Could you be more concrete about this?

KW: You are aware of yourself in this moment, yes?

Q: I think so.

KW: So if I say, Who are you?, you will start to describe yourself— you are a father, a mother, a husband, a wife, a friend; you are a lawyer, a clerk, a teacher, a manager. You have these likes and dislikes, you prefer this type of food, you tend to have these impulses and desires, and so on.

Q: Yes, I would list all the things that I know about myself.

KW: You would list the "things you know about yourself."

Q: Yes.

KW: All of those things you know about yourself are objects in your awareness. They are images or ideas or concepts or desires or feelings that parade by in front of your awareness, yes? They are all objects in your awareness.

Q: Yes.

KW: All those objects in your awareness are precisely not the observing Self. All those things that you know about yourself are precisely not the real Self. Those are not the Seer; those are simply things that can be *seen*. All of those objects that you describe when you "describe yourself" are actually *not* your real Self at all! They are just more objects, whether internal or external, they are not the real Seer of those objects, they are not the real Self. So when you describe yourself by listing all of those objects, you are ultimately giving a list of mistaken identities, a list of lies, a list of precisely what you ultimately *are not*.

So who is this real Seer? Who or what is this observing Self?

Ramana Maharshi called this Witness the I-I, because it is aware of the individual I or self, but cannot itself be seen. So what is this I-I, this causal Witness, this pure observing Self?

This deeply inward Self is witnessing the world out there, and it is witnessing all your interior thoughts as well. This Seer sees the ego, and sees the body, and sees the natural world. All of those parade by "in front" of this Seer. But the Seer itself cannot be seen. If you see anything, those are just more objects. Those objects are precisely what the Seer is not, what the Witness is not.

So you pursue this inquiry, Who am I? Who or what is this Seer that cannot itself be seen? You simply "push back" into your awareness, and you *dis-identify* with any and every object you see or can see.

The Self or the Seer or the Witness is not any particular thought—I can see that thought as an object. The Seer is not any particular sensation—I am aware of that as an object. The observing Self is not the body, it is not the mind, it is not the ego—I can see all of those as objects. What is looking at all those objects? What in you right now is looking at all these objects—looking at nature and its sights, looking at the body and its sensations, looking at the mind and its thoughts? What is looking at all that?

Try to feel yourself right now—get a good sense of being yourself—and notice, that self is just another object in awareness. It isn't even a real subject, a real self, it's just another object in awareness. This little self and its thoughts parade by in front of you just like the clouds float by through the sky. And what is the real you that is witnessing all of that? Witnessing your little objective self? Who or what is that?

As you push back into this pure Subjectivity, this pure Seer, you won't see it as an object—you can't see it as an object, because it's not an object! It is nothing you can see. Rather, as you calmly rest in this observing awareness—watching mind and body and nature float by—you might begin to notice that what you are actually feeling is simply a sense of freedom, a sense of release, a sense of not being bound to any of the objects you are calmly witnessing. You don't see anything in particular, you simply rest in this vast freedom.

In front of you the clouds parade by, your thoughts parade by, bodily sensations parade by, and you are none of them. You are the vast expanse of freedom through which all these objects come and go. You are an opening, a clearing, an Emptiness, a vast spaciousness, in which all these objects come and go. Clouds come and go, sensations come and go, thoughts come and go—and you are none of them; you are that vast sense of freedom, that vast Emptiness, that vast opening, through which manifestation arises, stays a bit, and goes.

So you simply start to notice that the "Seer" in you that is witnessing all these objects is itself just a vast Emptiness. It is not a thing, not an object, not anything you can see or grab hold of. It is rather a sense of vast Freedom, because it is not itself anything that enters the objective world of time and objects and stress and strain. This pure Witness is a pure Emptiness in which all these individual subjects and objects arise, stay a bit, and pass.

So this pure Witness is not anything that can be seen! The attempt to see the Witness or know it as an object—that's just more grasping and seeking and clinging in time. The Witness isn't out there in the stream; it is the vast expanse of Freedom in which the stream arises. So you can't get hold of it and say, Aha, I see it! Rather, it is the Seer, not *anything* that can be seen. As you rest in this Witnessing, all that you sense is just a vast Emptiness, a vast Freedom, a vast Expanse—a transparent opening or clearing in which all these little subjects and objects arise. Those subjects and objects can definitely be seen, but the Witness of them cannot be seen. The Witness of them is an utter *release* from them, an utter Freedom not caught in their turmoils, their desires, their fears, their hopes.

Of course, we tend to *identify* ourselves with these little individual subjects and objects—and that is exactly the problem! We identify the Seer with puny little things that can be seen. And that is the beginning of bondage and unfreedom. We are actually this vast expanse of Freedom, but we identify with unfree and limited objects and subjects, all of which can be seen, all of which suffer, and none of which is what we are.

Patanjali gave the classic description of bondage as "the identification of the Seer with the instruments of seeing"—with the little subjects and objects, instead of the opening or clearing or Emptiness in which they all arise.

So when we rest in this pure Witness, we don't see this Witness as an object. Anything you can see is *not* it. Rather, it is the absence of any subjects or objects altogether, it is the *release* from all of that. Resting in the pure Witness, there is this background absence or Emptiness, and this is "experienced," *not* as an object, but as a vast expanse of Freedom and Liberation from the constrictions of identifying with these little subjects and objects that enter the stream of time and are ground up in that agonizing torrent.

So when you rest in the pure Seer, in the pure Witness, you are invisible. You cannot be seen. No part of you can be seen, because you are not an object. Your body can be seen, your mind can be seen, nature can be seen, but you are not any of those objects. You are the pure source of awareness, and not anything that arises in that awareness. So you abide as awareness.

Things arise in awareness, they stay a bit and depart, they come and they go. They arise in *space*, they move in *time*. But the pure Witness does not come and go. It does not arise in space, it does not move in time. It is as it is; it is ever-present and unvarying. It is not an object out there, so it never enters the stream of time, of space, of birth, of death. Those are all experiences, all objects—they all come, they all go. But you do not come and go; you do not enter that stream; you are aware of all that, so you are not caught in all that. The Witness is aware of space, aware of time—and is therefore itself free of space, free of time. It is timeless and spaceless—the purest Emptiness through which time and space parade.

So this pure Seer is prior to life and death, prior to time and turmoil, prior to space and movement, prior to manifestation—prior even to the Big Bang itself. This doesn't mean that the pure Self existed in a time before the Big Bang, but that it exists prior to time, period. It just never enters that stream. It is aware of time, and is thus free of time—it is utterly timeless. And because it is timeless, it is eternal—which doesn't mean everlasting time, but free of time altogether.

It was never born, it will never die. It never enters that temporal stream. This vast Freedom is the great Unborn, of which the Buddha said: "There is an unborn, an unmade, an uncreate. Were it not for this unborn, unmade, uncreate, there would be no release from the born, the made, the created." Resting in this vast expanse of Freedom is resting in this great Unborn, this vast Emptiness.

And because it is Unborn, it is Undying. It was not created with your body, it will not perish when your body perishes. It's not that it lives on beyond your body's death, but rather that it never enters the stream of time in the first place. It doesn't live on after your body, it lives prior to your body, always. It doesn't go on in time forever, it is simply prior to the stream of time itself.

Space, time, objects—all of those merely parade by. But you are the Witness, the pure Seer that is itself pure Emptiness, pure Freedom, pure Openness, the great Emptiness through which the entire parade passes, never touching you, never tempting you, never hurting you, never consoling you.

And because there is this vast Emptiness, this great Unborn, you can indeed gain liberation from the born and the created, from the suffering of space and time and objects, from the mechanism of terror inherent in those fragments, from the vale of tears called samsara.

Q: I can get a brief taste of that as you talk about it.

KW: Most people can connect fairly quickly with the Witness. Living from that Freedom is a gentle exercise, and this is where meditation is very helpful.

Q: Any specific recommendations?

KW: Well, various types of meditation often aim for different transpersonal realms. Some aim for psychic experiences, some for the deity mysticism of the subtle realm, some for the formlessness and Freedom of the causal Witness, and some for nondual Unity or One Taste, which we will discuss in a moment.

My recommendation is simply to start with the acknowledged teachers in any of the great contemplative traditions. One might start by consulting the works of Father Thomas Keating, Rabbi Zalman Schachter-Shalomi, the Dalai Lama, Sri Ramana Maharshi, Bawa Muhaiyadeen, or any of the many widely acknowledged teachers in any of the great lineages.

Perhaps later on we can talk about the importance of an *integral practice* that takes the best of these great traditions and integrates them with the best of psychotherapy, to arrive at an "all-level, all-quadrant" transformative practice.

Q: Definitely. In the meantime, we are at fulcrum-9 and the Witness. How does that Witness relate to the causal unmanifest?

KW: The Witness is itself the causal unmanifest. It is itself pure Emptiness. And if, as a yogic endeavor, you actually keep inquiring intensely into the source, into the pure Subjectivity of this Seer, then all objects and subjects will simply cease to arise at all. And that would be nirvikalpa or *cessation*—an actual yogic state, a discrete state (it is, in fact, the fusion phase of fulcrum-9). This is pure *formless mysticism*—all objects, even God as a perceived form, vanish into cessation, and so deity mysticism gives way to formless mysticism.

Because all possible objects have *not yet arisen*, this is a completely *unmanifest* state of pure Emptiness. What you actually "see" in this state is infinite nothing, which simply means that it is too Full to be contained in any object or any subject or any sight or any sound. It is pure consciousness, pure awareness, prior to any manifestation at all—prior to subjects and objects, prior to phenomena, prior to holons, prior to things, prior to anything. It is utterly timeless, spaceless, objectless. And therefore it is radically and infinitely free of the limitations and constrictions of space and time and objects—and radically free of the torture inherent in those fragments.

It is not necessary to pursue the Witness in that particularly yogic fashion, but it can be done, and it does point up the unmanifest source of the Seer itself. This is why many traditions, like Yogachara Buddhism, simply equate Emptiness and Consciousness. We needn't get involved in all the technical details and arguments about that, but you get the general point—the Witness itself, pure Consciousness itself, is not a thing, not a process, not a quality, not an entity—it is ultimately unqualifiable—it is ultimately pure Emptiness.

Q: Why is it called the "causal"?

KW: Because it is the support or cause or creative ground of all junior dimensions. Remember that we saw, as Whitehead put it, that "the ultimate metaphysical principle is the creative advance into novelty." Creativity is part of the basic ground of the universe. Somehow, some way, miraculously, new holons emerge. I say out of Emptiness, but you can call that creative ground whatever you want. Some would call it God, or Goddess, or Tao, or Brahman, or Keter, or Rigpa, or Dharmakaya, or Maat, or Li. The more scientifically oriented tend to prefer to speak simply of the "self-transcending" capacity of the universe, as does Jantsch. That's fine. It doesn't matter. The point is, stuff emerges. Amazing!

Emptiness, creativity, holons—and that is exactly where we started our account in chapter 1. These holons arise as subject and object, in both singular and plural forms—that is, the four quadrants—and they follow the twenty tenets, which is simply *the pattern that manifestation displays* as it arises, a pattern that is a potential of Emptiness, a potential of the Dharmakaya, a potential of the Godhead. And with that pattern of twenty tenets, off we go on the evolutionary drive of holons returning to their source.

That pattern embodies a creative drive to greater depth, greater consciousness, greater unfolding, and that unfolding ultimately unfolds into its own infinite ground in pure Emptiness. But that Emptiness is not itself an emergent, it is rather the creative ground, prior to time, that is present all along, but finally becomes transparent to itself in certain holons that awaken to that Emptiness, to that Spirit, to that groundless Ground.

That same Emptiness, as Consciousness, was present all along as the interior depth of every holon, a depth that increasingly shed its lesser forms until it shed forms altogether—its depth goes to infinity, its time goes to eternity, its interior space is all space, its agency is the very Divine itself: the ground, path, and fruition of Emptiness.

The Nondual

Q: So this causal unmanifest—is it the absolute end point? Is this the end of time, the end of evolution, the end of history? The final Omega point?

KW: Well, many traditions take this state of cessation to be the ultimate state, the final end point of all development and evolution, yes. And this end state is equated with full Enlightenment, ultimate release, pure nirvana.

But that is not the "final story," according to the Nondual traditions. Because at some point, as you inquire into the Witness, and rest in the Witness, the sense of being a Witness "in here" completely vanishes itself, and the Witness turns out to be everything that is witnessed. The *causal* gives way to the *Nondual*, and formless mysticism gives way to nondual mysticism. "Form is Emptiness and Emptiness is Form."

Technically, you have dis-identified with even the Witness, and then integrated it with all manifestation—in other words, the second and third phases of fulcrum-9, which leads to fulcrum-10, which is not really a separate fulcrum or level, but the reality or Suchness of all levels, all states, all conditions.

And this is the second and most profound meaning of Emptiness—it is not a *discrete* state, but the reality of *all* states, the Suchness of all states. You have moved from the causal to the Nondual.

Q: Emptiness has two meanings?

KW: Yes, which can be very confusing. On the one hand, as we just saw, it is a discrete, identifiable state of awareness—namely, unmanifest absorption or cessation (nirvikalpa samadhi, ayn, jnana samadhi, nirodh, classical nirvana). This is the causal state, a discrete state.

The second meaning is that Emptiness is not merely a particular state among other states, but rather the reality or suchness or condition of all states. Not a particular state *apart* from other states, but the reality or condition of *all* states, high or low, sacred or profane, ordinary or extraordinary. Recall that on figure 9-1 we had Spirit as both the highest level ("causal") and the ever-present Ground of all levels ("nondual").

Q: We already discussed the discrete state; now the Nondual.

KW: Yes, the "experience" of this nondual Suchness is similar to the nature unity experience we earlier discussed, except now this unity is experienced not just with gross Form out there, but also with all of the subtle Forms in here. In Buddhist terms, this is not just the Nirmana-kaya—gross or nature mysticism; and not just the Sambhogakaya—subtle or deity mysticism; and not just the Dharmakaya—causal or formless mysticism. It is the Svabhavikakaya—the integration of all three of them. It is beyond nature mysticism, beyond deity mysticism, and beyond formless mysticism—it is the reality or the Suchness of each, and thus integrates each in its embrace. It embraces the entire spectrum of consciousness—transcends all, includes all.

Q: Again, rather technical. Perhaps there's a more direct way to talk about Nondual mysticism?

KW: Across the board, the sense of being any sort of Seer or Witness or Self vanishes altogether. You don't look at the sky, you are the sky. You can taste the sky. It's not out there. As Zen would say, you can drink the Pacific Ocean in a single gulp, you can swallow the Kosmos whole—precisely because awareness is no longer split into a seeing subject in here and a seen object out there. There is just pure seeing. Consciousness and its display are not-two.

Everything continues to arise moment to moment—the entire Kosmos continues to arise moment to moment—but there is nobody watching the display, there is just the display, a spontaneous and luminous gesture of great perfection. The pure *Emptiness* of the Witness turns out to be one with every *Form* that is witnessed, and that is one of the basic meanings of "nonduality."

Q: Again, could you be even more specific?

KW: Well, you might begin by getting into the state of the Witness—that is, you simply rest in pure observing awareness—you are *not* any object that can be seen—not nature, not body, not thoughts—just rest in that pure witnessing awareness. And you can get a certain "sensation" of that witnessing awareness—a sensation of freedom, of release, of great expanse.

While you are resting in that state, and "sensing" this Witness as a great expanse, if you then look at, say, a mountain, you might begin to notice that the sensation of the Witness and the sensation of the mountain are the same sensation. When you "feel" your pure Self and you "feel" the mountain, they are absolutely the same feeling.

In other words, the real world is not given to you *twice*—one out there, one in here. That "twiceness" is exactly the meaning of "duality." Rather, the real world is given to you *once*, immediately—it is one feeling, it has one taste, it is utterly full in that one taste, it is not severed into seer and seen, subject and object, fragment and fragment. It is a singular, of which the plural is unknown. You can taste the mountain; it is the same taste as your Self; it is not out there being reflected in here— that duality is not present in the immediateness of real experience. Real experience, before you slice it up, does not contain that duality—real experience, reality itself, is "nondual." You are still you, and the mountain is still the mountain, but you and the mountain are two sides of one and the same experience, which is the one and only reality at that moment.

If you relax into present experience in that fashion, the separate-self sense will uncoil; you will stop standing back from life; you will not have experience, you will suddenly become all experience; you will not be "in here" looking "out there"—in here and out there are one, so you are no longer trapped "in here."

And so suddenly, you are not in the bodymind. Suddenly, the body-mind has dropped. Suddenly, the wind doesn't blow on you, it blows through you, within you. You are not looking at the mountain, you are the mountain—the mountain is closer to you than your own skin. You *are* that, and there is *no you*—just this entire luminous display spontaneously arising moment to moment. The separate self is nowhere to be found.

The entire sensation of "weight" drops altogether, because you are not in the Kosmos, the Kosmos is in you, and you are purest Emptiness. The entire universe is a transparent shimmering of the Divine, of primordial Purity. But the Divine is not someplace else, it is just all of this shimmering. It is self-seen. It has One Taste. It is nowhere else.

Q: Subject and object are nondual?

KW: You know the Zen koan, "What is the sound of one hand clapping?" Usually, of course, we need two hands to clap—and that is the structure of typical experience. We have a sense of ourselves as a subject in here, and the world as an object out there. We have these "two hands" of experience, the subject and the object. And typical experience is a smashing of these two hands together to make a commotion, a sound. The object out there smashes into me as a subject, and I have an experience—the two hands clap together and experience emerges.

And so the typical structure of experience is like a punch in the face. The ordinary self is the battered self—it is utterly battered by the universe "out there." The ordinary self is a series of bruises, of scars, the results of these two hands of experience smashing together. This bruising is called "duhkha," suffering. As Krishnamurti used to say, in that gap between the subject and the object lies the entire misery of humankind.

But with the nondual state, suddenly there are not two hands. Suddenly, the subject and the object are one hand. Suddenly, there is nothing outside of you to smash into you, bruise you, torment you. Suddenly, you do not *have* an experience, you *are* every experience that arises, and so you are instantly released into all space: you and the entire Kosmos are one hand, one experience, one display, one gesture of great perfection. There is nothing outside of you that you can want, or desire, or seek, or grasp—your soul expands to the corners of the universe and embraces all with infinite delight. You are utterly Full, utterly Saturated, so full and saturated that the boundaries to the Kosmos completely explode and leave you without date or duration, time or location, awash in an ocean of infinite care. You are released into the All, as the All—you are the self-seen radiant Kosmos, you are the universe of One Taste, and the taste is utterly infinite.

So what is the sound of that one hand clapping? What is the taste of that One Taste? When there is *nothing outside of you* that can hit you, hurt you, push you, pull you—what is the sound of that one hand clapping?

See the sunlight on the mountains? Feel the cool breeze? What is not utterly obvious? Who is not already enlightened? As a Zen Master put it, "When I heard the sound of the bell ringing, there was no I, and no bell, just the ringing." There is no twiceness, no twoness, in immediate experience! No inside and no outside, no subject and no object—just immediate awareness itself, the sound of one hand clapping.

So you are not in here, on this side of a transparent window, looking at the Kosmos out there. The transparent window has shattered, your bodymind drops, you are free of that confinement forever, you are no longer "behind your face" looking at the Kosmos—you simply are the Kosmos. You *are* all that. Which is precisely why you can swallow the Kosmos and span the centuries, and nothing moves at all. The sound of this one hand clapping is the sound the Big Bang made. It is the sound of supernovas exploding in space. It is the sound of the robin singing. It is the sound of a waterfall on a crystal-clear day. It is the sound of the entire manifest universe—and you are that sound.

Which is why your Original Face is not *in here*. It is the sheerest Emptiness or transparency of this shimmering display. If the Kosmos is arising, you are that. If nothing arises, you are that. In either case, you are that. In either case, you are not in here. The window has shattered. The gap between the subject and object is gone. There is no twiceness, no twoness, to be found anywhere—the world is *never* given to you *twice*, but always only *once*—and you are that. You are that One Taste.

This state is not something you can *bring about*. This nondual state, this state of One Taste, is the very nature of every experience *before* you slice it up. This One Taste is not some experience you bring about through effort; rather, it is the actual condition of all experience *before* you do anything to it. This uncontrived state is *prior* to effort, prior to grasping, prior to avoiding. It is the real world *before* you do anything to it, including the effort to "see it nondually."

So you don't have to do something special to awareness or to experience in order to make it nondual. It starts out nondual, its very nature is nondual—prior to any grasping, any effort, any contrivance. If effort arises, fine; if effort doesn't arise, fine; in either case, there is only the immediacy of One Taste, prior to effort and non-effort alike.

So this is definitely not a state that is hard to get into, but rather one that is impossible to avoid. It has always been so. There has never been a moment when you did not experience One Taste—it is the only constant in the entire Kosmos, it is the only reality in all of reality. In a million billion years, there has never been a single second that you weren't aware of this Taste; there has never been a single second where it wasn't directly in your Original Face like a blast of arctic air.

Of course, we have often lied to ourselves about this, we have often been untruthful about this, the universe of One Taste, the primordial sound of one hand clapping, our own Original Face. And the nondual traditions aim, not to bring about this state, because that is impossible, but simply to *point it out* to you so that you can no longer ignore it, no longer lie to yourself about who you really are.

Q: So this nondual state—does this include the duality of mind and body, of Left and Right?

KW: Yes. The primordial state is prior to, but not other to, the entire world of dualistic Form. So in that primordial state there is no subject and object, no interior and exterior, no Left and no Right. All of those dualities *continue to arise*, but they are relative truths, not absolute or primordial truth itself. The primordial truth is the ringing; the relative truth is the "I" and the "bell," the mind and the body, the subject and the object. They have a certain relative reality, but they are not, as Eckhart would say, the final word.

And therefore the dilemmas inherent in those relative dualisms cannot be solved on the relative plane itself. Nothing you can do to the "I" or the "bell" will make them one; you can only relax into the prior ringing, the immediacy of experience itself, at which point the dilemma does not arise. It is not solved, it is dissolved—and not by reducing the subject to the object, or the object to the subject, but by recognizing the primordial ground of which each is a partial reflection.

Which is why the dilemmas *inherent* in those dualisms—between mind and body, mind and brain, consciousness and form, mind and nature, subject and object, Left and Right—cannot be solved on the relative plane—which is why that problem has *never* been solved by conventional philosophy. The problem is not solved, but rather dissolved, in the primordial state, which otherwise *leaves the dualisms just as they are*, possessing a certain conventional or relative reality, real enough in their own domains, but not absolute.

The Immediacy of Pure Presence

Q: Are there any orthodox or mainstream Western philosophers who recognize nonduality?

KW: I always found it fascinating that both William James and Bertrand Russell agreed on this crucial issue, the nonduality of subject and object in the primacy of immediate awareness. I think this is very funny, because if you can find something that these two agreed on, it might as well be coming straight from God, so I suppose we can embrace nonduality with a certain confidence.

Russell talks about this in the last chapters of his great book, *A History of Western Philosophy*, where he discusses William James's notion of "radical empiricism." We have to be very careful with these terms, because "empiricism" doesn't mean just sensory experience, it means experience itself, in any domain. It means immediate prehension, immediate experience, immediate awareness. And William James set out to demonstrate that this pure nondual immediateness is the "basic stuff" of reality, so to speak, and that both subject and object, mind and body, inside and outside, are all derivative or secondary. They come later, they come after the primacy of immediateness, which is the ultimate reality, as it were.

And Russell is quite right to credit James with being the first "mainstream" or "accepted" philosopher to advance this nondual position. Of course, virtually all of the mystical or contemplative sages had been saying this for a few millennia, but James to his eternal credit brought it crashing into the mainstream . . . and convinced Russell of its truth in the process.

James introduced this nondual notion in an essay called "Does 'Consciousness' Exist?" And he answered that consciousness does not exist, which has confused many people. But his point was simply that if you look at consciousness very carefully, it's not a thing, not an object, not an entity. If you look carefully, you'll see that consciousness is simply one with whatever is immediately arising—as we saw with the mountain, for example. You as a subject do not see the mountain as an object, but rather, you and the mountain are one in the immediacy of the actual experience. So in that sense, consciousness as a subjective entity does not exist—it's not a separate something that has an experience of a separate something else. There is just One Taste in the immediateness of experience.

So pure experience is not split into an inside and outside—there is no twiceness, no twoness, about it! As James characteristically put it, "Experience, I believe, has no such inner duplicity."

And notice that *duplicity* has the meaning of both "twoness" and "lying." The *twoness of experience is the fundamental lie*, the primordial untruthfulness, the beginning of ignorance and deception, the beginning of the battered self, the beginning of samsara, the beginning of the lie lodged in the heart of infinity. Each and every experience, just as it is, arrives as One Taste—it does not arrive fractured and split into a subject and an object. That split, that duplicity, is a lie, the fundamental lie, the original untruthfulness—and the beginning of the "small self," the battered self, the self that hides its Original Face in the forms of its own suffering.

Small wonder that D. T. Suzuki, the great Zen scholar, said that James's radical empiricism (or nondual empiricism) was as close as the West had gotten to "no-mind" or Emptiness. That's perhaps too strong, but you get the point.

Russell had a rather thin understanding of the fact that the great contemplative philosopher-sages—from Plotinus to Augustine to Eckhart to

Schelling to Schopenhauer to Emerson—had already solved or dissolved this subject/object duality. But aside from that misunderstanding, Russell introduces James's great accomplishment in a very clear fashion:

> The main purpose of this essay ["Does 'Consciousness' Exist?"] was to deny that the subject-object relation is fundamental. It had, until then, been taken for granted by philosophers that there is a kind of occurrence called "knowing," in which one entity, the knower or subject, is aware of another, the thing known or the object [the "two hands" of experience]. The knower was regarded as a mind or soul; the object known might be a material object, an eternal essence, another mind, or, in self-consciousness, identical with the knower. Almost everything in accepted philosophy was bound up with the dualism of subject and object. The distinction of mind and matter and the traditional notion of "truth," all need to be radically reconsidered if the distinction of subject and object is not accepted as fundamental.

To put it mildly. And then Russell adds, "For my part, I am convinced that James was right on this matter, and would on this ground alone, deserve a high place among philosophers."

Q: So they both caught a glimpse of nonduality.

KW: I think so, yes. It's fairly easy to catch at least a brief glimpse of nonduality. Most people can be "talked into it," as we were doing a moment ago, and at least get a little taste of it. And I think this is exactly what William James did with Bertrand Russell, in person, which is what Russell himself reports. Right after he says, "I am convinced that James was right on this matter," Russell adds, "I had thought otherwise until he persuaded me of the truth of his doctrine." I think James just pointed it right out to him! See the mountain? Where is your mind? Mind and mountain . . . nondual!

Q: So they were onto a taste of Zen? A taste of the Nondual?

KW: Well, a glimmer, a taste, a hint of the nondual—this is easy enough to catch. But for the Nondual traditions, *this is just the beginning*. As you rest in that uncontrived state of pure immediateness or pure freedom, then strange things start to happen. All of the subjective tendencies that you had previously *identified* with—all of those little selves and subjects that held open the gap between the seer and the seen—they all start burning in the freedom of nonduality. They all scream to the surface and die, and this can be a very interesting period.

As you rest in this primordial freedom of One Taste, you are no longer acting on these subjective inclinations, so they basically die of boredom, but it's still a death, and the death rattles from this liberation are very intense. You don't really have to do anything, except hold on—or let go—they're both irrelevant. It's all spontaneously accomplished by the vast expanse of primordial freedom. But you are still getting burned alive, which is just the most fun you can have without smiling.

Fundamentally, it doesn't matter what type of experience arises—the simple, natural, nondual, and uncontrived state is prior to experience, prior to duality, so it happily embraces whatever comes up. But strange things come up, and you have to stay with this "effortless effort" for quite some time, and die these little deaths constantly, and this is where real practice becomes very important.

Enlightenment

Q: You said nonduality doesn't reject dualism on its own level.

KW: No, that would miss the point. These dualisms—between subject and object, inside and outside, Left and Right—will still arise, and are *supposed* to arise. Those dualities are the very mechanism of manifestation. Spirit—the pure immediate Suchness of reality—manifests as a subject and an object, and in both singular and plural forms—in other words, Spirit manifests as all four quadrants. And we aren't supposed to simply evaporate those quadrants—they are the radiant glory of Spirit's manifestation.

But we are supposed to see through them to their Source, their Suchness. This One Taste has to permeate all levels, all quadrants, all manifestation. And precisely because this is the simplest thing in the world, it is the hardest. This effortless effort requires great perseverance, great practice, great sincerity, great truthfulness. It has to be pursued through the waking state, and the dream state, and the dreamless state. And this is where we pick up the practices of the Nondual schools.

Q: Does "Enlightenment" mean something different in these schools?

KW: Yes, in a sense. There are two rather different schools about this "Enlightened" state, corresponding to the two rather different meanings of "Emptiness" that we discussed.

The first takes as its paradigm the causal or unmanifest state of absorption (nirvikalpa, nirodh, ayn). That is a very distinct, very discrete, very identifiable state. And so if you equate Enlightenment with that state of cessation, then you can very distinctly say whether a person is "fully Enlightened" or not.

Generally, as in the Theravadin Buddhist tradition and the Samkhya yogic schools, whenever you enter this state of unmanifest absorption, it burns away certain lingering afflictions and sources of ignorance. Each time you fully enter this state, more of these afflictions are burned away. And after a certain number and type of these entrances—often four— you have burned away everything there is to burn, and so you can enter this state at will, and remain there permanently. You can enter nirvana permanently, and samsara ceases to arise in your case. The entire world of Form ceases to arise.

But the Nondual traditions do not have that as their goal. They will often use that state, and often master it. But more important, these schools—such as Vedanta Hinduism and Mahayana and Vajrayana Buddhism—are more interested in pointing out the Nondual state of Suchness, which is not a discrete state of awareness but the ground or empty condition of *all states*. So they are not so much interested in finding an Emptiness divorced from the world of Form (or samsara), but rather an Emptiness that embraces all Form even as Form continues to arise. For them, nirvana and samsara, Emptiness and Form, are not-two.

And this changes everything. In the causal traditions, you can very definitely say when a person is in that discrete state. It is obvious, unmistakable. So you have a clearly marked yardstick, so to speak, for your Enlightenment.

But in the Nondual traditions, you often get a quick introduction to the Nondual condition very early in your training. The master will simply point out that part of your awareness that is *already* nondual.

Q: How, exactly?

KW: Very similar to when we were talking about the Witness, and I sort of "talked you into" a glimpse of it; or even further with the non-dual One Taste of you and the mountain. The Nondual traditions have an enormous number of these "pointing out instructions," where they simply point out what is *already* happening in your awareness anyway. Every experience you have is *already* nondual, whether you realize it or not. So it is *not* necessary for you to *change your state of consciousness* in order to discover this nonduality. Any state of consciousness you have will do just fine, because nonduality is fully present in every state.

So *change of state* is *not* the point with the Nondual traditions. Recognition is the point. Recognition of what is always already the case. Change of state is useless, a distraction.

So you will often get an initiation taste, a pointing out, of this Non-dual state that is always already the case. As I said, I think this is exactly what James did with Russell, in a small way. Look at immediate awareness closely, and you will see that subject and object are actually one, are already one, and you simply need to recognize it. You don't have to engineer a special state in which to see this. One Taste is already the nature of any state, so pretty much any conscious state will do.

Q: It's simply pointed out.

KW: Yes. You've seen those newspaper puzzles, something like, "There are fifteen Presidents of the United States hidden in this picture of the ocean. Can you spot all fifteen?"

Q: The comedian Father Guido Sarducci has a joke on those—"Find the Popes in the Pizza."

KW: We'll get in trouble here! Maybe we better stick with presidents, who are used to being blankly humiliated.

The point in these games is that you are looking right at all the faces. You already have everything in consciousness that is required. You are looking right at the answer—right at the presidents' faces—but you don't recognize them. Somebody comes along and points them out, and you slap your head and say, Yes, of course, I was looking right at it.

Same with the Nondual condition of One Taste. You are looking right at it, right now. Every single bit of the Nondual condition is fully in your awareness right now. All of it. Not most of it, but absolutely all of it is in your awareness right now. You just don't recognize it. So somebody comes along and simply points it out, and you slap your head—Yes, of course, I was looking right at it all along.

Q: And this happens in the training?

KW: Yes. Sometimes right at the beginning, sometimes down the line a bit, but this transmission is crucial.

But the central point we were discussing is that, because this Nondual condition is the nature or suchness of any and all states—because this Emptiness is one with whatever Forms arise—then the world of Form will continue to arise, and you will continue to relate to Form. You will not try to get out of it, or away from it, or suspend it. You will enter it fully.

And since Forms continue to arise, then you are *never* at an *end point* where you can say, "Here, I am fully Enlightened." In these traditions, Enlightenment is an ongoing process of new Forms arising, and you relate to them as Forms of Emptiness. You are one with all these Forms as they arise. And in that sense, you are "enlightened," but in another sense, this enlightenment is *ongoing*, because new Forms are arising all the time. You are never in a *discrete* state that has no further development. You are always learning new things about the world of Form, and therefore your overall state is always evolving itself.

So you can have certain breakthrough Enlightenment experiences— satori, for example—but these are just the *beginning* of an *endless* process of riding the new waves of Form as they ceaselessly arise. So in this sense, in the Nondual sense, you are never "fully" Enlightened, any more than you could say that you are "fully educated." It has no meaning.

Q: Some of these Nondual traditions, particularly the Tantra, get pretty wild.

KW: Yes, some of them get pretty wild. They are not afraid of samsara, they ride it constantly. They don't abandon the defiled states, they enter them with enthusiasm, and play with them, and exaggerate them, and they couldn't care less whether they are higher or lower, because there is only God.

In other words, all experiences have the same One Taste. Not a single experience is closer to or further from One Taste. You cannot engineer a way to get closer to God, for there is only God—the radical secret of the Nondual schools.

At the same time, all of this occurs within some very strong ethical frameworks, and you are not simply allowed to play Dharma Bums and call that being Nondual. In most of the traditions, in fact, you have to master the first three stages of transpersonal development (psychic, subtle, and causal) before you will even be allowed to talk about the fourth or Nondual state. "Crazy wisdom" occurs in a very strict ethical atmosphere.

But the important point is that in the Nondual traditions, you take a vow, a very sacred vow, which is the foundation of all of your training, and the vow is that *you will not disappear into cessation*—you will *not* hide out in nirvana, you will not evaporate in nirodh, you will not abandon the world by tucking yourself into nirvikalpa.

Rather, you promise to ride the surf of samsara until all beings caught in that surf can see that it is just a manifestation of Emptiness. Your vow is to pass through cessation and into Nonduality as quickly as possible, so you can help all beings recognize the Unborn in the very midst of their born existence.

So these Nondual traditions do not necessarily abandon emotions, or thoughts, or desires, or inclinations. The task is simply to see the Emptiness of all Form, not to actually get rid of all Form. And so Forms continue to arise, and you learn to surf. The Enlightenment is indeed primordial, but this Enlightenment continues forever, and it forever changes its Form because new Forms always arise, and you are one with those.

So the call of the Nondual traditions is: Abide as Emptiness, embrace all Form. The liberation is in the Emptiness, never in the Form, but Emptiness embraces all forms as a mirror all its objects. So the Forms continue to arise, and, as the sound of one hand clapping, you are all those Forms. You are the display. You and the universe are One Taste. Your Original Face is the purest Emptiness, and therefore every time you look in the mirror, you see only the entire Kosmos.

PART THREE

BEYOND FLATLAND

14

Ascending and Descending

Q: In this final series of discussions, we want to bring all these pieces together into a truly integral view. We want to discuss an "all-level, all-quadrant" approach to consciousness, therapy, spirituality, and transformative practice. And we want to talk about the many obstacles in this integral view, obstacles such as flatland.

In order to do so, I wonder if you could give us the briefest possible summary of the overall discussion so far—a brief summary of the "big picture" up to this point.

KW: Okay. (But you can skip this section altogether if you hate summaries! Our narrative picks up immediately in the next section.)

A Brief Summary

KW: We started with Emptiness, creativity, holons. Or Spirit, creativity, holons. In other words, out of Emptiness, holons creatively emerge.

As they emerge, they evolve. This evolution, or Spirit-in-action, has certain features in common wherever it appears. These common features I have summarized as the twenty tenets, and we discussed a few of them. These are the patterns of manifestation.

For example, we saw that all holons have four capacities—agency and communion, self-transcendence and self-dissolution. Because of the self-transcending drive, new holons emerge. As they emerge, they emerge holarchically. They transcend and include. Cells transcend and include molecules, which transcend and include atoms, and so on.

Likewise, the self-transcending drive of the Kosmos produces holons of greater and greater depth. And we saw that the greater the depth of a holon, the greater its degree of consciousness, among other things.

But greater depth also means more things that can go wrong. Dogs get cancer, atoms don't. There is a dialectic of progress at every turn—hardly a sweetness-and-light affair!

Holons not only have an inside and outside, they also exist as individuals and as collectives. This means that every holon has four facets, which we called the four quadrants: intentional, behavioral, cultural, and social. These were indicated in figure 5-2.

So we followed the evolution of the four quadrants up to the human forms of those quadrants, at which point humans themselves begin to reflect on these quadrants, think about them, notice that they themselves are embedded in them. And in this attempt to gain knowledge about their own situation, humans generate various knowledge quests, quests for truth.

Since each of these four quadrants deals with a different aspect of holons, each of them has a different type of truth, a different validity claim. And humanity, through long and painful experimentation, slowly learned these validity tests—ways to ground knowledge in the realities of each quadrant. We saw these as truth, truthfulness, justness, and functional fit.

Since the two objective and exterior dimensions—the Right-Hand quadrants—can both be described in objective it-language, we simplified the four quadrants to the Big Three: I, we, and it. Studied, for example, in self, morals, science. Or art (self and self-expression), ethics, and objectivity. The Beautiful, the Good, and the True. In the spiritual domains: Buddha, Sangha, Dharma—the ultimate I, ultimate We, and ultimate It.

We could simplify the Big Three even further. The Left-Hand dimensions (the I and the we) can only be accessed by introspection and interpretation, whereas the Right Hand delivers itself up to perception and empiricism—and those are the Left- and Right-Hand paths. That is, the Right-Hand aspects are the exteriors of holons, and so they can be seen empirically. But the intentional and cultural—the Left-Hand quadrants—involve interior depth that can only be accessed by interpretation. Interpretation means, in the broadest sense, empathic resonance from within, as opposed to objective staring from without. *Surfaces can be seen, but depth must be interpreted.* And those are the Right- and Left-Hand paths.

But those are all just ways to talk about these four facets of any holon.

And the central point was, don't confuse these four quadrants. Simplify them, yes, but don't merely equate them, because these four quadrants, with their four different types of truth, are the basic facets of any holon, and reducing one to the others does not explain that quadrant but simply destroys it.

Therefore, as we followed the evolution of holons, we were careful to follow not only the exteriors of those holons—atoms, molecules, cells, organ systems, Gaia, etc.; we also followed their correlative interiors—sensations, images, concepts, rules, right up to subtle and causal occasions. In short, we saw this interior evolution go from prepersonal to personal to transpersonal.

And we saw that this interior evolution involves *ladder, climber,* and *view*: the ladder or basic levels or nested holarchy of consciousness; the climber or the self with a fulcrum at every stage (a 1-2-3 process of fusion/differentiation/integration); and the changing worldviews (archaic, magic, mythic, rational, etc.), each of which produces a different self-identity, needs, and moral sense.

Thus, we saw self-identity, needs, and moral response go from physiocentric to biocentric to egocentric to ethnocentric to worldcentric, the platform for all higher and truly spiritual developments. And we saw that an "accident" at any of these stages produces a pathology characteristic of the stage where the accident occurs (psychosis, borderline, neurosis, script, etc.).

And finally, we looked specifically at the four higher stages and fulcrums, the four transpersonal stages: the psychic, the subtle, the causal, and the nondual. We saw that each of these also has its own worldview and therefore its own type of mysticism, namely, nature mysticism, deity mysticism, formless mysticism, and nondual mysticism.

These higher stages are very rare, very difficult accomplishments. In the past, they were reached only by a small handful—the lone shaman, the yogi in the cave, the small sanghas and cloisters of the true seekers of wisdom. These deeper or higher states have never been anything near an average or collective mode of awareness. If we look at the evolution of the average mode, then we find something like figure 5-2, which stops at the centaur and vision-logic and a planetary federation with global or worldcentric morality—which is still an unrealized ideal for most.

If these higher or transpersonal stages emerge in our future collective evolution, then they will manifest in all four quadrants—intentional, behavioral, cultural, and social. And we are awaiting the possible forms of this future evolution, even if, individually, we pursue these higher states in our own case.

But the essential point is that at these higher or transpersonal stages, the Spirit that was present throughout the entire evolutionary process becomes increasingly conscious of its own condition. It has gone from subconscious to self-conscious to superconscious, unfolding more of itself and enfolding more of itself at every stage. Spirit slumbers in nature, begins to awaken in mind, and finally recognizes itself as Spirit in the transpersonal domains—but it is the same Spirit present throughout the entire sequence: the ground, path, and fruition of the whole display.

With Spirit's shocking Self-recognition, Forms continue to arise and evolve, but the secret is out: they are all Forms of Emptiness in the universe of One Taste, endlessly transparent and utterly Divine. There is no end limit, no foundation, no final resting place, only Emptiness and endless Grace. So the luminous Play carries on with insanely joyous regard, timeless gesture to timeless gesture, radiant in its wild release, ecstatic in its perfect abandon, endless fullness beyond endless fullness, this miraculously self-liberating Dance, and there is no one anywhere to watch it, or even sing its praises.

The Great Holarchy

Q: What you just summarized is one type of integral view, which includes all the quadrants (I, we, and it) as they evolve through all the levels (from matter to body to mind to soul to spirit). But that type of integral view tends to be denied in the West, and often in the East as well, because either some of the levels or some of the quadrants are left out.

KW: Yes, that's right. Especially in the modern West, we can't help but notice that all of the higher, transpersonal, spiritual levels of consciousness are looked upon with grave suspicion and even outright hostility. In fact, the worldview of scientific materialism, which is the "official" worldview of the modern West, aggressively denies not only the higher stages of consciousness development but the existence of consciousness itself. The only thing that is ultimately real is frisky dirt.

Q: Flatland.

KW: Yes, flatland. Either in the form of subtle reductionism, which reduces every interior or Left-Hand event to its exterior or Right-Hand correlate; or worse, gross reductionism, which reduces every Right-Hand system to Right-Hand atoms. In either case, the entire Left-Hand domains are denied irreducible reality: there is no consciousness, no mind, no soul, no spirit, no value, no depth, and no divinity found any-where in the disqualified universe, only a great web of interwoven "its" or, even worse, atomistic "its"—a truly insane worldview, wouldn't you say?

Q: We want to trace the historical rise of this flatland as carefully as we can, because otherwise a genuinely integral view will escape us. So why don't you set this up for us.

KW: Just for the moment, let's stick with the Upper-Left quadrant, with the individual *spectrum of consciousness*—these nine or so basic levels of consciousness. If you look at figure 14-1, you will see what is essentially the same basic spectrum, the Great Holarchy of conscious-ness, as it appears in both Plotinus and Aurobindo. And, of course, for both of them, this holarchy is not actually a stepladder, but a series of nested and enfolded dimensions. Figure 14-1 is just a sophisticated ver-sion of figure 2-2.

Now the really interesting point is that this Great Holarchy was, as Lovejoy put it, the dominant official philosophy of most of humankind, East and West, through the largest portion of its existence. In simplified forms we find a holarchy of earth, human, and sky (or heaven) even in the earliest foraging cultures. Chögyam Trungpa, for example, in his wonderful book *Shambhala: The Sacred Path of the Warrior*, makes this point very convincingly. This basic holarchy would later be elaborated into matter, body, mind, soul, and spirit (and in many cases that would be elaborated into even more subdivisions). But the point is that some-

Absolute One (Godhead)	Satchitananda/Supermind (Godhead)
Nous (Intuitive Mind) [subtle]	Intuitive Mind/Overmind
Soul/World-Soul [psychic]	Illumined World-Mind
Creative Reason [vision-logic]	Higher-mind/Network-mind
Logical Faculty [formop]	Logical mind
Concepts and Opinions	Concrete mind [conop]
Images	Lower mind [preop]
Pleasure/pain (emotions)	Vital-emotional; impulse
Perception	Perception
Sensation	Sensation
Vegetative life function	Vegetative
Matter	Matter (physical)
PLOTINUS	AUROBINDO

FIGURE 14-1. *The Great Holarchy according to Plotinus and Aurobindo.*

thing like this Great Holarchy has been part of the cultural background of most humans for most of our history.

That is, right up until the Enlightenment in the West. With the fundamental Enlightenment paradigm, all of reality—including the Great Holarchy—was mapped in empirical and monological terms. This was a well-intentioned but deeply confused attempt to understand consciousness and morals and values and meaning by putting them under the microscope of the monological gaze.

And do you know what happened? The interior depths completely disappeared from view. They could not be found with the monological gaze, and so they were soon pronounced nonexistent or illusory or derivative or epiphenomenal—all polite words for "not really real." All I's and all we's were reduced to mere its—atomistic or holistic, depending upon your prejudice—but all of which had only, at best, functional fit.

None of these interwoven its can be said to be better or deeper or higher or more valuable: just equally flat and endlessly faded surfaces scurrying about in objective systems, not one of which has the slightest clue as to value or depth or quality or goodness or beauty or worth.

Q: We have flatland.

KW: We have flatland. We looked at this as good news, bad news. The good news of modernity was that the Big Three were differentiated—art, science, morals. The bad news was that they had not yet been integrated, and this allowed an explosive science to colonize and dominate the I and the we domains.

Thus the downside of the Enlightenment was that it reduced all Left-Hand dimensions to their Right-Hand correlates, and it thought that a *simple mapping* of these empirical exteriors was all the knowledge that was worth knowing—the mirror of nature, the representation paradigm. This left out the mapmaker itself—the consciousness, the interiors, the Left-Hand dimensions—and resulted in nothing but the flat and faded surfaces of a brutally monochrome world.

And so, following John Locke, "the teacher of the Enlightenment," the great modern mapping game was afoot: map the entire Kosmos in empirical terms. And a century or so into this game of converting the entire Kosmos into objective its, the Enlightenment agenda awoke one morning to find to its utter horror that it was living in a thoroughly disqualified universe—a universe absolutely bereft of value, meaning, consciousness, quality, and worth. In mapping exterior correlates, it had gutted all interior depth, had eviscerated the interiors and laid them out to dry in the blazing sun of the monological gaze.

And so slowly, in an atmosphere of puzzled confusion, the bloodless corpse of the Enlightenment agenda was wheeled into the morgue—and the postmodern rebellion began. Postmodern, post-Enlightenment, post-empirical, post-whatever: something had gone profoundly, *profoundly*, wrong.

Q: The collapse of the Kosmos.

KW: Yes. The monological agenda had, in one sweeping action, completely collapsed the interior dimensions of being and consciousness and depth. It had, in other words, completely collapsed the Great Holarchy of consciousness. Whether prepersonal, personal, or transpersonal—you cannot find consciousness with the monological gaze. You cannot see it with a microscope, a telescope, a photographic plate. And so it must not exist. It must not be "really real."

And that is basically why it is *only* with the modern West that we do not have access to the Great Holarchy.

This-Worldly versus Otherworldly

Q: The history of this collapse is fascinating. And your historical research seems to challenge several longstanding myths about the Western tradition, starting with Plato.

KW: If you look at figure 14-1, it might be obvious that there are, so to speak, two major directions you can move in this Great Holarchy: you can ascend from matter to spirit, or you can descend from spirit to matter. Upward is very *transcendent*, downward is very *immanent*. Ascending is very *otherworldly*, descending is very *this-worldly*.

Q: This is where you introduce "Ascending" and "Descending" spirituality.

KW: Yes. And most people think of Plato as the Ascending or "otherworldly" philosopher, who saw this manifest world, this Earth and everything on it, as a pale shadow or copy of the eternal Forms of the other and real world.

Q: Ecophilosophers trace much of the West's "hatred" of this world to Plato.

KW: Yes, and those assumptions are quite incorrect. As Arthur Lovejoy points out, Plato actually describes two movements—what we are calling Ascent and Descent—and both of these movements are equally important in Plato.

The first movement, the Ascending movement, is a movement from the Many to the One, a movement where we see that behind the fleeting and shadowy forms of manifestation there is a single Source, a ground-less Ground, the Absolute, and we rise to an understanding of this absolute Good.

Q: We "ascend" in that sense.

KW: Yes. But the other movement is equally important in Plato, namely, the movement whereby the One empties itself into all creation, gives itself to all forms, so that all of creation itself is a perfect manifestation of Spirit. So *this world*, this very Earth, Plato called "a visible, sensible God."

Q: The "descent" of the One into the Many.

KW: Yes, exactly. Now it is indeed true that Plato gave the West most of its otherworldly philosophy. But, as Lovejoy is at pains to demonstrate, Plato *also* gave the West virtually all of the terms for its this-worldly exuberance and celebration, the celebration of the visible, sensible God. The entire manifest world was seen as a manifestation or embodiment of the Good, of the Absolute, and was to be celebrated as such! The *greater the diversity* in the world, the greater the spiritual Glory and Goodness.

And indeed, most of the this-worldly philosophies of the West have their origin in Plato. Listen to Lovejoy: "The most notable—and the less noted—fact about Plato's historic influence is that he did not merely give to European otherworldliness its characteristic form and phraseology and dialectic, but that he also gave the characteristic form and phraseology and dialectic to precisely the contrary tendency—to a peculiarly *exuberant kind of this-worldliness*."

And, as Lovejoy concludes, both of these currents—Ascending and Descending, or otherworldly and this-worldly, or transcendent and immanent—were united and integrated in Plato. As Lovejoy puts it, "The two strands in Plato's thought are here fused." Ascending and Descending are united and integrated—and that is Plato's final stance, as it were.

Now what happened in subsequent history is that these two strands were brutally torn apart. There was a violent rupture between the advocates of mere Ascent and the advocates of mere Descent. These two currents, which in fact ought to be united and integrated, were catastrophically fractured into the Ascenders versus the Descenders.

Q: The point would be to integrate *both* Ascending and Descending, and that would be part of an integral view.

KW: Yes, definitely. Whitehead's famous comment—that the Western tradition is basically a series of footnotes to Plato—may be true, but the footnotes were fractured. People tended to take their favorite "half" of Plato—the otherworldly or the this-worldly—but rarely did they take the whole.

We do not have to settle for the fractured footnotes to Plato. The Ascending and Descending currents were united in Plato, and they were likewise united in Plotinus.

Q: But things begin to "fall apart" after Plotinus.

KW: In a sense, yes. It is generally agreed that Plotinus was fleshing out the essentials of Plato in a more comprehensive fashion. And in Plotinus we have the Great Holarchy of Being, as presented in figure 14-1, and we have the two basic movements in this nested holarchy, namely, Ascending and Descending, or what Plotinus calls Reflux and Efflux. Spirit constantly effluxes or empties itself into the world, so that the entire world and all its inhabitants are perfect manifestations of Spirit. And likewise the world constantly returns or refluxes to Spirit, so that this entire world is itself spiritual to the core—the visible, sensible God.

According to Plotinus, each senior dimension in the Great Holarchy transcends and includes its junior, so that each and every thing and event, without exception, is perfectly nested in Spirit, in the One, which is therefore the seamless integration and union of Ascent and Descent, Reflux and Efflux, transcendence and immanence.

Q: You point out that this becomes very clear in Plotinus's attack on the Gnostics.

KW: Yes, that's right. Most of the Gnostics were mere Ascenders. Any form of Descent was, in fact, equated with evil. So the entire manifest world—*this* world—was thought to be illusory, shadowy, corrupted, sinful. Only by ascending to the One and shunning the Many could salvation be found.

If Plotinus—carrying the Platonic torch—were really otherworldly, you would expect him to join with the Gnostics and celebrate their merely Ascending agenda and attack all this-worldly endeavors. Instead, Plotinus began an absolutely devastating attack on the Gnostics, on these mere Ascenders, precisely because they couldn't balance the Ascending current with the equally important Descending current.

In other words, the Gnostics had found the causal One, but they didn't push through to the Nondual realization that the One and the Many are not-two, that Emptiness and Form are nondual, that this-worldly and otherworldly are One Taste, that the Ascending and Descending currents need to be integrated in the nondual Heart.

And so Plotinus tears into the Gnostics with an extraordinary and altogether convincing attack, and in some of the most beautiful spiritual prose ever written, reminds the Gnostics that this entire visible world is a manifestation of Spirit and is to be loved as Spirit. And if they, the Gnostics, really loved Spirit, as they proclaim, then they would love Spirit's children, whereas they merely despise them. In effect, Plotinus accuses the Gnostics of spiritual child abuse.

Q: You quote that attack in *Sex, Ecology, Spirtuality*. I wonder if you would read it for us.

KW: Plotinus is speaking:

> Do not suppose that a man becomes good by despising the world and all the beauties that are in it. They [the Gnostics] have no right to profess respect for the gods of the world above. When we love a person, we love all that belongs to him; we extend to the children the affection we feel for the parent. Now every Soul is a daughter of Spirit. How can *this world* be separated from the *spiritual* world? Those who despise what is so nearly akin to the spiritual world, prove that they know nothing of the spiritual world, except in name. . . .
>
> Let [any individual soul] make itself worthy to contemplate the Great Soul by ridding itself, through quiet recollection, of deceit [untruthfulness] and of all that bewitches vulgar souls. For it let all be quiet; let all its environment be at peace. Let the earth be quiet and the sea and air, and the heaven itself waiting. Let it observe how the Soul flows in from all sides into the resting world, pours itself into it, penetrates it and illumines it. Even as the bright beams of the sun enlighten a dark cloud and give it a golden border, so the Soul when it enters into the body of the heaven gives it life and timeless beauty and awakens it from sleep. So the world, grounded in a timeless movement by the Soul which suffuses it with intelligence, becomes a living and blessed being. . . .
>
> It [Soul/Spirit] gives itself to every point in this vast body, and vouchsafes its being to every part, great and small, though these parts are divided in space and manner of disposition, and though some are opposed to each other, others dependent on each other. But the Soul is not divided, nor does it split up in order to give life to each individual. All things live by the Soul *in its entirety* [i.e., ultimately there are no degrees, no levels, but simply pure Presence]; it is all present everywhere. The heaven, vast and various as it is, is one by the power of the Soul, and by

it is this universe of ours Divine. The sun too is Divine, and so are the stars; and we ourselves, if we are worth anything, are so on account of the Soul. Be persuaded that by it thou can attain to God. And know that thou wilt not have to go far afield. . . .

Wisdom and Compassion

Q: So that rather clearly shows the nondual orientation of Plotinus. You relate this integration of Ascent and Descent to the union of wisdom and compassion.

KW: Yes, we see this in both East and West. The Path of Ascent from the Many to the One is the *path of wisdom*. Wisdom sees that behind all the multifarious forms and phenomena there lies the One, the Good, the unqualifiable Emptiness, against which all forms are seen to be illusory, fleeting, impermanent. Wisdom is the return of the Many to the One. In the East: Prajna, or wisdom, sees that Form is Emptiness.

The Path of Descent, on the other hand, is the *path of compassion*. It sees that the One actually manifests as the Many, and so all forms are to be treated equally with kindness, compassion, mercy. Compassion or Goodness is, in fact, the very mechanism of manifestation itself. The One manifests as the Many through an infinite act of compassion and charity, and we embrace the Many with that same compassion and care. Compassion touches all manifestation with concern and gentle wonderment. In the East: Karuna, or compassion, sees that Emptiness is Form.

So we have: Wisdom sees that the Many is One, and Compassion sees that the One is the Many. Or in the East: Prajna sees that Form is Emptiness, Karuna sees that Emptiness is Form.

Q: Wisdom and Compassion—this is also Eros and Agape.

KW: Yes, ascending Eros and descending Agape, transcendence and immanence, the love that reaches up and the love that reaches down. . . .

The central historical point in all of this is that with the great Nondual systems, from Plotinus in the West to Nagarjuna in the East, we see an emphasis on *balancing and integrating these two movements*. The *Ascending* or *transcendental* current of wisdom or Eros or prajna is to be balanced with the *Descending* or *immanent* current of compassion or Agape or karuna; and the union of these two, the union of the One and the Many, of Emptiness and Form, of Wisdom and Compassion—their union in the nondual Heart of One Taste is the source and goal and ground of genuine spirituality.

God and Goddess

Q: This is also God and the Goddess—as Eros and Agape, Wisdom and Compassion, Ascent and Descent. . . .

KW: Yes, in a broad sense. If we ignore for the moment the more provincial and stage-specific notions of the horticultural Great Mother as a farming protectress, and the agrarian images of God the Father as a Big Daddy in the Sky—these mythic images are not very useful for an overall picture—and if we look instead to the broad understanding of God and Goddess, then the balanced picture that emerges is something like this:

If we wish to think in such terms, then the Masculine Face of Spirit—or God—is preeminently Eros, the Ascending and *transcendental* current of the Kosmos, ever-striving to find greater wholeness and wider unions, to break the limits and reach for the sky, to rise to unending revelations of a greater Good and Glory, always rejecting the shallower in search of the deeper, rejecting the lower in search of the higher.

And the Feminine Face of Spirit—the Goddess—is preeminently Agape, or Compassion, the Descending and *immanent* and manifesting current of the Kosmos, the principle of embodiment, and bodily incarnation, and relationship, and relational and manifest embrace, touching each and every being with perfect and equal grace, rejecting nothing, embracing all. Where Eros strives for the Good of the One in transcendental wisdom, Agape embraces the Many with Goodness and immanent care.

Q: Which you tie in with Tantra.

KW: Tantra, in the general sense, presents the ultimate Nondual reality as the sexual embrace of God and the Goddess, of Shiva and Shakti, of Emptiness and Form. Neither Ascent nor Descent is final, ultimate, or privileged, but rather, like the primordial yin and yang, they generate each other, depend upon each other, cannot exist without the other, and find their own true being by dying into the other, only to awaken together, joined in bliss, as the entire Kosmos, finding that eternity is wildly in love with the productions of time, the nondual Heart radiating as all creation, and blessing all creation, and singing this embrace for all eternity—an embrace that we are all asked to repeat in our own awareness, moment to moment, endlessly, miraculously, as the immediate presence of One Taste. This is the Nondual vision, this union of Reflux and Efflux, God and the Goddess, Emptiness and Form, Wisdom and Compassion, Eros and Agape, Ascent and Descent—perfectly and blissfully united in One Taste, the radical sound of one hand clapping.

Two Different Gods

Q: This is likewise the nondual integrative vision of Plotinus.

KW: Yes. But this union of Ascent and Descent would, in subsequent Western history, be often broken, with the otherworldly Ascenders and the this-worldly Descenders in constant and sometimes violent conflict. This subsequent war has been one of the central and defining conflicts in the Western mind.

Q: The war between the Ascenders and the Descenders.

KW: Yes. It's quite remarkable. Beginning with Augustine, and continuing right down to today, the Ascenders and the Descenders were in relentless and often brutal conflict, and this saddled the West with two *completely incompatible Gods*, as it were.

The God of the Ascenders was otherworldly to the core—my kingdom is not of this world. It was puritanical, usually monastic and ascetic, and it saw the body, the flesh, and especially sex, as archetypal sins. It sought always to flee the Many and find the One. It was purely *transcendental*, and was always pessimistic about finding happiness in this world. It shunned time in favor of eternity, and hid its face in shame from the shadows of this world.

The God of the Descenders counseled *exactly the opposite*. It fled from the One into the embrace of the Many. It was in love with the visible, sensible God, and sometimes Goddess. It was a God of pure embodiment, of pure *immanence*. It was fascinated with diversity, and found its glory in the celebration of this diversity. Not greater oneness, but greater variety was the goal of this God. It celebrated the senses, and the body, and sexuality, and earth. And delighted in a creation-centered spirituality that saw each sunrise, each moonrise, as the visible blessing of the Divine.

Q: In *Sex, Ecology, Spirituality* you trace the history of this war between the two Gods.

KW: Yes, that's right. In the West, during the millennium between Augustine and Copernicus, we see an almost exclusively *Ascending* ideal. Indeed, since this was an *agrarian* structure, there was a selection for male-biased spirituality, which consequently centered on Eros more than Agape, on Ascent more than Descent, on the One to the exclusion of, even hatred of, the Many.

And thus true salvation, true liberation, could not be found in this body, on this earth, in this lifetime. It was *otherworldly* to the core. Flesh is sin and sex is sin and earth is sin and body is sin, no matter what faint praise was given to creation itself. And so, of course, the root of sin was Eve in general—woman, body, flesh, nature, carnality: all of that becomes taboo in the deepest sense. Always, for the mere Ascenders, Descent is the Devil.

Q: In both the East and the West.

KW: Definitely. There is a constant tendency in agrarian societies, *wherever* they appear, to let the Ascending current pronounce this world evil or illusory, and to condemn earth, body, senses, sexuality (and woman). There were exceptions, of course, but this is the constant tendency in all agrarian structures: otherworldly to the core, with my kingdom not of this world, and an intense desire to find a nirvana away from the world of samsara. You find this from early Judaism to virtually all forms of Gnosticism to early Buddhism and most forms of Christianity and Islam.

And this was indeed the case in the West, especially, as I said, from the time of Augustine to the time of Copernicus. An almost exclusively Ascending ideal dominated European consciousness for a thousand years. The Way Up was the counsel that the Church gave for her perfections and her virtues, and lay not your treasures upon this earth was the one sure way to salvation—which means, find nothing in or on this earth to be treasured.

Oh, there was plenty of lip service given to the Goodness of God's creation (Goodness = Agape, Compassion, Descent), but the bottom line was that you could not gain liberation or salvation on this earth, in this life, and therein lies the entire story. Life was okay, but things got really interesting once you died. Once, that is, you got off this earth. This earth was not a place where realization could be found; this earth was simply a runway for the real take-off.

Q: All of which soon changed.

KW: Yes, all of which changed, and changed dramatically, with the Renaissance and the rise of modernity, culminating in the Enlightenment and the Age of Reason. And the simplest way to describe this entire period is that, at this point, *the Ascenders were out, the Descenders were in*.

And for mere Descenders, any form of Ascent is *always* despised. Ascent, in fact, becomes the new evil. Ascent is forever the Devil in the eyes of the Descended God.

So it is no surprise that from modernity forward, virtually any Ascent, of any variety, became the new sin. The rise of modernity, the rejection of Ascent, and the embrace of a purely Descended world—these came into being together.

And here we are on the trail of the modern West's denial of the transpersonal dimensions. Here we start to see exactly the beginning of the dismissal, or rejection, or marginalization, of the genuinely spiritual and transpersonal. Here we start to see the glorification of flatland, the embrace of the Descended grid. The eclipse of any sort of transcendental wisdom—the eclipse of any sort of Ascent—cast a shadow over the entire face of modernity, a shadow that is the signature of our times.

The Descended Grid

Q: This flatland, this Descended grid, has marked the entire modern and postmodern condition.

KW: In many ways, yes. As a general statement, yes. Salvation in the modern world—whether offered by politics, or science, or revivals of earth religion, or Marxism, or industrialization, or consumerism, or retribalism, or sexuality, or horticultural revivals, or scientific materialism, or earth goddess embrace, or ecophilosophies—salvation can be found only on this earth, only in the phenomena, only in manifestation, only in the world of Form, only in pure *immanence*, only in the Descended grid. There is no higher truth, no Ascending current, nothing *transcendental* whatsoever. In fact, anything "higher" or "transcendental" is now the Devil, is now the great enemy, is now the destroyer of the earthbound, sensory-drenched God and Goddess. And all of modernity and postmodernity moves fundamentally and almost entirely within this Descended grid, the grid of flatland.

Q: So this is not integrating Ascent and Descent . . .

KW: No, this is simply the dominance of the Descenders. And not just in "official" reality, but also in virtually every form of "counterculture" or "counterreality." The Descended grid is so entrenched, so unconscious, so background, so deeply ingrained, that even the "new paradigm" rebels often move completely within its clutches. It infects equally orthodox and avant-garde, conventional and alternative, industrialist and ecologist.

Q: That's exactly what I want to focus on next.

15

The Collapse of the Kosmos

Q: The modern and postmodern world moves within the Descended grid. So the obvious question is, why?

KW: The dialectic of progress took its first modern spill. Evolution hit a bump in the road and the whole car tilted on its side and began to skid down the road. The differentiation of the Big Three—consciousness, culture, and nature—began to career into the dissociation of the Big Three, and their subsequent collapse into the Big One of flatland.

Evolution, of course, is a self-correcting agenda, and it is in the process of slowly righting itself. As in the stock market, there is an overall and unmistakable upward trend, but this doesn't stop violent short-term fluctuations, both up and down—periods of growth and periods of depression. And starting in the eighteenth century, aspects of the cultural stock market hit a great depression, the likes of which we have rarely seen, and are just now beginning to overcome.

Q: So this collapse is not a reductionism that you find in previous cultures.

KW: That's basically correct; premodern cultures lack both the good news and the bad news of this differentiation, which sometimes confuses critics. Because earlier cultures did not differentiate the Big Three in the first place, they couldn't collapse and reduce them. The extraordinary *advance* of differentiating the Big Three allowed this extraordinary tragedy. The *dignity* of modernity began to slide into the *disaster* of modernity, and there, pretty much, is where the modern and postmodern world still rests: a fragmented lifeworld with self and culture and science at each other's throat, each struggling, not for integration, but domination, each trying to heal the fragmentation by denying reality to the other quadrants.

And so it came about that this great evolutionary leap forward brought its first great catastrophe, the dialectic of progress in its first modern form, blood all over the brand-new carpet.

The Dignity of Modernity

Q: So before we discuss this bad news, why don't you very quickly review the good news of modernity, since this seems to be where many critics get sidetracked.

KW: Yes, it's important to emphasize, because the antimodernists focus on the bad news and tend to forget the good news altogether.

Neither magic nor mythic is postconventional. But with the shift to reason and worldcentric morality, we see the rise of the modern liberation movements: liberation of slaves, of women, of the untouchables. Not what is right for me or my tribe, or my race, or my mythology, or my religion, but what is fair and right and just for all humans, regardless of race, sex, caste, or creed.

And thus, in a mere hundred-year period, stretching roughly from 1788 to 1888, slavery was outlawed and eliminated from every rational-industrial society on earth. In both the preconventional/egocentric and the conventional/ethnocentric moral stance, slavery is perfectly acceptable, because equal dignity and worth are *not* extended to all humans, but merely to those of your tribe or your race or your chosen god. But from a postconventional stance, slavery is simply wrong, it is simply intolerable.

This was the first time in history that a general societal type had eliminated slavery! Some earlier societies happened not to have slavery, but, as Gerhard Lenski's massive evidence demonstrates, no general type of society was ever free of it, until rational-industrialization.

This was true East and West, North and South—white men and black men and yellow men and red men enslaved their fellow men and women, and thought little of it. Some societies, such as early foraging, had relatively less slavery, but even foragers were not free of it altogether—in fact, they invented it.

In this regard, one of the social nightmares in America is that this country was formed right during the great transition period from agrarian slavery to industrial no-slavery. The Constitution, in fact, is still a largely agrarian document—slavery is so taken for granted it isn't even mentioned, and women are not counted as citizens (and none of that even has to be explained in the document itself!). But as the center of cultural gravity continued to switch from mythic-agrarian to rational-industrial, slavery was eliminated across the board, although its scars are still with us.

Q: Women were also "freed," so to speak.

KW: Yes, for almost identical reasons, we would see the rise of feminism and the women's movement on a culture-wide scale, generally dated, as we said, from Wollstonecraft in 1792, exactly the general beginning period of the numerous liberation movements.

This, too, was almost totally a product of rational-industrialization, and must be counted as one of modernity's many extraordinary achievements. Previously, where the Big Three weren't differentiated (where noosphere and biosphere were still indissociated), *biological* determinants, such as male physical strength, were often the dominant *cultural* determinants as well, because they weren't differentiated: male physical strength meant male cultural strength. If the mode of production did not demand much physical exertion—as in horticulture—then women lucked out, and the societies were relatively "equalitarian," although when push came to shove, women were always the shov-ee.

But with the differentiation of self and culture and nature (the differentiation of the Big Three), biological determinants became increasingly irrelevant. Biology was no longer destiny. Equal rights can *never* be achieved in the biosphere, where big fish eat little fish; but they can be achieved—or certainly aimed for—in the noosphere. And liberal feminism arose at this time in history, and not before this time, to announce this new and emergent truth—in the noosphere, women deserve equal rights—a truth centered in postconventional depth and worldcentric rationality.

Q: There was the whole movement of the democracies themselves.

KW: Yes, essentially the same phenomenon. The mythological worldview, quite contrary to the picture painted by many Romantics, was in virtually all cases shot through with dominator hierarchies. The mythic god is the god of a *particular* peoples—it is sociocentric and ethnocentric, not postconventional and worldcentric. It is the god of all peoples only if all peoples bow before that particular god. It is therefore "worldcentric" only by *forced conversion*, and, if necessary, *military conquest*, as the great mythic-imperial Empires of the Aztecs, Incas, Romans, Khans, and Ramses would make quite obvious. These dominator hierarchies generally have a single head: Pope or King or Cleopatra or Khan is on top, and stretching out beneath are various degrees of servitude. All of them conquered in the name of their mythic god or goddess, before whom all beings must bow.

The Age of Reason was therefore the Age of Revolution as well, revolution against mythic dominator hierarchies. This was a revolution not just in theory but in practice, in politics. One of the great themes of the Enlightenment was "No more myths!" because myths are precisely what divide and antagonize peoples, and set them against each other in ethnocentric ways, and inflict their cruelties on unbelievers in the name of a chosen god.

And so Voltaire's impassioned cry rang out across the continent: "Remember the cruelties!" Remember the cruelties inflicted on people in the name of the mythic god—remember the hundreds of thousands burned at the stake in order to save their souls; remember the Inquisition grotesquely inscribing its dogma on the flesh of the torture victim; remember the political inequalities inherent in mythic hierarchies; remember the brutality that in the name of compassion had crushed innumerable souls under its domineering march.

On the other hand, a postconventional moral stance extends equal opportunity to all peoples, regardless of race, sex, creed, belief, myth, or god. And again, although not everybody lives up to this postconventional or worldcentric ideal, it was indeed, beginning with modernity, firmly embedded in widespread social institutions that protected its intent. Thousands and thousands of men and women fought and died for this democratic vision of worldcentric tolerance and universal pluralism, under the slogan, "I may disagree with what you say, but I will defend to the death your right to say it."

This, too, was radically novel, on any sort of large scale. The early Greek democracies had none of this universalism. Let us remember that in the Greek "democracies," one out of three people were slaves, and women and children virtually so; the agrarian base cannot support emancipation of slaves. The city of Athens, like all city-states, had its own particular mythic god or goddess. And so the indictment handed down by the city of Athens began, "Socrates is guilty of refusing to recognize the gods of the State." It ended with, "The penalty demanded is death."

When asked, as was customary, if Socrates could suggest an alternative punishment, he suggested free meals for life.

But Socrates chose reason over myth, and drank the hemlock. Fifteen hundred years later, the world caught up with him, only this time the polis forced the gods to drink the hemlock, and from the death of those gods arose the modern democracies.

The Disaster of Modernity

Q: And we have, as good news, I suppose, the development of science itself.

KW: Yes, the differentiation of the Big Three allowed rational-empirical science to emerge unencumbered by blatant mythic dogmatisms. Empirical science—which means *rationality* tied to *empirical* observables through a hypothetico-deductive procedure—blossomed for the first time on any sort of culture-wide scale.

With empirical science there can be little quarrel, but with scientism . . . well, scientism is a different beast. And here we might as well start to look at the bad news, which was the *failure to integrate the Big Three*. Consciousness, morals, and science had indeed been freed from their magic and their mythic indissociation; each domain was set loose with its own power and its own truth and its own approach to the Kosmos, each of which had something *equally* important to say.

But by the end of the eighteenth century, the rapid, indeed extraordinary development of science began to throw the whole system off balance. The advances in the it-domain began to eclipse, and then actually *deny*, the values and truths of the I and the we domains. The Big Three began to collapse into the Big One: empirical science, and science alone, could pronounce on ultimate reality. Science, as we say, became scientism, which means it didn't just pursue its own truths, it aggressively denied that there were any other truths at all!

And thus, beginning especially, as I said, in the eighteenth century, the Left-Hand and interior dimensions were reduced to their Right-Hand empirical correlates. Only objective its with simple location were "really real"! The entire interior dimensions—in all holons, human and otherwise!—were completely gutted, and the ghost in the machine began its sad and lonely modern moan, a haunting cry made all the more plaintive in that it had not even the power to attract attention.

When only objective its with simple location are really real, then the mind itself is a *tabula* that was totally *rasa*, utterly blank until filled with *pictures* or representations of the only reality there was: objective and sensory nature. There is no real *Spirit*, there is no real *mind*, there is only empirical *nature*. No superconscious, no self-conscious, only subconscious processes scurrying endlessly, meaninglessly, in a vast system of interwoven its. The Great Holarchy utterly collapsed like a house of cards in an afternoon gust, and in its place we find only the *web of nature with its simple location.*

And thus, welcome to the modern, purely Descended world. All the truth that is fit to know is the truth of its, of mononature, of objective and empirical processes—and no Ascent of any variety is required. The Descended grid of flatland, the world of all proper troglodytes, hollow to the core.

Instrumental Rationality: A World of Its

Q: This seems to be the crux of the matter. How or why did science overrun the other domains?

KW: The extraordinary gains in empirical science—by Galileo, Kepler, Newton, Harvey, Kelvin, Clausius, Carnot—were being matched by the massive transformations wrought by industrialization. *Both of these were it-domain endeavors*, and so they fed on each other in a vicious spiral, pushing all other concerns by the wayside. In other words, the it-domain had two very powerful forces on its side—the accomplishments of empirical science and the power of industrialization.

The techno-economic base of a society (the Lower-Right quadrant) sets the *concrete forms* within which the culture moves and *can* move. The base doesn't determine the cultural superstructure in any sort of strong Marxist sense, but it does set various limits and possibilities (it's virtually impossible, for example, to outlaw slavery with an agrarian base, and equally impossible to vindicate women's rights).

Now the industrial base was a base of *instrumental productivity.* Of course, so was the bow and arrow, so was the hoe, so was the plow—but a steam engine? an internal combustion engine? In many ways the engine, the machine, was itself a simple evolution of productive capacity, stretching all the way back to the first rock used as a club or the first stick used as a spear. In that sense, there was nothing about industrialization that was a radical break with the past—men and women everywhere and at all times have tinkered with ways to secure their basic needs with instruments, with tools. But as the development of this quadrant became more and more complex, the sheer power of the machine, of the industrial base, brought instrumental productivity screaming to the fore.

Within the techno-economic base, a culture unfolds its possibilities.

And within the industrial base, an altogether productive and technical and *instrumental* mentality unfolded, a mentality that, almost of necessity, put a *premium on the it-domain*.

Now many critics—most critics, actually—tend to see a great number of problems with industrialization. It is supposed to be the cause of a mechanistic worldview; the destruction of an organic culture; the cause of an analytic and fragmented world; the displacement of social cohesion; the cause of ecological catastrophe; the ruin of religious sensibilities.

Those are important, but I don't think any of them are central. I think they are all derivative. Central is the pressure this productive base placed on consciousness to select for the it-domain. That is, the power of industrialization joined with the accomplishments of empirical science to select for a world where *its alone are real*. Everything else stems from that selection. All of those other problems stem from that problem.

The it-domain was growing like a cancer—a pathological hierarchy—invading and colonizing and dominating the I and the we domains. The *moral* decisions of the culture were rapidly being handed over to science and *technical* solutions. Science would solve *everything*. All problems in the I and the we domains were converted to technical problems in the it-domain. And thus science (theoretical and technical) would not only solve all problems, it would decide what was a problem in the first place—it would decide what was real and what was not.

Q: So the problem wasn't that the new science was analytic and divisive instead of holistic and systems-oriented.

KW: Absolutely not. The problem was that both atomistic science and holistic science were it-isms. Both contributed to the primary collapse. Atomistic its, holistic its—same basic nightmare.

Q: But we constantly hear, from the "new paradigm" folks, that we are living in a fractured world because the "old Newtonian" science was mechanistic, divisive, and atomistic, and these divisive concepts invaded society and caused its fragmentation; and that what is now required is for society to catch up with the new holistic sciences, from quantum physics to systems theory, and this will heal the divisions. And you're saying atomistic and holistic are both the culprit.

KW: Yes, that's right. When science pronounced its own mission to be the only real mission, it likewise pronounced the it-domain to be the only real domain. The empirical world of monological nature was the only real world. Humans were an inseparable part of this web of nature, and thus humans could also be known in an empirical, objective fashion.

You want consciousness? Don't *talk* to me, just cut into the brain and *look*! The monological gaze.

The idea was that the brain is part of nature, nature alone is real, so consciousness can be found in an empirical study of the brain—this is a horrible reduction to monological surfaces.

Q: But the brain *is* a part of nature!

KW: Yes, the brain is a part of nature, but the mind is not part of the brain. The mind, or consciousness, is the interior dimension, the exterior correlate of which is the objective brain. The mind is an I, the brain is an it. So, as we discussed earlier, the brain, like anything else in empirical nature, can be known by the monological gaze, by empiric-analytic investigation, but the mind can only be known by introspection, communication, and interpretation. You can look at a brain, but you must talk to a mind, and that requires not just observation but interpretation.

So when all aspects of holons were reduced to the great monological web of empirical its, then their interior dimensions were perfectly decimated. The interiors of plants and whales and wolves and chimps evaporate in the scorching blaze of the monological gaze. They are all just strands in the objective web—they have no lifeworld, they have no culture. And thus, if you reduce the Kosmos to the great web of empirical nature, you denature the interiors of nature as well. You only have empirical nature, monological nature, denatured nature, the hollow shell of the collapsed Kosmos: all I's and all we's reduced to interwoven its, reduced to the great web of simple location.

Of course, consciousness does not have simple location. Values, desires, states of consciousness, meaning, depth, peak experiences, spiritual illuminations—none of those have physical location in the exterior world of its. Consciousness exists in levels of its own interior space that are known from within, accessed by interpretation, and shared in mutual understanding guided by sincerity. And since *none* of those have simple location, then if you attempt to get at the interior beast by simply mapping its empirical-objective footprints, you will lose the very essence of the beast itself.

And then you will simply arrange your ontological holarchies based primarily on *physical* extension—*orders of magnitude* replace *orders of significance*, and so then the only "nests" you have are now based mostly on *size*: an atom is part of a bigger molecule is part of a bigger cell is part of a bigger organism is part of a bigger biosphere—and there is your holistic systems map.

At which point you have totally fallen into what Whitehead called the *fallacy of simple location*. Namely, if something can't be simply located in physical space, then it isn't "really real." You can locate Gaia, so it exists. You can locate cells, so they exist. You can locate the brain, so it exists. You can locate the biosphere, so it exists.

But you can't *simply locate* consciousness and values and meanings and morals in the same way. You can't point to them with your finger. You can't see them or find them anywhere in the great web of sensory nature. They become rambling and ridiculed ghosts in the machine, pathetic illusions in the organic system. They are merely personal tastes and subjective fantasies. The interiors *don't count* in a disqualified universe, the universe you can put your finger on.

The irony, of course, is that the universe you can put your finger on is the meaningless universe. So although consciousness and value and meaning are *intrinsic* to the *depth* of the Kosmos, they cannot be found in the cosmos. That is, they inhere in the Left-Hand dimensions of the Kosmos, not in the Right-Hand surfaces. And thus, if you are intent on only allowing the sensory surfaces, then you scrub the Kosmos clean of value and consciousness and meaning and depth, guaranteed.

And so it came about that the Great Holarchy was abandoned, essentially for the first time in history, because you couldn't put your finger on it. The ghost in the machine was indeed a ghost, because it had just committed suicide.

The Fundamental Enlightenment Paradigm

Q: So is this why theorists like Foucault have so sharply attacked the "sciences of man" that arose in the eighteenth century?

KW: Yes, very much so. Foucault beautifully summarized this monological madness with a perfect phrase: men and women, he said, became "objects of information, never subjects in communication." Foucault gave a perfect one-sentence summary of the entire nightmare of modernity. That is, human beings, like all holons, were studied only in their empirical and objective dimensions, and thus were reduced to mere its in the great interwoven web, with no depth and no intentionality and no personhood to speak of. The brutal world of the lab technician, slabs of meat each and all.

And thus, correlative with the rise of scientism, you have the rise of the "sciences of man," sciences that reduced human beings solely to objects of information. Also called "dehumanized humanism."

Q: Why did Foucault call that the "Age of Man"?

KW: Because "man" as an *object* of scientific investigation was "invented." Human beings became objects of monological rationality, something that had never happened before (because the Big Three had never been differentiated and then collapsed). In his own quirky way, Foucault would say that man had never existed before. Man was invented. And Foucault longed for "the end of man." So he concludes *The Order of Things* with the arresting metaphor, "One can certainly wager that man will be erased, like a face drawn in sand at the edge of the sea."

That's postmodernese for: the end of objectification. The end of this dehumanizing humanism, the end of "man," this *mere* objectification of the human person into monological its. To reduce all subjects to objects in the great interlocking web—this is actually power parading as knowledge, this is the tyranny of the monological gaze, this is the irony of flatland rationality, and this was one of Foucault's main targets.

So if you look at the major theorists and critics of the rise of modernity—such as Hegel, Weber, Habermas, Taylor, Foucault—a surprisingly consistent picture emerges. They all tend to agree on certain basic features of modernity: a disengaged subject surveying a holistic it-world, with knowledge being simply the empirical and objective representation or mapping of this holistic world (the representation paradigm, the mirror of nature). The subjective and intersubjective domains were thus *reduced* to empirical studies—I and we were reduced to interwoven its—and thus humans became "objects of information, never subjects in communication." This reduction of the Big Three to the Big One produced scientific materialism, dehumanized humanism, and the disqualified universe that still tends to dominate the modern and postmodern world.

No Spirit, No Mind, Only Nature

Q: So this is what you meant when you said that one broken God replaced the other.

KW: Yes, from an almost exclusively Ascending ideal, which had dominated Western consciousness for at least a thousand years, we get an almost exclusively Descended world, which has dominated modernity and postmodernity to this day. There is no translogical Spirit, and no dialogical mind; there is just monological nature. Surface nature, mononature, the world of sensory and material forms—this is the "God," this is the "Goddess," of the modern and postmodern world.

I have a handful of diagrams that might help explain this. If we go back to figure 2-2 (page 85), we will be reminded of the traditional Great Holarchy of Being, matter to body to mind to soul to spirit, with each level transcending and including its predecessors. Moving upward from the center (matter, the most fundamental) is the process of evolution (Reflux or Ascent, driven by Eros), and moving downward from spirit (the most significant) is involution (Efflux or Descent, driven by Agape). Each higher level is an emergent, marked by properties not found in its predecessors. Spirit is both the highest level (which transcends all, includes all), and the equally present Ground of each level (represented by the paper).

But what the traditional Great Nest failed to do, on any sort of significant scale, was to clearly differentiate the four quadrants. The material brain, for example, was simply placed, with all matter, on the bottom rung of existence, instead of seeing that the material brain is the exterior correlate of interior states of consciousness (so that the brain is not simply part of the lowest of all levels, but rather is the exterior correlate of some very high levels). Instead of seeing that consciousness is intimately associated with the material brain, consciousness seemed to hover above all matter, transcendental and metaphysical and completely otherworldly. (The discovery that states of consciousness have correlates in brain states—that all Left-Hand events have Right-Hand correlates—was a devastating blow to the Great Chain and all metaphysics as traditionally conceived, and rightly so, even though it went too far and contributed to the collapse of the Kosmos into nothing but scientific materialism.)

Likewise, the traditional Great Nest embodied little understanding of the profound ways that cultural contexts (Lower Left) mold all perception; of the ways that the techno-economic base (Lower Right) strongly influences individual consciousness; of the evolution of worldviews, individual consciousness, modes of production, and so on. In all these ways and more, the Great Chain was severely limited. (This did not stop individuals from using the Great Chain as a perfectly adequate map for individual spiritual development in the Upper-Left quadrant, which is what many did, including the likes of Plotinus. But it did severely limit the sensitivity of the Great Nest to those differentiated aspects of reality that we are calling the four quadrants.)

Q: But modernity did differentiate the four quadrants.

KW: Yes. All of this would change with modernity and the widespread differentiation of the Big Three. This can be represented as in figure 15-1 (and simplified as in figure 15-2), which is the Great Nest differentiated into the four quadrants (or the Big Three). This integral vision is what could have emerged, and what might yet still emerge, but what in fact did *not* emerge in any enduring way. Instead, the various levels and quadrants were all collapsed into their material (or empirical or objective) correlates, to result, soon enough, in flatland, in scientific materialism, in sensory mononature. Tracing this collapse of the Kosmos is the crux of our story at this point.

Q: You said it had to do with the fact that every Left-Hand event has a Right-Hand correlate, an "it" correlate. Coupled with industrialization and objective science, the "its" took over the world!

KW: Exactly. Every Left-Hand event does indeed have a Right-Hand or empirical correlate in the material (or objective) world—and thus it is always tempting to reduce the former (depths that require arduous interpretation) to the latter (surfaces that can be easily seen). What we called subtle reductionism.

This can be understood with reference to figure 15-3. Notice again that each level transcends and includes its predecessors. On the interior domains, we see that the theosphere (soul/spirit) transcends and includes

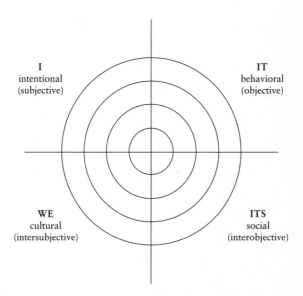

FIGURE 15-1. *The Great Nest with the Four Quadrants.*

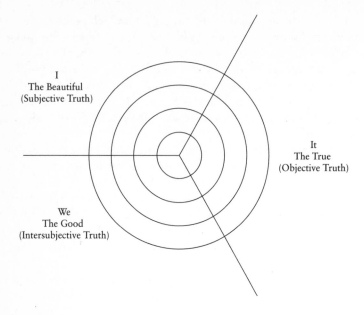

FIGURE 15-2. *The Big Three*

the noosphere (mind), which transcends and includes the biosphere (body). These are shorthand for the nine or so levels and fulcrums of interior consciousness development.

But just as important, each interior state of consciousness (from bodily consciousness to mental consciousness to spiritual consciousness) *has some sort of correlate in the material/objective brain and organism* (Upper Right). Thus, for example, even somebody who is having a spiritual experience (Upper Left) will show changes in objective brainwaves that can be measured on an EEG machine (Upper Right).

But conscious states, values, depth, and intentions cannot be reduced to material brainwaves because, although one value is better than another, one brainwave is not. You experience compassion and you know it is better than murder; while you are thinking that, your brain will be producing brainwaves that can be registered on an EEG. But, although you know that compassion is better than murder, there is nothing on the EEG machine that says, "This brainwave is more valuable; this brainwave is more moral; this brainwave is more beautiful." The EEG machine can *only* show that one brain state is *different* from another; it

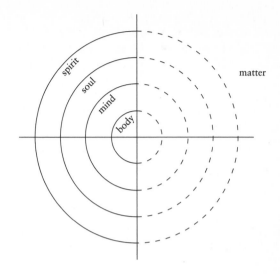

FIGURE 15-3. *Correlations of Interior (Consciousness)*
States with Exterior (Material) States

cannot say that one state is *better* than another. To make that judgment, you have to rely on interior consciousness, depth, and value recognition—holarchies of *quality*—while the EEG machine can only register holarchies of *quantity*. To reduce the Left to the Right is to reduce all quality to quantity, and thus, as we have seen, land directly in the disqualified universe, also known as flatland.

Q: Which is precisely what happened.

KW: Which is precisely what happened. As we saw, all Left-Hand and interior events were reduced to Right-Hand processes and objects and its. The rational Ego was left dangling in midair, cut off from its roots in its own body, cut off from spirit and the higher stages of its own interior development, and doing nothing but reflecting on the only reality of nature ("the mirror of nature"). Gone was spirit, and gone was mind as a real reality in itself, and all that was left was sensory nature, the empirical web of holistic its.

Q: In other words, flatland.

KW: Flatland, yes. This can be represented as in figure 15-4. The rational Ego is all that is left of the interior domains, and even its existence was challenged. The Eco—or Nature, or the Right-Hand world—is all that was believed to be ultimately real. The purely Descended world of flatland is now the ultimate reality.

Q: So you can see how the very differentiations of modernity allowed the dissociation and then the collapse into flatland. Good news, bad news.

KW: Yes, that's right. And so, once we finish our account of the historical rise of flatland, we can perhaps return to the central point: in order to have a truly *integral* view, we want to take the very best of the ancient wisdom (namely, it was "all-level," stretching from body to mind to soul to spirit) and combine that with the very best of modernity (namely, it was "all-quadrant," differentiating the Big Three), and thus arrive at an *all-level, all-quadrant* vision.

Q: Which would be something like figures 15-1, 15-2, and 15-3.

KW: Yes, that's right. For the moment, however, we are at the point that modernity embraced the "reality" of figure 15-4. Modernity fell in love with flatland, the Descended grid, the industrial ontology of a world of ITS.

The Voice of the Industrial Grid

Q: Now you were saying that the modern ecological crisis is primarily the result of the Descended grid.

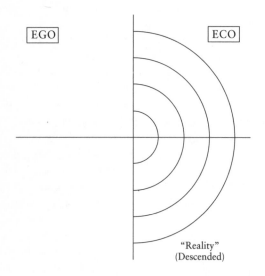

FIGURE 15-4. *Flatland*

KW: Anybody can say they are thinking "globally," but very few can actually take a worldcentric or postconventional perspective. As we saw, to *actually* live from a worldcentric or universal perspective requires five or six major interior stages of transformation and transcendence.

But if the entire Left Hand is ignored and devalued—if we ignore interiors and just rivet our eyes on a Right-Hand "global" map of Gaia or systems nature—we will ignore the actual path of getting people to that global or worldcentric stance. We will have a goal with no path. And we will have a map that denies and condemns Left-Hand transcendence, which is the actual path itself!

And all of that ignoring, all of that "ignorance," goes directly back to the subtle reductionism of the fundamental Enlightenment paradigm. We saw that rationality managed to differentiate the Big Three, but *industrialization* as much as anything collapsed them into the Big One of mononature, of empirical nature with its simple location, the world of figure 15-4.

In other words, this world of mononature is in fact a largely *industrial ontology*. The very notion that "empirical nature alone is real"—this is the modern Descended grid, and this grid is above all else the grid of industrial ontology. It is industrialization that *holds flatland in place*, that holds the objective world of simple location as the primary reality, that colonizes and dominates the interiors and reduces them to instrumental strands in the great web of sensory its. That "nature alone is real"—this is the voice of the industrial grid.

Q: Which is why you don't find this collapse in other cultures.

KW: That's right. Nature was either predifferentiated and egocentric, as in magic; or nature was devalued in favor of a mythic other world, as in mythology. Or, in the case of a Plotinus or a Padmasambhava, nature is an expression of Spirit, an embodiment of Spirit—Spirit transcends and includes nature.

But *never* in history had a differentiated nature simply been equated with the ultimate reality! Never had translogical Spirit and dialogical mind been so rudely reduced to monological nature. But with the modern industrial ontology, nature is the ultimate reality, nature alone is real.

Q: So *nature*, in that sense, is a *product* of industrialization.

KW: Yes, it appears so. As we were saying, that "nature alone is real"—this is the haunting voice of the industrial grid.

And then, with reference to Spirit, you will do one of two things: deny Spirit altogether, or claim nature is Spirit. The Enlightenment philosophers did the former, the Romantic rebellion and back-to-nature movement did the latter. *Both* thoroughly within this Descended grid of mononature, this rampant industrial ontology.

Q: Plotinus was turning in his grave?

KW: One can only imagine. Let me repeat that for Plato or Plotinus—or Emerson or Eckhart or Lady Tsogyal—nature is an *expression* of Spirit. In fact, for Plotinus, both mind and nature are expressions of Spirit, and Spirit *transcends* and *includes* both mind and nature in an integral embrace of One Taste. Or likewise with Buddhism: the Dharmakaya of Spirit gives rise to the Sambhogakaya of mind which gives rise to the Nirmanakaya of body and form and nature.

But to acknowledge *only* the Nirmanakaya? Only nature? This is the collapse of the Kosmos into empirical flatland. This is the palpable effect of the industrial ontology that began to invade and colonize and dominate the other domains—whereupon the *only* reality is nature.

Thus, only in the wake of Descended modernity could you have a Marx, a Feuerbach, a Comte. But likewise, only in the wake of modernity could you have the fully developed nature Romantics and ecophilosophers. They are all working the same side of the street, the same flatland, and finding their god, such as it is, in the Descended world of sensory nature, held secretly in place by the industrial grid. They are embracing the world depicted in figure 15-4.

Q: So this means that the Eco-Romantic movement is not a rebellion against industry but a product of industry.

KW: In many ways, yes. The belief that empirical nature is the ultimate reality—that *is* the industrial ontology. The Eco-Romantics rejected the industry but kept the ontology, and did so in the most loyal fashion. In other words, they rejected the superficial problem while embracing the deeper disaster. Like a battered kidnap victim, they fell in love with their captors.

The religion of Gaia, the worship of nature, is simply one of the main forms of industrial religion, of industrial spirituality, and it perpetuates that industrial paradigm.

Q: But the magical-foraging structure, for example, worshipped nature.

KW: No, that's not quite right. It simply wasn't differentiated from nature. That's an entirely different structure. *That* magical nature was animistically alive with egocentric impulse and undifferentiated feelings. The nature that the modern Eco-Romantics adore is necessarily a differentiated nature. Modern Romantics do not actually think that the clouds move because the clouds are following them, and they do not think the volcano exploded because it is mad at them personally (unless they're severely regressed to borderline pathology).

No, the modern nature worshipped by the Eco-Romantics is a fully differentiated nature. And that nature is the supreme reality for them. In other words, they worship the nature that was disclosed by the differentiation of the Big Three. And they think that this nature is the only reality. That is, they have made a god out of the modern collapse of the Big Three to the Big One; they have made a god of monological nature. Mononature, and mononature alone, is real. It is their God, their Goddess.

And that *collapse* of the Big Three to the Big One, we were saying, was largely the result of industrialization. The *collapse* was *held in place* by the *power* of industrialization.

In other words, the nature worshipped by the Eco-Romantics is the flatland nature of industrialization. It is the *same* mononature. The worship of Gaia is a product, and an action, of industrialization, and this worship of Gaia perpetuates the empirical-industrial paradigm. It perpetuates the primary reality of the sensorimotor world. It perpetuates the collapse of the Kosmos.

And this modern Descended grid is destroying Gaia, because it guts the interior dimensions where mutual accord and intersubjective wisdom can actually be found. The religion of Gaia is simply one of the ways the modern Descended grid reproduces itself. We might say, the cunning of the Descended grid. The modern Descended grid is destroying Gaia, and the religion of Gaia is simply one of its basic strategies.

Q: Now there's irony.

KW: Well, you know, modernity, irony.

The essential point is that the Descended grid actually destroys each of the Big Three—destroys mind and culture and nature—because it perpetuates their dissociation, their lack of integration, so that the torn fragments continue to bleed to death. Not just Gaia or nature, but also consciousness and culture are all devastated by their fragmentation and reduction.

It follows—yes?—that the ecocrisis is in large measure the result of the continued dissociation of the Big Three. We cannot align nature and culture and consciousness; we cannot align nature and morals and mind. We are altogether fragmented in this modernity gone slightly mad.

Yet it is the integration of the Big Three, and not the privileging of any one domain, that is our salvation, if such indeed exists. It is an integral vision that holds our promise. But as long as we continue to live within the Descended grid of flatland, then this integration is effectively

prevented. The Eco-Romantic solution—back to nature!—is thus no solution at all, but merely the perpetuation of the Descended grid, the
industrial grid.

Q: They are definitely anti-transcendence.

KW: Yes, since Descenders generally believe that transcendence or
Ascent of any form is evil, they think that transcendence destroys Gaia.
Those who make this claim, I believe, are confusing the mythic form of
dissociative "transcendence" (which indeed is earth-denying) with transcendence in general, which is simply the form of interior development
and evolution of consciousness—which is the actual path of earth-sav-
ing! But once that confusion is made, then these critics do tend to become very vocal about this, as you say. Transcendence ruins Gaia!
Transcendence is the beginning of all evil!

This is the modern industrial grid speaking through their mouths.
Despite the best of intentions, they are caught in the all-pervading industrial ontology of the modern and postmodern flatland. They think transcendence is destroying Gaia, whereas transcendence is the only way
fragments can be joined and integrated and thereby saved. They confuse
transcendence and repression; they confuse differentiation and dissociation; they confuse actualization hierarchies with dominator hierarchies.
No transcendence! Just get closer to nature—closer to the Descended
grid—precisely the cause of the problem, not the cure.

It is in that Descended grid that the modern and postmodern world
now moves—or flounders. This Descended grid determines our goals,
our desires, our consumption, our salvation. It largely governs the mainstream culture as well as the counterculture. The conformist and the
avant-garde equally sing its praises. It upholds the champions of modernity and equally tucks the haters of modernity into its unsuspected fold.
It is fully behind the Ego assaults and equally embraces the Eco movements. It dashes to hell any Ascent at all, and whispers in the ear of each
and all: I am here for you.

Modernity smashes its head against the iron bars of this Descended
grid, and calls the spilled blood knowledge. It wails with the anguish of
those self-inflicted wounds, and calls that anguish authenticity. It com-
mits itself to a deadening embrace of this flattened grid, and calls that
death grip passion. And it wishes, above all else, to prove its dedication
to this merciless Descent, and calls that servitude salvation. The Descended grid has sunk its unrelenting claws into everything that moves.

And—for the greatest irony in today's world—those in whom the
claws are sunk most deeply are made to sing its praises most loudly.

16

The Ego and the Eco

Q: We are in search of a more integral vision, an "all-level, all-quadrant" vision. This would unite the best of ancient wisdom (all-level) with the best of modernity (all-quadrant). One of the primary roadblocks to this integral vision is the embrace of the purely Descended world, the world of flatland.

KW: Yes, I believe so. Of course, individuals can always adopt an integral view for themselves. But the hope is that one would have some sort of support for this holistic and integral vision from the culture at large.

Q: Some sort of widespread "post-flatland" view.

KW: Yes, that's right. And various sorts of "post-flatland" rebellions actually began shortly after the Enlightenment—rebellions against the flatland view of the Enlightenment. Understanding these attempts at a post-flatland view will bring us right up to the present, and to the possibility of a truly integral worldview.

Q: The post-Enlightenment or postmodern rebellions. These began sometime between the eighteenth and nineteenth centuries.

KW: Yes. The profound contradictions in the fundamental Enlightenment paradigm soon generated a series of world-shaking developments, pitting the positive gains of modernity against its ugly underbelly. The *dignities* of modernity clashed with the *disasters* of modernity, and we are all still living in the smoking ruins of that extraordinary battle. A battle we could call the Ego versus the Eco.

Ego versus Eco

Q: In the battle between the rational Enlightenment—which you simply refer to as "the Ego camps"—and nature Romanticism—which you call "the Eco camps"—for all their differences, you maintain that both of them were thoroughly caught in the modern Descended grid.

KW: Yes. Particularly under the onslaught of industrialization, the purely Descended worldview was crashing down with a vengeance. The great web of interwoven its was settling over the modern and postmodern mind like a wet blanket.

Small wonder, then, that what both the rational Enlightenment and nature Romanticism had in common was this purely industrial ontology as an ultimate reference point. Both of them were fundamentally oriented to flatland, to the Right-Hand world of empirical, sensory, objective nature, which was the "really real" world. Both of them, in other words, thoroughly accepted the world as depicted in figure 15-4. But with a difference: the Ego camps wanted to stand back from nature and map it in a disinterested, rational, calculating, scientific fashion, whereas the Eco camps wanted to get closer to nature with feelings and sympathetic communion.

So the difference is that where the Ego-Enlightenment approached the flat and Descended world with rational and industrious calculation, the Eco-Romantics approached it through feeling, sentiment, and emotion. In feelings, we could become one with flatland, one with nature, one with the world of form, and this "oneness" with the phenomenal world, with the Descended world, was thought to be salvation. The nature Romantics didn't want to control flatland, they wanted to become one with it.

The Flatland Twins

Q: Since both Ego and Eco are caught in flatland, why even bother with their squabbles?

KW: Because both of them maintained that they were overcoming the problems inherent in the dissociation of the Big Three, whereas both of them were actually contributing to the disaster.

Q: So what was the difference between them? Because they sharply disagreed on many issues.

KW: Yes. Within the purely Descended grid, they moved in two diametrically opposed directions.

The rational Ego camp—the basic Enlightenment camp, from Descartes to Locke to Fichte—generally had a desire to control, calculate, even subdue the world of nature. The life in nature was solitary, poor, nasty, brutish, and short—and at any rate, quite amoral—and so they understandably felt that the job of the rational Ego was to extricate itself from this brutish and amoral net. The job of the Ego was to *disengage* from the net of nature. Hence this rational Ego is often referred to as the disengaged self, the unencumbered self, the autonomous self, and so on (which we can see in figure 15-4: the "autonomous" Ego dangling in midair).

The Eco-Romantic rebellion found this intolerable, primarily because it introduced a massive dualism or rift between the ego and the world of nature. The founders of the broad Eco-Romantic rebellion—in various ways, Rousseau, Herder, the Schlegels, Schiller, Novalis, Coleridge, Wordsworth, Whitman—wanted above all else to introduce what they felt was some measure of wholeness, harmony, union between self and world. And especially they wanted to see the self and nature united in a broad current of cosmic Life. Not a distancing representation, but a sympathetic insertion into this great web of nature, the ultimate reality toward which all actions and all knowledge must be geared. In short, they wanted oneness with themselves by finding a oneness with nature.

But note, it's the same nature. It's the same sensorimotor nature of the Ego camps, only now approached with an entirely different intent—not to control it or calculate it or dominate it, but rather to become one with it, and thus find "wholeness" in themselves as well.

Q: They were both enthralled with the voice of sensory nature.

KW: Yes. This is why Charles Taylor is able to demonstrate (in his massive *Sources of the Self*) that the Enlightenment and Romantic versions of nature were *both* based on the same modern conception of nature, namely, nature as a great interlocking order or system of empirical processes that is itself the ultimate or foundational reality. The Ego would "reflect" on this reality (the "mirror of nature"), and the Eco would become one with it—but it was the same IT in both cases.

Q: So we have the Ego-Enlightenment on the one hand, and the Eco-Romantic rebellion on the other.

KW: In the most general sense, yes. With the collapse of the Kosmos, there emerged from the shattered debris these two crippled survivors. Whereupon there then commenced an extraordinary battle between these two camps, both despising each other, both convinced they had the solutions to modernity's dissociations, and yet both thoroughly locked within the same Descended grid that was in fact the cause of the problem—and a grid that was never once seriously questioned.

The Ego's Truth

Q: So this war. . . .

KW: The problem was that both the Ego and the Eco camps had undeniable truths that they had latched on to—scraps of truth that had managed to survive the collapse of the Kosmos—and their respective truths were so important and so crucial that neither side would let go of them, understandably.

Q: Start with the important truths of the Ego camp.

KW: The reason that the Ego camps, particularly as they began to evolve away from empiricism and toward Kant and Fichte—the reason they wanted to "get out" of nature was primarily the fact that in sensory nature, there are no conscious moral values. In the Right-Hand world of its, there are no Left-Hand morals!

In the interior or Left-Hand domains, we saw that the human being is at first biocentric and egocentric, lost in its own impulses and incapable of taking the role of other. As egocentric gives way to sociocentric, the human being starts to treat others of its group with the same courtesy it extends to itself. And then with worldcentric morality, the human being attempts to treat all humans with equal dignity or at least equal opportunity. (And with further development into the World Soul, all sentient beings are extended this courtesy, even if they can't respond.)

The rational Ego camps, at their best, represented a postconventional and worldcentric morality, a universal pluralism, and, as we saw, this was part of the dignity of the democratization movements of the Enlightenment. And they were quite right to point out that worldcentric morality exists *nowhere in the world of sensory nature*.

Of course, there is plenty of altruism in nature, but only as an unconscious display of functional fit and genetic inclusion. A consciously worldcentric moral stance is found only in humans, and, as a matter of fact, this worldcentric stance is reached only by a relatively small number of highly developed humans (greater depth, less span).

To reach this higher and relatively rare stance of universal care, I must rise above my natural *biocentric* impulses (sex and survival), my *egocentric* wishes, and my *ethnocentric* proclivities—and stand instead as a relatively *worldcentric* locus of moral awareness that insists on universal compassion. And that freedom from shallower engagements is exhilarating, because it has plugged me into a higher or deeper or truer self.

I am, of course, summarizing Immanuel Kant. And this was part of the extraordinary and exhilarating appeal of Kant. It is only by rising above my egocentric impulses, and my natural desires, and my conformist or ethnocentric perspectives—all of which Kant called "heteronomy"—it is only by rising above these shallower stances, only by taking a deeper or higher perspective, a worldcentric perspective, that I find my own highest aspirations and my own truest self. (We would say, I have evolved to at least fulcrum-5 or 6).

It is only *then* that I become capable of universal care and universal compassion, which is a freedom from the shallowness of these lesser engagements. It is only by Ascending, only by *transcending* these lower orders, that I rise above these baser instincts and find a more universal and tolerant stance. If I reduce reality to the Right-Hand world of mononature, I lose all of that!

For an entire age, Kant stood for moral freedom in worldcentric awareness, precisely by beginning to transcend the merely Descended world, the flatland world where only its and surfaces and valueless objects rule. And this indeed was the beginning of the major *modern* current of Ascent and transcendental awareness, which attempted to break out of the Descended grid of empirical nature, where conscious morals cannot be found.

Kant was outraged—or at any rate, rudely awakened from his dogmatic slumber—by Hume's perfectly mindless empiricism, and Kant responded with what many consider to be the finest and most sophisticated philosophy the West has ever produced. Whatever we decide about that, Kant's transcendental idealism was certainly impressive by any standards, and almost all modern transcendental currents, to the extent that they could be heard at all, would trace a large part of their heritage to Kant—Fichte, Schelling, Hölderlin, Hegel, Schopenhauer, Nietzsche, Bradley, Husserl, Heidegger. . . . Kant, we might say, was the first important modern to do noble and heroic battle with the trolls and troglodytes.

And so there was the Ego's enduring truth. Only in the Left-Hand currents of the Kosmos can we find a higher and wider stance that allows universal tolerance and compassion to flourish. Only with a Left-Hand path can compassion be introduced into the Right-Hand world.

The Ego's Problem

Q: But you said the Ego camps, including Kant, had some severe limitations.

KW: Well, there's a very big problem in all this. Granted that everything Kant said is true enough; granted that this worldcentric moral stance is found nowhere in the categories that frame sensory nature, but only in practical or ethical mind; and granted that nature in that sense is something that must be transcended. But then how do you *integrate* mind and nature? How do you not only *transcend* but also *include* nature? What about this split between mind and nature? The split between Left and Right? The split between Ego and Eco? Not just their differentiation but their dissociation? Because this split is also a split *within my own being*—my mind and my body are split as well. Mind is split from external nature and from internal nature. And what about *that*? Is the price of morality dissociation?

And Kant had no final answer to this, although he attempted to heal the split between the knowledge of morals and the knowledge of nature via aesthetics. Note that he is *trying to integrate the Big Three*—aesthetics, morals, science—which are still flying apart, and Kant cannot pull them together, try as he might.

We saw that the great *advance* of modernity was to differentiate the Big Three, and this Kant does admirably—his three great critiques deal with science, ethics, and art. But we also saw that the great *failure* of modernity was its incapacity to integrate the Big Three, and in this failure Kant was no exception, as critics (such as Hegel) would soon point out.

So in the wake of Kant—that is, in the wake of modernity—we are faced with the massive conundrum: mind and morals and nature, and how could they ever be united? Not re-united!, because they were *never* united or integrated in the first place (because they had never been differentiated in the first place). This differentiation was utterly new, and so was the dissociation—and *that* was the blood all over the brand-new carpet.

Here was the nightmare of the industrial wasteland, a nightmare humanity had never before seen, a nightmare Kant spots and brilliantly works, but a nightmare from which he cannot awaken us.

The Ego and Repression

Q: So apart from the Ego's truth, there was still this massive rift between mind and nature.

KW: Yes. And here we find the major, and I think very accurate, criticism of the Ego camps. Granted they introduced a measure of transcendence, but, *as always*, transcendence can simply go too far and become *repression*.

The rational Ego wanted to rise above nature and its own bodily impulses, so as to achieve a more universal compassion found nowhere in nature, but it often simply repressed these natural impulses instead: repressed its own biosphere; repressed its own life juices; repressed its own vital roots. The Ego tended to *repress* both external nature and internal nature (the id). And this repression, no doubt, would have something to do with the emergence of a Sigmund Freud, sent exactly at this time (and never before this time) to doctor the dissociations of modernity. (This dissociation is well represented in figure 15-4, where the Ego is dangling in midair, cut off from its own body and from the exterior world.)

All of these dualisms understandably vexed the Romantics no end. The Ego seemed to be introducing splits and dualisms and dissociations everywhere, and the Romantics wanted above all else to find instead a *wholeness* and *harmony* and *union*.

The Ego was quite happy to continue mapping the world in an objective and monological fashion, which, of course, disenchanted the world in the process. The detached and disengaged Ego would simply map this world of empirical nature with representational knowledge. If the Ego *disenchanted* nature in the process, so much the better! It is precisely by disenchanting nature that the Ego frees itself! The disenchantment of the world—fine with me, said the Ego, fine with me.

But the Eco camps were absolutely alarmed, and pointed out that this disenchantment was fast becoming disembowelment. Repression, dissociation, desiccation. There is what the rational Ego has brought us! A disenchanted world. And the Eco camps arose directly in response to this wretched disenchantment, and they took it upon themselves to re-enchant the world.

The wild, fabulous, amazing, and extraordinary attempt at re-enchantment had finally begun.

The Re-enchantment of the World

Q: So the Eco camps began with a criticism of the rational Ego.

KW: Yes, basically. Most of the Romantic criticisms could be summarized as an extreme uneasiness with the Ego's *repressive* tendencies. The rational Ego—that great autonomous master of its universe—had in fact simply sealed out and ignored its prepersonal roots as well its transpersonal illuminations. It had cut off, or pretended to cut off, its subconscious juices as well as its superconscious inspirations. And so for all of its wonderful accomplishments, the autonomous Ego had nonetheless left massive roadkill everywhere on the highway to rational heaven.

And it was especially this *repression* that the Romantic rebellion would focus on.

Q: The criticism was true.

KW: Yes, there is much truth to that criticism, and this is where the Romantic camps attacked. They found this repressive split between morals and nature, or mind and nature, or mind and body, or Ego and Eco—those are all the same split—they found this split to be intolerable. They understandably wanted *wholeness* and *unity*. So where Kant and Fichte would talk endlessly of the *autonomy* of the self from nature and nature's baser instincts, the Romantics would talk endlessly of *uniting* with nature in some sort of vital and expressive union, in some great *unitary* stream of Life and Love.

The desirability and necessity of healing this split between morals and nature—this was the great truth the Romantics came to announce, and it is a truth that is as enduring in its own way as the Kantian notion of the necessity for transcendence.

Q: But something has to give.

KW: Yes, at this historical point we reach total gridlock, complete philosophical gridlock, an utter standoff between the Ego and the Eco camps. How can you possibly reconcile these two positions? How can you reconcile the necessity to rise above nature with a necessity to become one with it?

This is still the crucial problem, isn't it? How can you reconcile Ego and Eco? This is still the critical dilemma in today's world, yes?

The Ego camp, we just saw, had no satisfactory answer. But the Eco-Romantic solution was notoriously just as unsatisfactory, by almost everybody's account, and their "solution" of the "one Life stream" was vigorously attacked by the Ego camps. How, the Ego camps sarcastically asked, can you unite with nature, become one with nature, act only on nature's impulses, and yet still preserve the worldcentric and postconventional morality that we have all fought so hard to secure?

The Romantic response was lame in the extreme, and centered mostly on defining "nature" in two very different and utterly contradictory ways, and they simply switched back and forth between these two definitions as suited their purposes.

Back to Nature

Q: The Romantics had two different definitions of nature?

KW: Yes. First they maintained, in true Descended fashion, that empirical nature is the one reality, the all-inclusive and all-embracing reality. This, of course, is the modern Descended grid, and the Romantics swallowed it hook, line, and sinker. And yet culture, they maintained, has grievously *deviated* from this nature, it has *split* from this nature, it has lost touch with the great life stream, it is ruining nature.

Q: The ecophilosophers still maintain that.

KW: Yes, but look at the two very different and contradictory definitions of nature hidden in that statement. First, nature is supposed to be the one single reality of which all organisms, including the human, are part. In this sense, nature is absolutely *all-inclusive*, nothing is outside of it. It is the ultimate and all-embracing reality, and everything that occurs is an activity of this ultimate reality.

But two, culture is supposed to have *deviated* from this nature. Culture has to some degree split itself from nature. Culture, in fact, is ruining nature. So now we have *two* natures: a nature that you can't deviate from, versus a nature that you can. And clearly they can't be the same thing. They sneaked in two natures.

So what is the relation of this Nature with a capital N that embraces *everything*, versus this nature that is *different* from culture because it is getting ruined by culture?

Q: The big Nature is supposed to include and unify culture and nature.

KW: Yes, and so again, what is the relation of Nature and nature? See, this was the whole problem.

The entire Romantic movement crashed and went up in flames over this internal contradiction. What the best of the Romantics were trying to say is that Nature with a big N is Spirit, is the entire Kosmos (both Left and Right), because Spirit does indeed *transcend* and *include* both culture and nature. And that is fine, that is true enough.

But because the Romantics were caught in the incredibly pervasive Descended grid, they simply identified Nature with nature. They identified Spirit with sensory nature. They identified Spirit with the visible, sensible, Right-Hand world, taken as a whole. They identified Spirit with the great web of nature.

And here they went up in smoke, a spectacularly narcissistic, egocentric, flamboyant explosion—because the closer you get to preconventional nature, the more egocentric you become. And in search of Nature, the Romantics headed back to nature.

The Eco and Regression

Q: So the collapse of the Kosmos is the same as the collapse of Nature to nature.

KW: Yes, that's right. Now, if you are Ego and deny any sort of spiritual reality anyway, then fine, you'll simply map this empirical nature in a disengaged fashion, no problem. You are a happy, mindless, mapping fool.

But if you are tender-hearted, and if you are open to spiritual experiences—and yet you are still inadvertently trapped in the industrial ontology—then you will simply equate Spirit with sensory nature. Your spiritual *intuition* is probably very genuine, but your *interpretation* occurs within the orbit of the industrial grid. The only reality there is—Right-Hand empirical nature—must *therefore* be the ultimate spiritual reality as well.

So even if you have a direct experience of the World Soul, or even the Nondual—pow!, it's interpreted as coming from sensory nature. The industrial grid, operating preconsciously, beats you to the interpretation, and you are secretly caught in that flatland framework.

And thus instead of *moving forward* in *evolution* to the emergence of a Nature or Spirit (or World Soul) that would indeed unify the differentiated mind and nature, you simply recommend "back to nature." Not forward to Nature, but back to nature.

Q: This regressive trend is characteristic of many Romantic movements, down to today's ecophilosophers.

KW: In many cases, yes. And here is where this regressive move becomes so historically important, becomes an incredibly influential current in the modern and postmodern world:

If nature or the biosphere is the only fundamental reality—if it is actually "spirit"—then, the Romantics announced, anything that *moves away from nature* must be *killing* spirit. Culture moves away from nature, and so culture must be killing spirit. So if sensory nature is the ultimately Real, then *culture* must be the original Crime.

And we are not simply talking about the fact that culture can go too far and repress nature; we are not talking about the fact that the mind can repress the body's impulses—granted all of that is true enough. The Romantic objection was much deeper and much stronger. Something about culture itself necessarily disrupted nature, and since nature is the sole spiritual reality, something about culture per se was antispiritual. Culture, in fact, was the original Crime against a primal Paradise of natural freedom and spiritual abundance.

This "spiritual insight" is the core of most Eco-Romantic movements, then and now. And yet this "insight" is not really spiritual in any profound sense; it is an interpretation framed largely within the secret requirements of the industrial grid. It is simply one of the numerous hidden ways that the modern Descended grid defends itself against any transcendence, defends itself against any genuine spirituality. It is a defense mechanism of a worldview that wishes to maintain the outrageous lie that finite nature alone is real. And so it must present this nature as being Spirit, and it must present anything that deviates from nature as being the devil.

And with this "insight" began the extremely influential movements of "back to nature," of "the noble savage," of a "Paradise Lost," of a primal Eden that had been disrupted and distorted by the horrible Crime of Culture.

To find a purer reality, a truer self, a more genuine feeling, and a fairer community, we must get back prior to the Crime of Culture and rediscover a historical past in which this Crime had not occurred. And once we find this Paradise Lost, we must, as a social agenda, make it the Promised Land by reverting to or incorporating the original, primal, pristine way of life into the modern world.

And here begins the retro-Romantic slide.

Paradise Lost

Q: This slide seems to appear in many different areas, from the original Romantics to many of the modern ecophilosophers.

KW: Well, it's very easy to see how it got started. Modernity had managed to differentiate the Big Three for the first time in history—and this included differentiating mind and nature. But because modernity could not yet integrate them, the Big Three tended to drift into dissociation, and this the Romantics rightly reacted to with alarm. This reaction was completely understandable; quite noble, in fact, and I believe we can all applaud the Romantics for trying to do *something* about it.

Since this dissociation was so alarming, the Romantics did the obvious but, it now appears, naive thing—they thought the problem was the differentiation itself: we simply never should have differentiated the Big Three to begin with. Failing to see that differentiation is the *necessary prelude* to *integration*, the Romantic solution was to simply head back to those days prior to the differentiation. Not prior to the *dissociation*—which would have been right—but prior to the differentiation itself!—which was the regressive slide. The only way to cure the problems of the oak is to go back to being an acorn!

And the only way to do that is to get back to the good ole days when culture and nature were undifferentiated, back to humanity's acornness, back prior to this horrible Crime that humanity had committed against nature. History was therefore depicted as a series of horrifying errors that led humanity further and further away from the original pristine state where mind and nature were "one," conveniently overlooking the fact that this original "pristine state" had none of the disasters of modernity precisely because it had none of the dignities either. For the Romantics, the oak was somehow a horrible violation of the acorn, and humanity's job was to rediscover and get back to its acornness.

Q: Whereas the real solution might be, what?

KW: We can probably all agree that typical or conventional culture is not often imbued with a great deal of genuine spirituality. But the remedy is to go post-conventional, not pre-conventional. The remedy is to go post-conventional in Spirit, not pre-conventional in nature. Spirit transcends and includes both culture and nature, and thus integrates and unifies both.

But if you recommend going back to the pre-conventional state, back to acornness, back to the original "pristine" state of nature, then you have not integrated the differentiations, you have simply obliterated them by regressing to a point before they emerged at all. You recommend magical indissociation or mythic immersion, hypocritically taking advantage of the dignities and freedoms of modernity while you endlessly complain about how rotten it all is.

This is not translogical Spirit; it is certainly not the dreaded dialogical culture; it is pure, simple, monological nature—which, by my sneaky dual definition, I have now proclaimed to be Spirit or Nature. I will get away from the Crime of Culture. I will get back to Paradise Lost. I will find the noble savage in myself. I will discover the original Eden, when none of modernity's differentiations plagued me with the burden of distinguishing my ego from reality at large. And I will then possess a damning indictment of modernity: I have found the Paradise Lost which will be the Promised Land, if only modernity will listen to me and get back to a mute and dumbfounded nature.

And in this regression from noosphere to biosphere, you are indeed released from the disasters of modernity, by releasing yourself from the dignity and the demands as well. You have cured the *repression* by *regression*.

Q: But you *can* have strong spiritual experiences in nature. This is very common. And I think that is what the nature Romantics meant by Spirit.

KW: Yes, indeed you can, but the source of these spiritual feelings is not nature itself. You might stare for hours at a sunset, and suddenly disappear into the World Soul, and feel yourself at one with all nature. This is well and good. But nature is not the source of this intuition. Worms and rats and foxes and weasels do not stare for hours at the sunset, and marvel at its beauty, and transcend themselves in that release—even though their senses are in many cases much sharper than ours, even though they see nature more clearly than we! No, nature is not the *source* of this Beauty; nature is its destination. The *source* is transcendental Spirit, of which nature is a radiant expression.

And thus when, in nature, you can relax your egoic grasping and stand as an opening or clearing in awareness—and nature is an inviting place to do so—then through that clearing might come pouring the power and the glory of the World Soul, and you are temporarily struck perfectly dead by the wonder and the beauty of it all—a beauty that takes your breath away, takes your self away, all at once—a beauty that bestows new splendor on the setting sun and renders nature insanely vivid in its display.

But if you are committed to *interpreting* this spiritual experience in a completely Descended pattern—if you are caught in the industrial grid—then you will ascribe this Spirit to simple nature itself. You will mistake the effect for the cause. You will fail to see that you got to this World Soul intuition precisely by developing from sensory-biocentric to egocentric to sociocentric to worldcentric to World Soul, each of which transcends and includes.

Thus, struck by the beauty of the World Soul that you have mistakenly reduced to sensory nature, you will recommend—not that we go from nature to culture to Spirit—but that we simply get back to nature, even though the weasel sitting next to you doesn't seem to be seeing the same thing in nature that you are—wonder why that is?

And because you now think that the World Soul or Spirit is a simple sensory impact—is nature itself—you will then start to think, not that culture is a necessary part of an evolution *on its way* to a *conscious* apprehension of Spirit as true Self, but rather that culture *hides* and *distorts* this sensory nature in which your "real self" supposedly resides. Culture is not *on the way* to the true Self, it is simply a crime against the "true self" of your biocentric feelings.

In short, you will start recommending, not that we move forward to fulcrum-7 and the Eco-Noetic Self, but that we move back to fulcrum-2 and the biocentric or ecocentric or ecological self.

Q: But when I look around me, it certainly appears that everything is a part of nature. My organism is part of nature, the landscapes, the clouds, the lakes and forests, human beings and other animals—everything is part of nature. So why couldn't an ecological approach include everything?

KW: That's just the point—when you look *around* you (the Right-Hand world). If you look *within* you (the Left-Hand world), you will find a different story, the story of the growth and evolution of consciousness itself. Those *interior* stages of growth do indeed have correlates in the world of empirical nature, just as depicted in figure 15-3. But if you reduce those interiors to their exterior correlates—reduce everything to ecology or nature or the sensorimotor world—then you land squarely in the world of interwoven its, otherwise known as flatland (just as shown in figure 15-4). A truly integral approach, on the other hand, would include both the Ego and Eco, or interiors and exteriors, or Left and Right—as we will see—but in the meantime, we are focusing on exactly those approaches that believed that "everything is part of nature," as you put it.

Q: I inadvertently bought the flatland grid.

KW: Yes, and so did the Romantics, then and now. And that tends to be regressive because it ignores the interior hierarchies and leaves us only with the sensory and material world, which pulls us into our own preconventional, egocentric levels.

Q: You said this regression was converted into a critique of modernity.

KW: Yes, the real difficulty in this approach is that it misses altogether the actual cause of modernity's problems. The real problem was the dissociation of the Big Three and their collapse to the Big One of mononature—the industrial ontology. The Romantics spotted and rejected the nastiness of industry, but not the ontology of industry. They thus attacked the superficial problem while enthusiastically promoting the deeper problem, the real nightmare.

Because the startling fact is that ecological wisdom does not consist in understanding how to live in accord with nature; it consists in understanding how to get humans to agree on how to live in accord with nature.

This wisdom is an intersubjective accord in the noosphere, not an immersion in the biosphere. No representation of the biosphere whatsoever will produce this wisdom. It can be found on none of the maps of exterior surfaces and sensory marvels; it is a path of intersubjective accord based upon mutual understanding grounded in sincerity; it has its own developmental stages, with its own logic; it can be found nowhere in empirical nature.

But if preconventional biosphere is your Goddess, then you must get back closer to sensory nature in order to be saved. And since modernity differentiated this nature, you must get back prior to that differentiation. You must in all ways go premodern.

Q: The regressive slide.

KW: Yes. And thus, where the Ego camps were perpetuating what amounted to *repression*, the Eco camps were advocating what amounted to *regression*. Repression and regression were—and are—the twin engines of the flatland game, the twin machines of industrial ontology.

The Way Back Machine

Q: The Eco-Romantics were often very specific about the lost glories of the past.

KW: Yes. Beginning in the eighteenth century, and continuing down to today, you have the Eco-Romantics basically setting their Way Back machine to the period where they felt that culture was the least differentiated from nature. The great search for Paradise Lost had begun.

Not the search for a timeless Spirit that we have alienated in this present moment by our contracting and grasping tendencies, but the search for a "spirit" that was fully present at some past time—some past historical or prehistorical period—but was then "killed" by the great Crime of Culture, or the crime of the patriarchy, or one sort of crime or another.

Q: The original Romantics were fond of Greece.

KW: Yes, for the early Romantics, such as Schiller, ancient Greece was by far the favorite stop on the Regress Express, because mind and nature were supposed to be a "unity" (they were indeed undifferentiated to any great extent). And never mind that for precisely that reason one out of three Greeks were slaves, and women and children might as well have been. There were few of the disasters of modernity, it is true—and few of the dignities either.

Ancient Greece is now quite out of favor with the Romantics, mostly because, being *agrarian*, it was patriarchal. So the Romantics set their Way Back machine one stage further back, and they arrived at *horticultural* societies. These are now by far the favorite haunt of the ecofeminists. These societies, as we saw, were often matrifocal, ruled by the Great Mother.

And let us delicately ignore the central ritual of many horticultural societies—the ritual human sacrifice, which was required, among other things, to ensure crop fertility. Let us likewise forget that, according to Lenski's massive data, an astonishing 44 percent of these societies engaged in frequent warfare and over 50 percent in intermittent warfare (which rather puts to rest the notion of the peace-loving Great Mother societies); that 61 percent had private property rights; that 14 percent had slavery; and 45 percent had bride price. These horticultural societies were anything but "pure and pristine," as the ecomasculinists themselves have pointed out.

Q: They prefer foraging.

KW: Yes, the ecomasculinists (deep ecologists) have pushed yet one stage *further back* and arrived at foraging cultures as the "pure and pristine state." And, in fact, according the ecomasculinists, the ecofeminists' beloved horticulture is not truly close to nature in a pure way, because those societies depended upon farming, which is actually a rape of the land. Hunting and gathering, now that's pure and pristine.

And let us ignore the data that show that 10 percent of these societies had slavery, 37 percent had bride price, and 58 percent engaged in frequent or intermittent warfare. This must be the pure and pristine state— because there is no further back! This *must* be it! And so I will now ignore every single unpleasant thing about any of these societies, and they will be the noble savage, period.

Although logically, of course, the thing to do is push back to apes, because they have no slavery, bride price, war, and so on. I mean, why not get serious about this retrogression and really carry it to its conclusion: everything past the Big Bang was a Big Mistake. This is the logic you get locked into if you confuse differentiation and dissociation; you think every differentiation is a mistake—you think the oak is a crime against the acorn.

And so the search for the pure and pristine state would go, pushing further and further back—scraping more and more layers of depth off the Kosmos in search of a pristine state in which the Romantic insertion into nature could occur. You cure the repression by regression. You cure the disease by getting rid of the depth. By, that is, becoming more shallow.

The Great Battle of Modernity: Fichte versus Spinoza

Q: So this historical gridlock between the Ego camps and the Eco camps. The Ego wanted to subdue the Eco, the Eco wanted to get rid of the Ego.

KW: Yes. The gridlock was, do you *transcend* nature so as to find moral freedom and autonomy, or do you become *one* with nature so as to find unity and wholeness? Are you transcendental Ego or immanent Eco?

That is, pure Ascent or pure Descent?

This fundamental problem, this recalcitrant dualism! This two-thousand-year-old battle between the Ascenders and the Descenders—the single battle that has most defined the entire Western tradition—has simply reappeared in its *modern* form as the battle between the Ego and the Eco.

And this millennia-old rivalry soon found its archetypal champions in Fichte and Spinoza.

Q: Very briefly.

KW: Very briefly: Fichte attempted to overcome the split between Ego and Eco by absolutizing the Ego, the path of Ascent. It was in the pure I, the pure transcendental Self, that liberation was to be found. And the more of the pure Ego, and the less of the Eco, then the better for everybody, said Fichte, as he bowed at the altar of the Ascending God.

The Eco-Romantics, of course, were headed in exactly the opposite direction, under the gaze of exactly the other God. They would overcome this split between Ego and Eco by absolutizing the Eco, absolutizing the path of Descent. And thus the Eco camps would find their archetypal champion in an imaginatively interpreted Spinoza (they imagined that by Nature Spinoza meant nature—but never mind, he would do just fine!). Pure freedom thus resides in a total immersion in the Great System of nature, the pure Eco. The more of the Eco, and the less of the Ego, the better for everybody, said the Romantics, as they eagerly bowed at the earth-bound altar of the purely Descending God.

Q: So we have this standoff between Ego and Eco, Fichte and Spinoza.

KW: Yes, and this wasn't a minor side issue. This was exactly the end limit of the two-thousand-year-old battle at the heart of the West's attempt to awaken. And it was an agonizing problem because everybody vaguely intuited that both camps were at least partially right. But how?

So the cry everywhere went up: We must integrate Fichte and Spinoza! Or Kant and Spinoza. Or Kant and Goethe. Variations on the same theme. This really was an obsession for an entire age, particularly toward the end of the eighteenth century.

Q: So who won?

KW: Well, it all came to the same thing: how can you transcend nature for moral freedom and yet become one with nature for wholeness? Autonomy versus wholeness. Which do you want? Freedom from nature, or freedom as nature? How can you possibly have both? How can you integrate Ascending and Descending? These fractured footnotes to Plato! Where is your salvation to be found? Where is your God to be located?

Q: In the midst of this battle came a person you are obviously quite fond of, and who perhaps solved the dilemma. In *Sex, Ecology, Spirituality,* you introduce this person by reading a letter from someone who attended the lectures. Mind if I read that letter?

KW: Go ahead.

17

The Dominance of the Descenders

Q: "Schelling is lecturing to an amazing audience, but amidst so much noise and bustle, whistling, and knocking on the windows by those who cannot get in the door, in such an overcrowded lecture hall, that one is almost tempted to give up listening to him if this is to continue. During the first lectures it was almost a matter of risking one's life to hear him. However, I have put my trust in Schelling and at the risk of my life I have the courage to hear him once more. It may very well blossom during the lectures, and if so one might gladly risk one's life— what would one not do to be able to hear Schelling?

"I am so happy to have heard Schelling's second lecture— indescribably. The embryonic child of thought leapt for joy within me when he mentioned the word 'actuality' in connection with the relation of philosophy to actuality. I remember almost every word he said after that. Here, perhaps, clarity can be achieved. This one word recalled all my philosophical pains and sufferings.—And so that she, too, might share my joy, how willingly I would return to her, how eagerly I would coax myself to believe that this is the right course—Oh, if only I could!— now I have put all my hope in Schelling. . . ."

KW: Yes, the letter is from Søren Kierkegaard, during Schelling's Berlin lectures of 1841. Attending those lectures, beside Kierkegaard, were Jakob Burkhardt, Michael Bakunin, and Friedrich Engels, collaborator of Karl Marx.

Q: So can you summarize his central point, especially about integrating mind and nature?

KW: Schelling began by saying that, if it is true that the Enlightenment had succeeded in differentiating mind and nature, it had also tended to forget the transcendental and unifying Ground of both, and thus it tended to *dissociate* mind and nature—the disaster of modernity.

This dissociation of mind and nature, Ego and Eco, with mind "mirroring" nature in scientific inquiry—what we saw as the representation paradigm—this dissociation was, of course, well under way. Representation had, Schelling pointed out, introduced a rift or cleavage between nature as external object and the reflecting self as subject—which also, he said, made humans *objects* to themselves—dehumanized humanism, as we earlier put it. And when representation is made an end in itself, it becomes "a spiritual malady," he said.

In this he was in agreement with the Romantics. In fact, Schelling was one of the principal founders of Romanticism, although he also moved quite beyond it, largely by refusing regression to nature. That is, Schelling realized that the dissociation could not be overcome by a *return* to the immediacy of feeling, "to the childhood, as it were, of the human race." There was no going back to Eco-nature, and Schelling knew it.

Rather, he maintained, we have to go forward *beyond* reason in order to discover that mind and nature are both simply different movements of one absolute Spirit, a Spirit that manifests itself in its own successive stages of unfolding. As Schelling's colleague Hegel would soon put it, Spirit is not One apart from Many, but the *very process* of the One expressing itself through the Many—it is infinite activity expressing itself in the *process of development itself*—or, as we would now say, Spirit expresses itself in the entire process of evolution.

Evolution: The Great Holarchy Unfolds in Time

Q: So this developmental or evolutionary notion was not new with Darwin.

KW: Far from it. The Great Chain theorists, beginning as early as Leibniz, began to realize that the Great Chain could best be understood as a holarchy that is not given all at once, but rather unfolds over enormous stretches of historical and geographical time—starting with matter, then the emergence of sensation in life forms, then perception, then impulse, then image, and so on.

And thus, about a century before Darwin, it was widely accepted in educated circles that the Great Chain had actually unfolded or developed over vast time. And—this was crucial—since the Great Chain contained no "gaps" or holes (because the plenitude of Spirit fills all empty spaces), the research agenda was to find any "missing links" in evolution.

Q: That's where the term actually came from?

KW: Yes, any missing links in the Chain. And so there began a massive search for the "missing links" between various species. So widespread was this understanding, so common and so taken for granted, that even the notorious circus promoter P. T. Barnum could advertise that his museum contained "the Ornithorhincus, or the connecting link between the seal and the duck; two distinct species of flying fish, which undoubtedly connect the bird and the fish; the Mud Iguana, a connecting link between reptiles and fish—with other animals forming connecting links in the Great Chain of animated Nature." That's two decades before Darwin published *Origin of Species*!

Q: That's hilarious.

KW: It's also fascinating. All of this looking for the missing links. It was behind the search for microorganisms, whose existence Leibniz had already deduced solely on the basis of the Great Chain—microorganisms simply *had* to be there to fill in certain apparent gaps in the Chain. It was behind the belief in life on other planets, which Giordano Bruno had deduced on the basis of the Great Chain. And the missing links between species—all of this was based, not initially on empirical or scientific evidence, but directly on the belief in the Great Chain.

Q: A Neoplatonic idea.

KW: Yes, all of this, in one way or another, goes back to Plotinus. Spirit is so full and complete, he said, that when it empties itself into creation, it leaves no place untouched—it leaves no holes or gaps or missing links. And Plotinus's Great Holarchy is the way these links or levels connect and include and nest each other, all the way from matter to God.

Now, if you take that Great Holarchy, exactly as presented by Plotinus (fig. 14-1), and if you realize that it unfolds in time—unfolds over vast stretches of time—then you basically have today's general understanding of the major stages of evolution. Evolution does indeed proceed from matter to sensation to perception to impulse to image to symbol, and so on.

Except, of course, we moderns, committed to a Descended grid, have no higher stages of evolution beyond reason, and we interpret the entire Great Chain in merely empirical and natural terms—which is precisely why we can't understand or explain the self-transcending drive of this evolution that has nonetheless become our modern god!

But the central point is that Plotinus temporalized equals evolution. And this was all worked out and widely accepted a century before Darwin. Schelling wrote the transcendental philosophy around 1800. We have P. T. Barnum's advertisement around 1840. Darwin published around 1860, decades after people were already going to museums to see the "missing links."

What Darwin and Wallace contributed to this already-accepted notion was the theory, not of evolution, but of evolution by natural selection—which, it turns out, can't explain macroevolution at all! Which is why Wallace always maintained that natural selection itself was not the cause but the *result* of "Spirit's manner and mode of creation," and even Darwin was most reluctant to remove Spirit from the nature of evolution.

And so, if you had to pick two of the philosophers who, after Plato, had the broadest impact on the Western mind, they very well might be Plotinus and then Schelling. For this reason alone: Plotinus gave the Great Holarchy its fullest expression, and Schelling set the Great Holarchy afloat in developmental time, in evolution. And if there is one idea that dominates the modern and postmodern mind at large, it is evolution.

And we are at the point, historically, that it is beginning to be understood that the Great Holarchy evolved over time. And standing at that crucial watershed is Schelling.

Evolution: Spirit-in-Action

Q: I take it that for Schelling, development or evolution was still a spiritual movement.

KW: It's hard to understand any other way, and Schelling knew it. Spirit is present at each and every stage of the evolutionary process, *as the very process itself*. As Hegel would soon put it, the Absolute is "the process of its own becoming; it becomes concrete or actual only by its development."

Q: Here is a quote from Hegel: "That the history of the world, with all the changing scenes which its annals present, is this process of development and the realization of Spirit—only *this* insight can reconcile Spirit with the history of the world—that what has happened, and is happening every day, is not only not 'without God', but is essentially God's work."

KW: Yes, which is why Zen would say, "That which one can deviate from is not the true Tao."

Schelling's point is that nature is not the only reality, and mind is not the only reality. *Spirit is the only reality.* But in order to create the manifest world, Spirit must go out of itself, empty itself, into manifestation. Spirit descends into manifestation, but this manifestation is nevertheless Spirit itself, a form or expression of Spirit itself.

So Spirit first goes out of itself to produce nature, which is simply *objective* Spirit. At this point in evolution Spirit is still *un-self-conscious*. Thus the whole of nature Schelling refers to as *slumbering Spirit*. Nature is not a mere inert and instrumental backdrop for mind, as the Ego camps maintained. Rather, nature is a "self-organizing dynamic system" that is "*the objective manifestation of Spirit*"—precisely Plato's "visible, sensible God," but now set developmentally afloat.

So nature is most definitely not a static or deterministic machine. For Schelling, nature is "God-in-the-making." The very processes of nature are *spiritual processes*—they are *striving* for spiritual awakening—because they are objective Spirit striving to actualize itself (Eros).

And so here Schelling is acknowledging the major contention of the Eco-Romantics—nature indeed is *not* a mechanical and doltish backdrop; *nature is spiritual to the core*. But slumbering Spirit, because Spirit has not yet become self-conscious, the Kosmos has not yet begun to consciously *reflect on itself*.

With the emergence of mind, Spirit becomes self-conscious, which, among other things, introduces conscious morals into the world, morals found nowhere in nature. And these morals represent an advance in consciousness over what can be found in slumbering nature. And here Schelling is acknowledging the rational-Ego camps and their undeniable contributions.

Spirit is starting to awaken to itself. Spirit seeks to know itself through symbols and concepts, and the result is that the universe begins to think about the universe—which produces the world of reason and, in particular, the world of conscious morals. Thus, says Schelling, where nature is *objective Spirit*, mind is *subjective Spirit*.

But unlike the Ego camps, Schelling is insisting that the Ego itself is simply one moment in the overall arc of Spirit's self-actualization. He refuses to stop with either the Eco or the Ego schools. Schelling is heading for the Nondual.

But he freely concedes that at this historical point—where mind and nature become differentiated—there does indeed appear to be a massive rift in the world, namely, between the reflecting mind and the reflected nature. But unlike the radical Ego camps, who want the mind to be supreme, and unlike the pure Eco camps, who want nature to be supreme, Schelling sees that both of them are necessary but partial moments on the way to a Spirit that will transcend and include them both, and thus awaken to its own supreme identity.

Q: So with modernity we are temporarily stuck with this battle between mind and nature, between Ego and Eco.

KW: Yes, this painful birth of modernity's acute self-consciousness is a necessary part of Spirit's awakening. We moderns must go through the fire. And no other period has had to face this fire on a collective scale. Going backward simply avoids the fire, it does not transform it.

So Schelling insists that instead of going back prior to this split, we rather must go forward beyond the Ego and beyond the Eco, both of which pretend to be "absolute." But these two "apparent absolutes," as he calls them, are *synthesized* in the third great movement of Spirit, which is the transcendence of *both* nature and mind and thus their radical union.

Q: With Fichte and Spinoza in mind.

KW: Exactly. With the pure Ego and the pure Eco in mind. This *nondual* synthesis, according to Schelling, is also the identity of subject and object in one timeless act of self-knowledge, of Spirit *directly knowing itself* as Spirit, a direct mystical intuition, says Schelling, that is *not mediated* through *any forms*, whether those forms be the *feelings* of objective nature or the *thoughts* of subjective mind.

And here we have an unmistakable and profound glimpse of the formless and nondual groundless Ground, the pure Emptiness of One Taste. Schelling would often refer to the "indifference" and the "Abyss," precisely in the lineage of Eckhart and Boehme and Dionysius. "In the ultimate dark Abyss of the divine Being, the primal ground or Urgrund, there is no differentiation but only pure identity." What we have been calling the Supreme Identity.

Thus, for Schelling (and for his friend and student Hegel), Spirit goes out of itself to produce objective nature, awakens to itself in subjective mind, and then recovers itself in pure Nondual awareness, where subject and object are one pure immediacy that unifies both nature and mind in realized Spirit.

And so: Spirit knows itself objectively as *nature*; knows itself subjectively as *mind*; and knows itself absolutely as *Spirit*—the Source, the Summit, and the Eros of the entire sequence.

Glimmers of the Nondual

Q: These three broad movements can also be referred to as subconscious, self-conscious, and superconscious.

KW: Or prepersonal, personal, and transpersonal; or prerational, rational, and transrational; or biosphere, noosphere, and theosphere, not to put too fine a point on it.

Q: So how exactly does this vision integrate the gains of both the Ego and the Eco without just forcing them together?

KW: Schelling's key insight was that the Spirit that is *realized* in a conscious fashion in the supreme identity is in fact the Spirit that was *present all along* as the *entire process* of evolution itself. All of Spirit, so to speak, is present at every stage, as the process of unfolding itself. But at each stage Spirit unfolds more of itself, realizes more of itself, and thus moves from slumber in nature to awakening in mind to final realization as Spirit itself. But the Spirit that is *realized* is the same Spirit that was present all along, as the entire process of its own awakening.

So, to answer your question specifically, Schelling could integrate Ego and Eco—Fichte and Spinoza, autonomy and wholeness—because, he pointed out, when you realize your supreme identity as Spirit, then you are *autonomous* in the fullest sense—because nothing is outside you—and therefore you are also *whole* or *unified* in the fullest sense—because nothing is outside you. Full autonomy and full wholeness are one and the same thing in the supreme identity.

So men and women don't have to sacrifice their own autonomy or will because their will ultimately aligns itself with the entire Kosmos. The entire Kosmos is something your deepest Self is doing, and you *are* that Kosmos in its entirety. Full autonomy, full wholeness.

This is a profound integration of Ego and Eco, of Ascent and Descent, of transcendence and immanence, of Spirit *descending* into even the lowest state and *ascending* back to itself, but with Spirit nonetheless fully present at each and every stage as the process of its own self-realization, a divine play of Spirit present in every single movement of the Kosmos, yet finding more and more of itself as its own Play proceeds, dancing fully and divine in every gesture of the universe, never really lost and never really found, but present from the start and all along, a wink and a nod from the radiant Abyss.

Always Already

Q: And what exactly separated this vision from the Eco-Romantic vision?

KW: The pure Romantics, then and now, would never admit that mind and Spirit transcend nature, because nothing transcends nature.

There is *only* nature, and mind and Spirit are somehow the same as this nature, or the sum total of this nature, or strands in the web of this nature.

And so most of all, the Eco-Romantics could not understand that "that which you can deviate from is not the true Tao." The ecophilosophers keep telling us what we have *deviated* from, which shows that they are aware of nature, but not Nature. They do not seem to have understood the true Tao or Spirit.

According to the Idealists—and the Nondual sages everywhere—the extraordinary and altogether paradoxical secret is that the Final Release is *always already* accomplished. The "last step" is to step off the cycle of time altogether, and find the Timeless there *from the start*, ever-present from the very beginning and at *every point* along the way, with no deviations whatsoever.

"The Good," says Hegel, "the absolutely Good, is eternally accomplishing itself in the world; and the result is that it need not wait upon us, but is *already in full actuality accomplished*."

I have one last quote for you, from Findlay, one of Hegel's great interpreters: "It is by the capacity to understand this that the true Hegelian is marked off from his often diligent and scholarly, but still profoundly misguided misinterpreter, who still yearns after the showy spectacular climax, the Absolute coming down . . . accompanied by a flock of doves, when a simple return to utter ordinariness is in place [cf. Zen's "ordinary mind"]. Finite existence in the here and now, *with every limitation*, is, Hegel teaches, when rightly regarded and accepted, identical with the infinite existence which is everywhere and always. To live on Main Street is, if one lives in the right spirit, to inhabit the Holy City."

As Plotinus knew and Nagarjuna taught: always and always, the other world is this world rightly seen. Every Form is Emptiness *just as it is*. The radical secret of the supreme identity is that there is only God. There is only the Kosmos of One Taste, always already fully present, always already perfectly accomplished, always already the sound of one hand clapping. And the very belief that we *could* deviate from this is the arrogance of the egoic delusion, the haunting mask of divine egoism gloating over the smoking ruins of its own contracting tendencies. We can preserve nature, but Nature preserves us.

The Fading of the Vision

Q: The Idealist vision almost completely faded within a few decades.

KW: Yes. The Descended grid ate Idealism alive and spat out Gaia-centric salvation, whether in the form of Marxism or ecocentrism or capitalism—the same grid, and the same wobbling between the only two choices available: control nature (Ego), become one with nature (Eco).

Q: So is it a matter of simply trying to bring back some form of Idealism?

KW: Not really, because evolution moves on. We have a different techno-economic base now, and Idealism as it was proposed would not now functionally fit. There will be a new type of Idealism, we might say, but the coming Buddha will speak digital. Which I suppose is another conversation.

In any event we can't simply stop with Schelling or any of the Idealists. Granted that the summary I gave of Spirit-in-action is valid—and I believe it is—nevertheless, none of the Idealists really understood the four quadrants very well, and their grasp of the actual details and stages of the transpersonal domains was rather thin. I believe we can summarize these shortcomings in two simple points.

The first was a failure to develop any truly *contemplative practices*— that is, any true paradigms, any reproducible exemplars, any actual *transpersonal practice*. Put differently: no yoga, no meditative discipline, no experimental methodology to reproduce in consciousness the transpersonal insights and intuitions of its founders.

The great Idealist systems were thus mistaken for metaphysics, or more of the same ole "mere representation" philosophy that had no actual referent, and that Kant had thoroughly demolished. And because the Idealists lacked a transpersonal practice, this harsh criticism was in many ways true, alas. Idealism tended to degenerate into monological metaphysics, and so it rightly suffered the fate of all mere metaphysics— that is, of all systems that merely *map* the world and don't sufficiently provide interior technologies to change the mapmaker.

Q: So the first failure was that they had no yoga—no transpersonal practice to reproduce their insights.

KW: That's right, no way to reproduce transpersonal awareness in a practicing community. No way to concretely disclose a deeper self (I or Buddha) in a deeper community (We or Sangha) expressing a deeper truth (It or Dharma). But yes, put simply, no yoga.

Q: And the second major failure?

KW: Although profound intuitions into the genuinely transpersonal domains were clearly some of the major, I would say *the* major, driving forces behind the Idealist movement, these intuitions and insights were often expressed almost totally in and through *vision-logic*, and this burdened Reason with a task it could never accomplish. Particularly with Hegel, the transpersonal and transrational Spirit becomes wholly *identi-*

fied with vision-logic or mature Reason, which condemns Reason to collapsing under a weight it could never carry.

"The Real is Rational and the Rational is Real"—and by "rational" Hegel means vision-logic. And this will never do. Vision-logic is simply Spirit as it appears at the centauric stage.

In 1796, Hegel wrote a poem for Hölderlin, which says in part: "For *thought cannot grasp* the soul which forgetting itself plunges out of space and time into a presentiment of infinity, and now re-awakens. Whoever wanted to speak of this to others, though he spoke with the tongues of angels, would feel the poverty of words."

Would that Hegel had remained in poverty. But Hegel decided that Reason could and should develop the tongues of angels.

This would have been fine, *if* Hegel also had more dependable practices for the developmental unfolding of the higher and transpersonal stages. Zen masters talk about Emptiness all the time! But they have a *practice* and a *methodology*—zazen, or meditation—which allows them to ground their intuitions in experiential, public, reproducible, fallibilist criteria. Zen is not metaphysics! It is not mere mapping.

The Idealists had none of this. Their insights, not easily reproducible, and thus not fallibilistic, were therefore dismissed as "mere metaphysics," and gone was a priceless opportunity that the West, no doubt, will have to attempt yet again if it is ever to be hospitable to the future descent of the World Soul.

Q: It's amazing the Idealists accomplished as much as they did.

KW: Isn't it? I keep thinking of this story: After World War II, Jean-Paul Sartre visited Stalingrad, the site of the extraordinary battle that in many ways was the turning point of the war. At that site the Russians had put up an absolutely heroic defense; over three hundred thousand German soldiers died. After surveying the site, Sartre kept saying, "They were so amazing, they were so amazing." Sartre, of course, was very sympathetic with the communist cause, so somebody finally said, "You mean the Russians were so amazing?" "No, the Germans. That they *got this far*."

I keep thinking of that phrase when I think of the Idealists. That they got this far.

The Dominance of the Descenders

Q: Yet they, too, were defeated. There is a famous phrase, that after Hegel everybody was saying "back to Kant!"

KW: Yes, which eventually meant: back to rationality and its grounding in the senses. In other words, back to mononature, back to the Right-Hand world.

The collapse of Idealism left the Descenders virtually unchallenged as the holders and molders of modernity. After some extraordinary gains for the Left-Hand dimensions in terms of consciousness and transpersonal Spirit, the Idealist current was snapped up by the industrial grid and converted, via Feuerbach and Marx, into a strongly materialistic and "naturalistic" conception. It's almost impossible to escape the modern Descended grid, and after absolutely heroic attempts by the Idealists, they were hounded out of town by the troglodytes.

And so Feuerbach, a student of Hegel, would soon announce that *any* sort of spirituality, *any* sort of Ascent, was simply a projection of men and women's human potentials onto an "other world" of wholly imaginative origin. And, according to Feuerbach, it is exactly this projection of human potential onto a "divine" sphere that cripples men and women and is the true cause of self-alienation.

He is, of course, confusing the old mythic otherworldliness with higher and interior transpersonal potentials, but it is exactly this confusion that allows him to embrace the Descended grid and maintain that nature alone is real.

Karl Marx and Friedrich Engels were paying very close attention. "*Apart from nature and human beings,*" Engels would write, "nothing exists; and the higher beings which our religious fantasy created are only the fantastic reflection of our own essence. The enthusiasm was general; we were all for the moment followers of Feuerbach."

And the entire modern and postmodern world is, in effect, the followers of Feuerbach.

The Internet

Q: But what about systems like the Internet, the computer network that now links millions and millions of people in an information exchange? Is that merely Descended? Isn't that global? And doesn't that point the way to global consciousness?

KW: What good is it if Nazis have the Net? You see the problem? The Net is simply the *exterior* social structure—the Lower-Right quadrant. But what goes through the Net—well, that involves *interior* consciousness and morals and values, which are rarely addressed by those who simply maintain the Net is a global consciousness. A horizontally extended Net is not the same as a vertically developed consciousness. Merely pushing the horizontal extension is flatland at its worst and most Descended and possibly most destructive.

The Net is simply part of the new techno-economic base (the Lower-Right quadrant), and as such, it is itself *neutral* with regard to the *consciousness* that uses it. All Right-Hand structures are neutral, value-free. What computer technology (and the Information Age) means is that the techno-base can *support* a worldcentric perspectivism, a global consciousness, *but does not in any way guarantee it*. As we have seen, cognitive advances are necessary but not sufficient for moral advances, and the cognitive means usually run way ahead of the willingness to actually climb that ladder of expanding awareness. The Net offers the possibility, but does not guarantee it.

Which is why the Net itself cannot be equated with global consciousness per se. What good is it if millions of people at moral stage 1 have the means of extending their egocentric morality? What good is it if Nazis have the Net?

All of that is overlooked when people simply focus on the holistic net of simple location. You focus on the exterior grid and ignore the interiors that are running through that grid. The flatland idea is that the Internet is global, so the consciousness using it must be global. But that's not true at all.

Most people, alas, are still at preconventional and conventional modes of awareness, egocentric and ethnocentric. And no systems map, and no Internet, will automatically change this. Neither a global holistic map, nor a global Internet, will in itself foster interior transformation, and often just the opposite, contributing to arrest or even regression. A great number of the Infobahn males are digital predators—egocentric computer warriors that couldn't care less about intersubjective cooperation and mutual recognition. So much for global consciousness. When worldcentric means are presented to less-than-worldcentric individuals, those means are simply used (and abused) to further the agenda of the less-than-worldcentric individual. The Nazis would have loved the Net. The neo-Nazis certainly do. The FBI reports that hate-group activity has dramatically skyrocketed, thanks to the Net, which allows these people to find one another.

Q: So, as usual, we need to include *development* in both Left-Hand and Right-Hand in order to achieve truly global consciousness.

KW: Yes, that's exactly the point.

The Religion of Gaia

Q: But what about such problems as overpopulation, ozone depletion, and so on? Those are immediate threats to Gaia—to us all—and the Eco-Romantics do attack those head on.

KW: Gaia's main problems are not industrialization, ozone depletion, overpopulation, or resource depletion. Gaia's main problem is *the lack of mutual understanding and mutual agreement in the noosphere* about how to proceed with those problems. We cannot rein in industry if we cannot reach mutual understanding and mutual agreement based on a worldcentric moral perspective concerning the global commons. And we reach that *worldcentric* moral perspective through a difficult and laborious process of interior growth and transcendence. In short, global problems demand global consciousness, and global consciousness is the product of five or six major interior stages of development. Simply possessing a global map won't do it. A systems map will not do it. An ecological map will not do it. Interior growth and transcendence, on the other hand, *will* do it.

But the Descended grid rejects transcendence altogether. And therefore it despises Gaia's only source of genuine salvation. This *hatred of transcendence* is the cunning of the Descended grid. This is how the Descended grid perpetuates its love affair with flatland. This is how it perpetuates the colonization of the I and the we by holistic chains of its. This is how it perpetuates the bitter fragmentation of the Good and the True and the Beautiful, and sets mind and culture and nature at fundamental odds, each not a trusted friend but a profound threat to the others, spiteful in regard, intent upon revenge.

And so of course the crude and obvious rational-Ego camps are contributing to the despoliation of Gaia, in their attempts to control and dominate nature. But it is the final irony of modernity that the religion of Gaia is also caught in the same Descended grid, and it is that grid that is the fundamental destructive force. The religion of Gaia has pledged allegiance to the grid that is killing Gaia.

And so the horrifying truth of the modern condition slowly dawns: The hatred of transcendence is the way the flatland grid reproduces itself in the consciousness of those it is destroying.

18

An Integral Vision

Q: I want to conclude these discussions by focusing on four topics: how we interpret our spiritual intuitions; environmental ethics; future world developments; and the integral vision itself.

The Writing on the Wall

Q: First, you maintain that many people are indeed having profound spiritual intuitions, but many of these people are not interpreting these intuitions very well.

KW: These spiritual intuitions are often very true and very real, I believe, but these intuitions are *interpreted*—they are *unpacked*—in less than graceful ways. We are all immersed in the modern Descended grid, to one degree or another, with its massive *dissociation* between self, culture, and nature. So spiritual intuitions often come crashing down into this dissociated grid, with less than happy results.

Q: For example?

KW: I might have an experience of Kosmic consciousness, or perhaps an intuition of the all-embracing World Soul, but I might interpret this *solely* in the terms of finding my Higher Self. I then think that if I find my Higher Self or higher consciousness, then all other problems will simply work themselves out wonderfully. I am doing the old Fichte move—the pure Self will solve everything—and I tend to ignore the *behavioral* and *social* and *cultural* components that are also necessary for transformation. I tend to get caught up in a very narcissistic orientation—find my True Self, the world will take care of itself.

Or I might take the other extreme—I have this experience of Kosmic consciousness, or maybe the World Soul, I feel one with the world, and I then decide the world that I am one with is simply sensory nature, mononature. I am indeed sensing a oneness with the mountain, with the ocean, with all life. But caught in the modern grid, I will ignore the subjective and intersubjective space that allowed me to develop to the point where I could be one with the mountain, and so I will think that this "oneness" involves nature alone.

So I will decide that if we all can just become one with Gaia, one with the pure Eco, then all our major problems will be solved. I present a nice systems map of the world, and tell everybody that they must agree that we are all strands in the Great Web, disregarding the massive interior changes in consciousness that are necessary to even be able to grasp a systems view in the first place. I am doing the old Spinoza move: insertion into the great immanent system will save us all, overlooking the fact that I can become one with the great immanent system only by a laborious process of inner transcendence (which involves six or seven fulcrums of development, at least).

This modern dissociation is so firmly entrenched in the collective psyche that when a genuine spiritual intuition descends, it descends into the *interpretive grid* of this modern fragmentation. The original spiritual intuition carries a sense of wholeness, but if I *interpret* this intuition merely in terms of my favorite quadrant, then I try to reproduce the wholeness by making my favorite fragment cover all the bases.

Q: So the intuition can be genuine, but the interpretation can get fouled up.

KW: Yes, that's the central point. As we said, surfaces can be seen, but all *depth* must be *interpreted*. And how we interpret depth is crucially important for the birth of that depth itself. Graceful and well-rounded interpretations of Spirit facilitate Spirit's further descent. Gracefully unpacking the intuition, interpreting the intuition, facilitates the emergence of that new spiritual depth.

On the other hand, ungraceful interpretations tend to prevent or abort further spiritual intuitions. Frail or shallow or fragmented interpretations derail the spiritual process. Usually this happens because the interpretations are drawn from only one quadrant—they do not equally honor and unpack all four quadrants, they do not honor and integrate the Big Three. And since Spirit manifests as all four quadrants—or simply the Big Three—then some aspect of Spirit gets denied or distorted or overemphasized, which sabotages Spirit's full expression and derails the spiritual process in its broader unfolding. We neglect the Beautiful, or the Good, or the True—we neglect the I, or the we, or the it domains—we neglect self, or culture, or nature—and thus send Spirit crashing into the fragments of our self-contracting ways.

The Superman Self

Q: So both the Ego and the Eco are trapped in ungraceful interpretations.

KW: Very often, yes. On the Ego side, as we were saying, many individuals intuit Spirit and yet unpack that intuition, interpret that intuition, solely or merely in terms of the Higher Self, the Inner Voice, archetypal psychology, Gnosticism, vipassana, the care of the Soul, interior Witnessing, the Universal Mind, pure Awareness, Enneagram patterns, transcendental Consciousness, or similar such *Upper-Left quadrant terms*. And however true that aspect of the intuition is, this unpacking leaves out, or seriously diminishes, the "we" and the "it" dimensions. It fails to give a decent account of the types of community, social service, cultural activity, and *relationships* in general that are the intersubjective forms of Spirit. It ignores or neglects the changes in the techno-economic infrastructures and the social systems that are the objective forms of Spirit. It centers on the intentional, but ignores the behavioral and cultural and social—it ignores the other three quadrants, or at least relegates them to very inferior and secondary status.

The "Higher Self" camp is thus notoriously immune to social concerns. Everything that happens to one is said to be "one's own choice"— the hyperagentic Higher Self is responsible for *everything* that happens—this is the monological and totally disengaged Ego gone horribly amuck in omnipotent self-only fantasies. This simply *represses* the networks of rich social and cultural communions that are just as important as agency in constituting the manifestation of Spirit.

The idea seems to be that if I can just contact my Higher Self, then everything else will take care of itself. But this fails to see that Spirit manifests always and simultaneously *as all four quadrants of the Kosmos*. Spirit, at any level, manifests as a self in a community with social and cultural foundations and objective correlates, and thus any *Higher* Self will inextricably involve a *wider* community existing in a *deeper* objective state of affairs. Contacting the Higher Self is not the end of all problems but the beginning of the immense and difficult new work to be done in all quadrants.

Q: But these approaches really do maintain that you create your own reality.

KW: You don't create your own reality; psychotics create their own reality. I know, the point is that a genuinely spiritual Self does manifest its own reality. So here's an old story from Vedanta Hinduism.

A man goes to an enlightened sage and asks, of course, for the meaning of life. The sage gives a brief summary of the Vedanta view, namely, that this entire world is nothing but the supreme Brahman or Godhead, and further, your own witnessing awareness is one with Brahman. Your very Self is in a supreme identity with God. Since Brahman creates all, and since your highest Self is one with Brahman, then your highest Self creates all. So far, this definitely looks like New Age city.

Off goes the gentleman, convinced that he has understood the ultimate meaning of life, which is that his own deepest Self is actually God and creates all reality. On the way home, he decides to test this amazing notion. Heading right toward him is a man riding an elephant. The gentleman stands in the middle of the road, convinced that, if he's God, the elephant can't hurt him. The fellow riding the elephant keeps yelling, "Get out of the way! Get out of the way!" But the gentleman doesn't move—and gets perfectly flattened by the elephant.

Limping back to the sage, the gentleman explains that, since Brahman or God is everything, and since his Self is one with God, then the elephant should not have hurt him. "Oh, yes, everything is indeed God," said the sage, "so why didn't you listen when God told you to get out of the way?"

It is true that Spirit creates all reality, and to the extent you identify with Spirit, you do indeed find that you are within that creative activity. But that creative activity *manifests in all four quadrants*, not *just* in or from your own particular awareness. But if you interpret spiritual awareness *merely* as a Higher Self, then you will ignore God in the other quadrants—you will ignore the elephant, or think it isn't real, or isn't important—you will ignore the cultural and social and behavioral work that desperately needs to be done in those domains in order to *fully* express the Spirit that you are.

But ignoring all of that, sooner or later you will get flattened by some sort of elephant. You will get ill, or lose a job, or fail in a relationship—some sort of elephant will run you over—and you will feel massive guilt because if you were really in touch with your true Self, the elephant wouldn't be able to hurt you. When all it really means is, you weren't listening to God in all quadrants.

Q: These approaches maintain that the more you contact higher consciousness or Higher Self, the less you worry about the world.

KW: Yes, the Real Self is Superman! And Superman never worries! And conversely, if you are "worried" or "concerned" about the poverty or injustice or anguish of the world, then this shows that you haven't found the true Self.

And in fact, it is just the opposite: the more you contact the Higher Self, the *more* you worry about the world, as a component of your very Self, the Self of each and all. Emptiness is Form. Brahman is the World. To *finally* contact Brahman is to *ultimately* engage the World. If you really contact your Higher Self, one of the first things you will want to do is not ignore the elephant but feed the elephant. That is, work in all four quadrants to help manifest this realization, and treat each and every holon as a manifestation of the Divine.

With the supreme identity, you are established in radical Freedom, it is true, but that Freedom *manifests* as compassionate activity, as agonizing concern. The Form of Freedom is sorrow, unrelenting worry for those struggling to awaken. The Bodhisattva weeps daily; the tears stain the very fabric of the Kosmos in all directions. The Heart moves into those places where Spirit remains unheralded and unheard; the work is a passion, an agony; it is always fully accomplished, and thus never ending.

But if you keep interpreting Spirit as simply a higher or sacred Self— ignoring Spirit in the other quadrants—then that is going to abort further realization. It won't just hurt others, it will profoundly sabotage your own spiritual development. It will cut off further realizations of Spirit's all-pervading presence. You will just keep retreating into your interior awareness, until that well runs dry, and you end up despising the manifest world because it "detracts" from your "real" self.

On the other hand, a more graceful unpacking facilitates further and deeper intuitions, intuitions touching the I and the We and the It domains: not just how to *realize* the higher Self, but how to see it *embraced* in culture, *embodied* in nature, and *embedded* in social institutions.

Realized, embraced, embodied, embedded: a more graceful interpretation covering all four quadrants, because Spirit itself manifests as all four quadrants. And this more graceful interpretation facilitates the birth of that Spirit which is demanding the interpretation. Graceful interpretation midwifes Spirit's birth, Spirit's descent. The more adequately I can interpret the intuition of Spirit, the more that Spirit can speak to me, the more the channels of communication are open, leading from communication to communion to union to identity—the supreme identity.

The Great-Web Gaia Self

Q: Whereas the other typical approach, the Eco approach, also tends to get caught in dissociated interpretations, but at the other extreme.

KW: Yes. There are many good souls who have a profound intuition of Spirit but unpack that intuition in merely "it" terms, describing Spirit as the sum total of all phenomena or processes interwoven together in a great unified system or net or web or implicate order or unified field—the Lower-Right quadrant.

All of which is true enough, but all of which leaves out entirely the interior dimensions of "I" and "we" as disclosed in their own terms. This less-than-adequate interpretation is unfortunately quite monological, flatland through and through.

It is the old Spinoza move, the other pole—the Eco pole—of the fundamental Enlightenment paradigm, in the form of the Romantic rebellion. It thinks that the enemy is atomism and mechanism, and that the central problem is simply to be able to prove or demonstrate once and for all that the universe is a great and unified holistic System or Order or Web. It marshals a vast amount of scientific evidence, from physics to biology to systems theory—all monological!—and offers extensive arguments, all geared to objectively proving the holistic nature of the universe. It fails to see that if we take a bunch of egos with atomistic concepts and teach them that the universe is holistic, all we will actually get is a bunch of egos with holistic concepts.

Precisely because this monological approach, with its unskillful interpretation of an otherwise genuine intuition, ignores or neglects the "I" and the "we" dimensions, it doesn't understand very well the exact nature of the inner transformations and the stages of inner transcendence that are absolutely necessary in order to be able to find an identity that embraces the All in the first place. *Talk* about the All as much as we want, nothing fundamentally changes.

And this world of empirical nature—the *biosphere*—becomes one's God, one's Goddess. Not Nature, but nature, is the great beloved.

Thus, however true the original intuition of Spirit is—and I do not doubt that it is true—it is not facilitated by these fragmented interpretations. Those interpretations, taken in and by themselves, *block* the transformative event. Those interpretations, driven originally by a true intuition of the very Divine, do not facilitate the further descent of that Divine. Those interpretations are unskillful to midwife the birth of Spirit.

Q: So they actually prevent further realizations.

KW: If I keep interpreting my Kosmic consciousness experience as a oneness with sensory nature, I sabotage Spirit in the other quadrants. I keep pushing the flatland Gaia map. And I find that people might buy the map, but nothing really fundamental is changing. They aren't really transforming. All they do is become ideologues, and try to get other people to buy the flatland map.

And I become very depressed, hollow-eyed. I say the reason I am so depressed is that Gaia is being destroyed—unaware of the hand I am playing in that downward spiral. Embracing the industrial ontology of simple location, I hug and kiss the spokes of the wheel that is grinding Gaia to her demise.

At its end limit, this approach, as we saw, fosters regression, both individual regression to biocentric and egocentric stances, and cultural regression to tribal or horticultural ideals. Reducing the Kosmos to flat-land sensory nature, and then trying to become one with that nature in biocentric immersion, leads to profoundly regressive, preconventional, body-bound, narcissistic glorification. This was the entire lesson of the Romantic slide!—the closer you get to preconventional nature, the more egocentric you become. Again, profound spiritual intuitions, when interpreted ungracefully, lead to less than happy results.

Q: You were saying that ecological wisdom doesn't consist in how to live in accord with nature, but how to get subjects to agree on how to live in accord with nature. In other words, how to integrate the Big Three.

KW: Yes. People are not born wanting to take care of Gaia. That noble state of global care is the *product* of a long and laborious and difficult process of growth and transcendence (involving, as we saw, over a half-dozen interior stages or fulcrums). But, like the multicults, the typical Eco-approaches condemn the actual path of transcendence that produced the noble state.

This then completely sabotages others getting to that state, and turns everybody loose to slide to their own lowest possibilities. This has already happened with the multicults, and with many Eco-approaches as well. Indeed, the multicults and ecotheorists have often joined hands to promote the retribalization of American culture.

Q: But the basic idea of the multicults is to honor individual differences.

KW: Yes, but that can *only* be done under the *protection* of the worldcentric stance of universal pluralism, which itself does not emerge until the postconventional stages (stages 5 and 6 and higher). And thus, without demanding and fostering ways for people to develop and evolve to these higher stages, we merely encourage them to act out their shallower engagements, and thus few people actually aspire to the worldcentric stance that alone allows the protection.

Instead, every sort of retribalization, fragmentation, preconventional, egocentric, and ethnocentric shallowness—all of those "diversities" are glorified as part of the decentered worldcentric stance, whereas they are exactly what prevent and sabotage that stance, and lead it by the hand into increasingly regressive engagements and the politics of narcissism, which, if it actually succeeds, will destroy the worldcentric stance that protected the pluralism in the first place. And this in turn will open the door to actual oppression, ethnocentric wars, imperialistic nightmares—we will lose all the liberation movements secured by the good news of the Enlightenment and its worldcentric tolerance.

You simply end up fostering a lack of growth, a lack of development, a lack of transcendence, a lack of evolution. You foster a culture of regression, a politics of narcissism. And this, you will happily tell yourself, has finally freed you from that horrible oppression known as modernity.

Beyond the Postmodern Mind

Q: Speaking of which, you realize that most of the world's great wisdom traditions are, in various ways, against modernity. Modernity is viewed as the great antireligious movement, the great movement of rational secularization, which "killed" God.

KW: Killed the *mythic* God, yes. But Spirit is in the overall process, not in any favored epoch or period or time or place. Reason has more depth than mythology, and thus actually represents a further unfolding of Spirit's own potentials. The rational denial of God contains more Spirit than the mythic affirmation of God, simply because it contains more depth. The very movement of modernity is a collective increase in Spirit's freedom, evidenced, among many other things, in the great liberation movements that define the very core of modernity.

So I might eulogize, for example, the glorious mythic-agrarian Empires, which were drenched in the blessings of my favorite mythic God, and I might worship that God as being the epitome of Freedom and Benevolence and Mercy. But I can do so only by ignoring the fact that the temples and the monuments to that God, the great pyramids and stone cathedrals, were built on the broken backs of slaves, of women and children accorded the grace of animals; the great monuments to that mythic God or Goddess were inscribed on the tortured flesh of millions.

Spirit as great Freedom is one thing; Spirit actually manifested as political democracies, quite another. Reason frees the light trapped in mythology and sets it loose among the oppressed, which actually undoes their chains on earth, and not merely in some promised heaven.

All of this eulogizing of past epochs, and hatred of the present, mostly stems from confusing the average mode with the most advanced modes in those cultures. That approach simply compares the most advanced modes of past epochs with the most disastrous aspects of modernity, and so of course finds nothing but devolution.

But this is just a typical example of what you were saying, which is that most of the great religious traditions are profoundly uneasy with modernity and postmodernity. Modernity, in various ways, is viewed as the Great Satan.

And my central point is that that idea is very confused. I believe that many traditional religious thinkers simply have not clearly *understood* modernity.

Q: Haven't understood modernity, how exactly?

KW: Every great epoch of human evolution seems to have one central idea, an idea that dominates the entire epoch, and summarizes its approach to Spirit and Kosmos, and tells us something altogether profound. And each seems to build upon its predecessor. These ideas are so simple and so central, they can be put in a sentence.

Foraging: *Spirit is interwoven with earthbody.* Foraging cultures the world over sing this profound truth. The very earth is our blood and bones and marrow, and we are all sons and daughters of that earth—in which, and through which, Spirit flows freely.

Horticulture: *But Spirit demands sacrifice.* Sacrifice is the great theme running through horticultural societies, and not just in the concrete form of actual ritual sacrifice, although we certainly see it there as well. But the central and pervading notion is that certain specific human steps must be taken to come into accord with Spirit. Ordinary or typical humanity has to get out of the way, so to speak—has to be sacrificed—in order for Spirit to shine forth more clearly. In other words, there are steps on the way to a more fully realized Spiritual awareness.

Agrarian: *These spiritual steps are in fact arrayed in a Great Chain of Being.* The Great Chain is the central, dominant, inescapable theme of every mythic-agrarian society the world over, with few exceptions. And since most of "civilized history" has been agrarian history, Lovejoy was quite right in stating that the Great Chain has been the dominant idea in most of civilized culture.

Modernity: *The Great Chain unfolds in evolutionary time.* In other words, evolution. The fact that Spirit was usually left out of the equation is simply the disaster of modernity, not the dignity nor the definition of modernity. Evolution is the one great background concept that hangs over every single modern movement; it is the God of modernity. And, in fact, this is a tremendously spiritual realization, because, whether or not it consciously identifies itself as spiritual, the fact is that it plugs humans into the Kosmos in an unbroken fashion, and further, points to the inescapable but frightening fact that humans are co-creators of their own evolution, their own history, their own worldspaces, because:

Postmodernity: *Nothing is pregiven; the world is not just a perception but also an interpretation.* That this leads many postmodernists into fits of aperspectival madness is not our concern. That nothing is pregiven is the great postmodern discovery, and it plugs humans into a plastic Kosmos of their own co-creation, Spirit become self-conscious in the most acute forms, on the way to its own superconscious shock.

Q: So those are the great defining ideas of each epoch. And your point about the antimodern religious thinkers . . .

KW: Yes, is that they are all too often trapped in the agrarian worldview. They have not come to terms with the form of Spirit in either its modern or its postmodern modes. With eyes turned from the wonders and dignities of modernity, they sing the songs of yesterday's marvels. Many traditional religious thinkers don't even think evolution has occurred!

They have not grasped Spirit in its manifestation as modernity; they have not seen that evolution is, as Wallace put it, the "manner and mode of Spirit's creation." They have not grasped the essence of modernity as the differentiation of the Big Three, and so they have missed the dignities of the modern liberation movements, of the abolition of slavery, of the women's movement, of the liberal democracies, each of which sent Spirit singing through a new mode of freedom unheard of in mythic-agrarian times. They think that because modernity introduced its own disasters, evolution itself must be rejected, failing to grasp the dialectic of progress.

And they have likewise often not grasped Spirit in its manifestation as postmodernity. Nothing is pregiven. But to the agrarian mind, everything is simply and everlastingly pregiven, static, unyielding to the advances of time or the unfolding of development. The entire world is simply pregiven by the mythic God, and salvation depends upon strictly following the given commandments that are forever etched in stone. To disagree with the agrarian worldview, there is eternal sin. And never mind that that worldview is ethnocentric, racist, sexist, patriarchal, and militant, for it has been gloriously spoken by the mythic God.

And so yes, to the extent the "religious authorities" are anchored in the agrarian worldview, they of course despise modernity, despise evolution, despise the process that is in fact working to undermine their own authority.

And yet their identification of Spirit with the static and pregiven agrarian worldview is exactly what prevents the modern and postmodern world from acknowledging Spirit. Modernity will *never* accept Spirit if Spirit means merely mythic-agrarian.

On the other hand, to adopt an integral vision, and see Spirit operating in all levels in all quadrants, is to acknowledge and honor Spirit's past manifestations, *and* to recognize and honor Spirit's Presence in the accomplishments of modernity and postmodernity.

World Transformation and the Culture Gap

Q: Do you think there is a major world transformation now in progress?

KW: Haltingly, jerkily, in fits and starts. We are seeing, and have been seeing since approximately World War II, the slow shift from rational-industrial society to vision-logic informational society. This is not a spiritual New Age transformation, but it is quite profound nonetheless.

If for the moment we use the Lower-Right quadrant as an indicator, there have been six or seven major transformations in human evolution—from foraging to horticultural to early agrarian to advanced agrarian to early industrial to late industrial to early informational. So we are right on the edge of one of the half-dozen or so major, profound, worldwide transformations in the formation of the human species. These are often simplified to three major transformations—farming, industry, information—so that today is the beginning of the "third wave."

But remember, we must, in my opinion, analyze this transformation in terms of all four quadrants (at least), or we'll miss the factors actually responsible for it. This transformation is being driven by a new techno-economic base (informational), but it also brings with it a new world-view, with a new mode of self and new intentional and behavioral patterns, set in a new cultural worldspace with new social institutions as anchors. And, as usual, specific individuals may, or may not, live up to these new possibilities.

Q: So go around the quadrants.

KW: A new center of gravity is slowly emerging—the vision-logic information society, with an existential or aperspectival worldview (Lower Left), set in a techno-economic base of digital information transfer (Lower Right), and a centauric self (Upper Left) that must integrate its matter and body and mind—integrate the physiosphere and biosphere and noosphere—if its behavior (Upper Right) is to functionally fit in the new worldspace.

And this is a very tall order. Because the really crucial point is that a new transformation places a new and horrible *burden* on the world. It is hardly cause for undiluted celebration! Every new emergent and transformative development brings a new demand and a new responsibility: the higher must be integrated with the lower. Transcend and include. *And the greater the degree of development, the greater the burden of inclusion.*

Q: That's a problem.

KW: That's a big problem. And the real nightmare is this: even with a new and higher worldview available, every human being still has to *start its own development at square 1*. Everybody, without exception, starts at fulcrum-1, and has to grow and evolve through all the lower stages in order to reach the new and higher stage made available.

So even a person born into a grand and glorious and global vision-logic culture *nevertheless* begins development at the physiocentric, then biocentric, then egocentric levels, then moves to the sociocentric levels, then moves to the postconventional and worldcentric levels. There is no way to avoid or circumvent that general process. Even if you write a huge three-volume novel, you are still using the same letters of the alphabet you learned as a child, and you can't write the novel without the childhood acquisitions!

And the more vertical levels of growth there are in a culture, the more things there are that can go horribly wrong. As I was saying, the greater the depth of a society, the *greater the burden* placed on the education and transformation of its citizens. The greater the depth, the more things that can go massively, wretchedly, horribly wrong. The more levels, the more chances for lying (pathology). Our society can be sick in ways that the early foragers literally could not even imagine.

Q: So societies with greater depth face increasingly greater problems.

KW: Yes, in all four quadrants! So where many people talk of the coming transformation and get all ecstatic and giddy at the thought, I tend to see another chance for a huge nightmare coming right at us.

Q: I wonder if you could give a few examples.

KW: It is sometimes said that one of the major problems in Western societies is the gap between the rich and the poor. This is true. But that is a flatland way to look at it—merely quantified as a money gap. And as alarming as that exterior gap between individuals is, there is a more worrisome gap—an *interior* gap, a culture gap, a gap in consciousness, a gap in depth.

As a society's center of gravity puts on more and more weight—as more individuals move from egocentric to sociocentric to worldcentric (or higher)—this places a huge burden on the society's need to *vertically integrate* those individuals at different depths in their own development. And the greater the depth of a culture's center of gravity, the greater the demand and the burden of this vertical integration.

Thus, the "economic gap" between rich and poor is bad enough, but much more crucial—and much more hidden—is the *culture gap*, the "values gap," the "depth gap," which is the gap between the depth offered as a potential by the culture, and those who can actually unfold that depth in their own case.

As always, the new and higher center of gravity *makes possible*, but does *not guarantee*, the availability of the higher or deeper structures to its individual citizens. And as a society's center of gravity puts on more and more weight, there are more and more individuals who can be left behind, marginalized, excluded from their own intrinsic unfolding, disadvantaged in the cruelest way of all: in their own interior consciousness, value, and worth.

This creates an *internal tension* in the culture itself. The gap between the "haves" and the "have nots" refers not just to money but to consciousness, morals, depths. This internal tension in a culture can be devastating. And the potential for this culture gap or consciousness gap becomes *greater* with *every* new cultural transformation. Ouch!

Q: That's similar to what you were saying about individual pathology as well.

KW: Yes, the gap between the individual's main self or center of gravity and the "small selves" that remain dissociated and excluded. The internal tension, the internal civil war, drives the individual bonkers.

Just so with society and culture at large. The greater the cultural depth, then the greater the possibility of the culture gap, the gap between the average depth offered by the culture and those who can actually unfold to that depth. And this likewise creates an internal tension that can drive the culture bonkers.

Q: This is another reason cultures such as foraging had fewer internal problems.

KW: Yes.

Q: Any suggestions for solutions?

KW: Well, in a sense, the culture gap is not our real problem. The real problem is that we are not allowed to even think about the culture gap. And we are not allowed to think about the culture gap because we live in flatland. In flatland, we do not recognize degrees of consciousness and depth and value and worth. Everybody simply has the same depth, namely, zero.

And since we recognize no depth in flatland, we can't even begin to recognize the depth gap, the culture gap, the consciousness gap, which will therefore continue to wreak havoc on developed and "civilized" countries, until this most crucial of all problems is first recognized, then framed in ways that allow us to begin to work with it.

Q: So before we can discuss the solutions, we have to at least recognize the problem.

KW: Yes, and everything in flatland conspires to prevent that recognition. This culture gap—this massive problem of vertical cultural integration—cannot be solved in flatland terms, because flatland denies the existence of the vertical dimension altogether, denies interior transformation and transcendence altogether, denies the nine or so interior stages of consciousness development that is truly part of a culture's human capital, but is not even entered on the ledgers of flatland.

Q: So how does this relate to the worldwide transformation now haltingly in progress?

KW: The hypothesis, recall, is that modernity differentiated the Big Three, and postmodernity must find a way to integrate them. If that integration doesn't occur, then the twenty tenets won't mesh, evolution won't purr, and some sort of massive and altogether unpleasant readjustment will very likely result.

And the point is, you cannot integrate the Big Three in flatland. In flatland, they remain dissociated at best, collapsed at worst. And no system that we are aware of has ever gone limping into the future with these types of massive internal dissociations. If these chaotic tensions do not lead to self-transcendence, they will lead to self-dissolution. Those are the two gruesome choices evolution has always offered at each vertical emergent.

And we are very close to seeing the culture gap lead to cultural collapse, precisely because flatland will not acknowledge the problem in the first place.

Environmental Ethics: Holonic Ecology

Q: So do you think that the *culture gap* problem is more urgent than the *environmental crisis*?

KW: They're the same thing; they are exactly the same problem.

Egocentric and ethnocentric couldn't care less about the global commons—unless you scare them into seeing merely how it affects their own narcissistic existence—whereupon you have simply *reinforced* exactly the self-centric survival motives that are the cause of the problem in the first place. You just reinforce all of that with ecological scare tactics.

No, it is only at a global, postconventional, worldcentric stance (fulcrum 5, 6, and higher) that individuals can recognize the global dimensions of the environmental crisis and, more important, possess the moral vision and moral fortitude to proceed on a global basis. Obviously, then, a significant number of individuals must reach a postconventional and worldcentric level of development in order to be a significant force in global care and ecological reform.

In other words, it is only by effectively dealing with the culture gap that we can effectively deal with the ecological crisis—they're the same gap, the same problem.

Q: As you earlier put it, global problems demand global consciousness for their solution, and global consciousness is the product of at least a half-dozen interior stages of growth. Without interior growth, the problems remain.

KW: Yes, the culture gap and the environmental crisis are two of the major problems bequeathed to us by flatland. The religion of flatland denies degrees of vertical depth and interior transcendence which alone can bring humans into worldcentric and global agreement about how to proceed with protecting the biosphere and the global commons.

Q: In one of our earlier discussions, you briefly outlined an environmental ethics that would emerge if flatland were rejected. Perhaps we could go into that.

KW: Discussions of environmental ethics usually center on what is known as axiology, the theory of values. And there are four broad schools of environmental axiology.

The first is bioequality—all living holons have equal value. A worm and an ape have equal value. This is quite common with deep ecologists and some ecofeminists.

The second approach involves variations on animal rights—wherever there is any sort of rudimentary feelings in animals, we should extend certain basic rights to those animals. This school therefore attempts to draw an evolutionary line between those living forms that don't possess enough feelings to worry about—insects, for example—and those that do—such as mammals. Different theorists draw that line in different places, based on how far down one can reasonably assume that feelings or sensations exist. The lowest serious suggestion so far is shrimp and mollusks. (Of course, if you push it all the way down, this reverts to bioequality, and all living holons have equal rights.)

The third school is hierarchical or holarchical, and often based on Whitehead's philosophy (Birch and Cobb, for example). This approach sees evolution as a holarchical unfolding, with each more complex entity possessing more rights. Human beings are the most advanced and thus possess the most rights, but these rights do not include the right to instrumentally plunder other living entities, since they, too, possess certain basic but significant rights.

The fourth school involves the various stewardship approaches, where humans alone have rights, but those rights include the care and stewardship of the earth and its living inhabitants. Many conventional religious theorists take this approach as a way to anchor environmental care in a moral imperative (Max Oelschlaeger, for example).

My own particular approach to environmental ethics did not set out to synthesize those various schools, although I believe it ends up incorporating the basics of each of them.

Q: So those are four schools of value. Your approach is also based on different *types* of value.

KW: Yes. These are Ground value, intrinsic value, and extrinsic value. Briefly:

All holons have equal *Ground value*. That is, all holons, from atoms to apes, are perfect manifestations of Emptiness or Spirit, with no higher or lower, better or worse. Every holon, just as it is, is a perfect expression of Emptiness, a radiant gesture of the Divine. As a manifestation of the Absolute, all holons have equal Ground value. All Forms are equally Emptiness. And that's Ground value.

But every holon, besides being an expression of the *absolute*, is also a *relative* whole/part. It has its own relative *wholeness*, and its own relative *partness*.

As a *whole*, every holon has *intrinsic value*, or the value of its own particular wholeness, its own particular depth. And therefore the greater the wholeness—or the greater the depth—then *the greater the intrinsic value*. Intrinsic value means it has value in itself. Its very depth is valuable, because that depth *enfolds* aspects of the Kosmos into its own being. The more of the Kosmos that is enfolded into its own being—that is, the greater its depth—then the greater its intrinsic value. An ape contains cells and molecules and atoms, embraces them all in its own internal makeup—greater depth, greater wholeness, greater intrinsic value.

So even though an ape and an atom are both perfect expressions of Spirit (they both have equal Ground value), the ape has more depth, more wholeness, and therefore more intrinsic value. The atom also has intrinsic value, but relatively less. (Less value does not mean no value!) We also saw that the greater the depth of a holon, the greater its degree of consciousness, so it comes to much the same thing to say that the ape is more intrinsically valuable than the atom because it is more conscious.

But every holon is not only a whole, it is also a part. And as a *part*, it has *value for others*—it is part of a whole upon which other holons depend for their existence. So as a part, each holon has *extrinsic value*, instrumental value, value for other holons. The more it is a part, the more extrinsic value it has. An atom has more extrinsic value than an ape—destroy all apes, and not too much of the universe is affected; destroy all atoms, and everything but subatomic particles is destroyed— the atom has enormous extrinsic value, instrumental value, for other holons, because it is an instrumental part of so many other wholes.

Q: You also tie this in with rights and responsibilities.

KW: Yes. Rights and responsibilities are often used in the same breath, but without understanding why they are inseparably linked. But they are inherent aspects of the fact that every holon is a whole/part.

As a *whole*, a holon has *rights* which express its relative autonomy. These rights are simply a *description* of the conditions that are necessary to sustain its wholeness. If the rights aren't met, the wholeness dissolves into subholons. If the plant doesn't receive water, it dissolves. *Rights* express the *conditions* for the *intrinsic value* of a holon to exist, the conditions necessary to sustain its wholeness, sustain its *agency*, sustain its depth.

But further, each holon is also a part of some other whole(s), and as a *part*, it has *responsibilities* to the maintenance of that whole. Responsibilities are simply a *description* of the conditions that any holon must meet in order to be a part of the whole. If it doesn't meet those responsibilities, then it cannot sustain its functional fit with the whole, so it is ejected (or actually destroys the whole itself). If the responsibilities aren't met, then it ceases to be a part of the whole. *Responsibilities* express the *conditions* for the *extrinsic value* of a holon to exist, the conditions necessary to sustain its partness, sustain its *communion*, sustain its span. If any holon wants to be part of a whole, it has to meet certain responsibilities. Not, it would nice if it met these responsibilities; it *must* meet them or it won't sustain its communions, its cultural and functional fit.

Q: So agency and communion, intrinsic value and extrinsic value, rights and responsibilities, are twin aspects of every holon, because every holon is a whole/part.

KW: Yes, in a nested holarchy of expanding complexity and depth. Because human beings have relatively more depth than, say, an amoeba, we have more *rights*—there are more conditions necessary to sustain the wholeness of a human—but we also have many more *responsibilities*, not only to our own human societies of which we are parts, but to all of the communities of which our own subholons are parts. We exist in networks of relationships with holons in the physiosphere and the biosphere and the noosphere, and our relatively greater rights absolutely demand relatively greater responsibilities in all of these dimensions. Failure to meet these responsibilities means a failure to meet the conditions under which our holons and subholons can exist in communion—which means our own self-destruction.

Again, it's not that it would be nice if we met these responsibilities; it is a condition of existence. It is mandatory, or our communions will dissolve, and us with them. But, of course, we often seem to want to claim the rights without owning the responsibilities. We want to be a *whole* without being a *part* of anything! We want to do our own thing!

Q: The culture of narcissism, you were saying.

KW: Yes, the culture of narcissism and regression and retribalization. We are in an orgy of seeking egoic rights with no responsibilities. Everybody wants to be a separate whole and demand rights for their own agency, but nobody wants to be a part and assume the responsibilities of the corresponding communions.

But, of course, you can't have one without the other. Our feeding frenzy of rights is simply a sign of fragmentation into increasingly egocentric "wholes" that refuse also to be parts of anything other than their own demands.

Q: Does either the Ego or the Eco approach overcome these problems?

KW: I don't think so. One of the great difficulties with the modern flatland paradigm—in both Ego and Eco versions—is that the notions of rights and responsibilities were both horribly collapsed, often beyond recognition.

Q: For example.

KW: In the Ego-Enlightenment version of flatland, we have: the disengaged and autonomous Ego assigns autonomy only to itself. That is, the rational Ego alone is a self-contained wholeness, and so the rational Ego alone has *intrinsic value* and therefore *rights*. All other holons are simply *parts* of the great interlocking order, so all other holons have merely part value, *extrinsic value*, instrumental value—and no rights at all. They are all instrumental to the Ego's designs. And so the disengaged Ego can do its own thing, and push the environment around any way it wants to, because everything else is now only instrumental to the Ego.

In the Eco-Romantic version, the great interlocking web is still the only basic reality, but it, and not the reflecting Ego, is now assigned autonomy value. Since the Great Web is the ultimate reality, then the Great Web alone has wholeness value or *intrinsic value*, and all other holons (human and otherwise) are now merely *instrumental* to its autopoietic maintenance. That is, all other holons are merely parts or strands in the Web, so they have merely *extrinsic* and instrumental value. In other words, what critics have called ecofascism. The Great Web alone has *rights*, and all other holons are ultimately subservient parts. And if you are speaking for the Great Web, then you get to tell us all what to do, because you alone are speaking for intrinsic value.

This approach gets further complicated because the Eco-Romantics, unlike the Ego camps, were often in search of genuine spiritual values and harmony. But, like most movements of modernity and postmodernity, their spiritual intuitions were interpreted in purely flatland terms, unpacked in Descended terms.

So they immediately confused *Ground value* with *intrinsic value*, and arrived at the stance of "bioequality." That is, they confused Ground value (all holons have the same absolute value, which is true) with intrinsic value (all holons have the same relative value, which is false), and thus they arrived at "bioequality." In other words, no differences in intrinsic value between any holons—no difference in intrinsic value between a flea and a deer. This industrial ontology ironically runs through many of the ecological movements.

Q: So we want to honor all three values.

KW: Yes, I think so. A truly "holonic ecology" would honor all three types of value for each and every holon—Ground value, intrinsic value, and extrinsic value. We want our environmental ethics to honor all holons without exception as manifestations of Spirit—and also, at the same time, be able to make pragmatic distinctions about the differences in intrinsic worth, and realize that it is much better to kick a rock than an ape, much better to eat a carrot than a cow, much better to subsist on grains than on mammals.

Q: You said this holonic ecology ends up incorporating the essentials of the four main schools of environmental ethics. How can we do this?

KW: With the believers in bioequality, we can agree that all holons possess equal Ground value, and honor the spiritual insight that many of these theorists are attempting to express. But not all holons have equal intrinsic value, so we can agree with the animal rights activists and the Whiteheadians that there is a hierarchy or holarchy of consciousness, and the higher a sentient being is on that holarchy, the less right you have to sacrifice it for your needs. Finally, we can agree with the stewardship schools in the sense that humans, because they generally possess the greatest depth, therefore possess the greatest responsibility (or stewardship) for the biosphere's welfare.

Q: How does this work in concrete terms? What are the pragmatic implications?

KW: Our first pragmatic rule of thumb for environmental ethics is: in pursuit of our vital needs, consume or destroy as little depth as possible. Do the least amount of harm to consciousness as you possibly can. Destroy as little intrinsic worth as possible. Put in its positive form: protect and promote as much depth as possible.

But we can't stop with that imperative alone, because it covers only depth but not span; only agency and not communion; only wholes, and not parts. Rather, we want to protect and promote *the greatest depth for the greatest span*. Not just preserve the greatest depth—that's fascist and anthropocentric—and not just preserve the greatest span—that's totalitarian and ecofascist—but rather preserve the greatest depth for the greatest span.

The Basic Moral Intuition

Q: You call this the Basic Moral Intuition.

KW: Yes. The Basic Moral Intuition is "protect and promote the greatest depth for the greatest span." I believe that is the actual form of spiritual intuition, the actual structure of spiritual intuition.

In other words, when we intuit Spirit, we are actually intuiting Spirit as it appears in all four quadrants (because Spirit manifests as all four quadrants—or, in short, as I and we and it). Thus, when I am intuiting Spirit clearly, I intuit its preciousness not only in myself, but in all other beings as well, for they share Spirit with me (as their own depth). And thus I wish to protect and promote that Spirit, not just in me, but in all beings as such, and I am moved, if I intuit Spirit clearly, to *implement* this Spiritual unfolding in as many beings as possible: I intuit Spirit not only as I, and not only as We, but also as a drive to implement that realization as an Objective State of Affairs (It) in the world.

Thus, precisely because Spirit actually manifests as all four quadrants (or as I, we, and it), then Spiritual intuition, when clearly apprehended, is apprehended as a desire to extend the depth of I to the span of We as an objective state of affairs (It): Buddha, Sangha, Dharma. Thus, protect and promote the greatest depth for the greatest span.

I believe that is the Basic Moral Intuition given to all holons, human and otherwise; but the greater the depth of a holon, the more clearly it will intuit that Ground and the more fully it will unpack that Basic Moral Intuition, extending it to more and more other holons in the process.

Q: Depth across span.

KW: Yes. The idea is that in attempting to promote the greatest depth for the greatest span, we must make pragmatic judgments about differences in intrinsic worth, about the degree of depth that we destroy in an attempt to meet our own vital needs—better to kill a carrot than a cow. Alan Watts hit it right on the head when someone asked him why he was a vegetarian. "Because cows scream louder than carrots."

But that must be carried across span as well, which prevents a dominator hierarchy. To give a stark example, if it came to killing a dozen apes or killing Al Capone, I'd have to say Al. There's nothing sacrosanct about being a human holon. That in itself is meaningless. That in itself is truly anthropocentric in the worst possible sense.

I hope you can get the general picture of holarchical ethics preserving not just depth, but depth across span, all set in a prior Ground value. Resting in Emptiness, promote the greatest depth for the greatest span. Such, I believe, is the pattern of the tears shed by Bodhisattvas everywhere.

An Integral Vision

Q: So in all of these cases—the problems with the culture gap, with vertical integration, with environmental ethics—they all hinge on a rejection of flatland.

KW: Definitely. We were talking about the possibility of a coming transformation, which in many ways is already in motion. But I don't believe this new transformation can harmoniously proceed without integrating the Big Three. The dissociation of the Big Three was the gaping wound left in our awareness by the failures of modernity, and the new postmodern transformation will have to integrate those fragments or it will not meet the demands of the twenty tenets—it will not transcend and include; it will not differentiate and integrate; it will not be able to evolve further; it will be a false start; evolution might very well erase it. We cannot build tomorrow on the bruises of yesterday.

Among numerous other things, this means a new form of society will have to evolve that integrates consciousness, culture, and nature, and thus finds room for art, morals, and science—for personal values, for collective wisdom, and for technical knowhow.

And there is no way to do this without going beyond flatland. Only by rejecting flatland can the Good and the True and the Beautiful be integrated. Only by rejecting flatland can we attune ourselves with Spirit's radiant expression in all its verdant domains. Only by rejecting flatland can we arrive at an authentic environmental ethics and a council of all beings, each gladly bowing to the perfected grace in all. Only by rejecting flatland can we come to terms with the devastating culture gap, and thus set individuals free to unfold their own deepest possibilities in a culture of encouragement. Only by rejecting flatland can the grip of mononature be broken, so that nature can actually be integrated and thus genuinely honored, instead of made into a false god that ironically contributes to its own destruction. Only by rejecting flatland can we set the global commons free in communicative exchange that is decentered from egocentric and ethnocentric and nationalistic imperialism, racked with wars of race and blood and bounty. Only by rejecting flatland can we engage the real potentials of vision-logic, which aims precisely at integrating physiosphere and biosphere and noosphere in a radical display of its own intrinsic joy. Only by rejecting flatland can the techno-base of the Infobahn be made servant to communion rather than master of digital anarchy, and in this way the Net might actually announce the dawn of global convergence, not global fragmentation. Only by rejecting flatland can a World Federation or Family of Nations emerge in a holarchical convergence around the World Soul itself, committed to the vigorous protection of that worldcentric space, the very form of Spirit's modern voice, glorious in its compassionate embrace.

And thus—to return to specifically spiritual and transpersonal themes—only by rejecting flatland can those who are interested in spirituality begin to integrate the Ascending and Descending currents. In flatland you can only be an Ascender or a Descender. You either deny any existence to flatland altogether (the Ascenders), or you try to make it into God (the Descenders).

Q: So we really have come full circle here, right back to the archetypal battle at the heart of the Western tradition—the Ascenders versus the Descenders.

KW: Yes. The purely Descended approaches absolutely despise the Ascending paths, and blame them for virtually all of humanity's and Gaia's problems. But not to worry, the loathing is mutual: the Ascenders maintain the Descenders are simply caught in self-dispersal and outward-bound ignorance, which is the real source of all humanity's turmoils.

The Ascenders and the Descenders, *after two thousand years*, still at each other's throat—each still claiming to be the Whole, each still accusing the other of Evil, each still perpetrating the same fractured insanity it despises in the other. The Ascenders and the Descenders—still crazy after all these years.

Q: The point is to integrate and balance the Ascending and Descending currents in the human being.

KW: Yes, the point is to bring these two currents into some sort of union and harmony, so that both wisdom and compassion can join hands in finding a Spirit that both transcends and includes this world, a Spirit eternally prior to this world and yet embracing this world and all its beings with infinite love and compassion, and care and concern, and the tenderest of mercies, and glory in the glance.

And however much the flurry of Descended religions help us to recognize and appreciate the visible, sensible God and Goddess, nonetheless, taken in and by themselves, they place an infinite burden on Gaia that poor finite Gaia cannot sustain. It might be sustainable growth, but it is unsustainable spirituality. And we desperately need both. The Ascending currents of the human being also have to be engaged, and activated, and cultivated, for it is only in being able to transcend our own limited and mortal egos that we can find that common Source and Ground of all sentient beings, a Source that bestows new splendor on the setting sun and radiates grace in each and every gesture.

Both the mere Ascenders and the mere Descenders, in tearing the Kosmos into their favorite fragments, are contributing to the brutality of this warfare, and they simply try to convert and coerce the other by sharing their diseases and waving their wounds. But it is in the union of the Ascending and the Descending that harmony is found, and not in any brutal war between the two. Only when both are united, we might say, can both be saved.

Q: Which brings us directly to the integral vision itself.

KW: Yes, to some sort of holistic and integrated view. I have concentrated on an approach that attempts to honor and include the very best of premodernity (the Great Nest of Being), the best of modernity (the differentiation of the Big Three), and the best of postmodernity (the integration of the Big Three)—to arrive at a truly "all-level, all-quadrant" approach.

Q: To arrive at an integral vision that can be summarized as in figures 15-1, 15-2, and 15-3, for example (pp. 299–301).

KW: Yes, that's right. Never before in history has this type of all-level, all-quadrant approach been possible, because never before were all the pieces of the puzzle available. Premodernity was all-level but not all-quadrant. Modernity was all-quadrant but not all-level (and that got even worse when the quadrants collapsed into flatland). Postmodernity, which set out to pick up the pieces and integrate the quadrants, instead fell into the intense gravitational field of flatland and ended up more fragmented than ever.

But the pieces are all present, and what is now required is a vision capable of weaving them together in a genuinely holistic fashion. This is what "all-level, all-quadrant" attempts to do. And if this type of integral vision succeeds, it will have immediate applications in business, education, medicine, health care, politics, cultural studies, psychology, human development—the list is truly endless, it seems.

Q: People can start to build this integral vision themselves by applying the four quadrants to whatever field they are in.

KW: That's true. In medicine, for example, you can see that any effective care would have to take into account, not just the objective medicine or physical treatment that you give the person (UR), but also the person's subjective beliefs and expectations (UL), the cultural attitudes, hopes, and fears about sickness (LL), and the social institutions, economic factors, and access to health care (LR), all of which have a causal effect on the course of a person's illness (because all four quadrants cause, and are caused by, the others). You can do the same analysis with law, education, business, politics, environmental ethics, schools of feminism, prison reform, philosophical systems, and so on.

And this will pay off in the most concrete of ways. If the four quadrants are real, then any health care system that includes all of them will be more effective (and therefore more cost efficient). Any business that takes them into account will be more efficient and thus more profitable. Any educational system will be more effective; politics will be more responsive; spirituality will be more transformative. And so on.

That is the first step of implementing a more integral vision—namely, moving from a one-quadrant approach to an *all-quadrant* approach. The second step is to move from all-quadrant to *all-level, all-quadrant*.

Q: Which would trace out the various waves and streams of development in each of the quadrants.

KW: Yes, that's right. We have especially focused on development in the Upper-Left quadrant—the nine or so fulcrums spanning the entire spectrum of consciousness, with their different needs, motivations, values, worldviews, self-identities, and so on, moving from matter to body to mind to soul to spirit. But those developments have correlates in all the other quadrants, and thus you can follow those as well. Not just, what will medicine look like if it includes all four quadrants, but what will medicine look like if it also spans the entire spectrum of consciousness in each of the quadrants? Not just, what can you do for healing if you use matter and body, but what can you do for healing if you use mind and soul and spirit as well? What would a full-spectrum medicine look like? Likewise, what would a full-spectrum education look like? Full-spectrum economy? Full-spectrum politics? Business? Marriage? Cinema? Art?

Q: Following the full spectrum in each of the quadrants. The I and the We and the It domains all evolve from body to mind to soul to spirit. Thus, all-quadrant, all-level.

KW: Yes. And we might especially want to remember, when we include soul and spirit in an integral view, that we do so in both Ascending and Descending ways. We want to include the liberating movement of wisdom that takes us from body to mind to soul to spirit, but also the incarnational movement of compassion and healing that brings soul and spirit down and into body, earth, life, and relationships—both God and Goddess equally honored.

This also opens up an enormous number of research projects—there are a thousand graduate theses on how to implement an all-level, all-quadrant approach. (For specific recommendations for following the levels and lines in each of the quadrants, see *Integral Psychology*.) But there are also all the small, daily ways that you can implement your own integral vision as well.

Q: Such as personal transformation and spiritual practice. Since an integral transformative practice would be all-level, all-quadrant, what would that actually involve?

KW: Here are some approaches where you can follow up on this if you like. Tony Schwartz, *What Really Matters: Searching for Wisdom in America*; Michael Murphy and George Leonard, *The Life We Are Given: A Long-Term Program for Realizing the Potential of Body, Mind, Heart, and Soul*; and my own *One Taste*.

The general idea is simply that we need to exercise body, mind, soul, and spirit—and to do so in self, culture, and nature.

Q: An integral vision.

KW: Yes, an integral vision. And the final result is simply to awaken to who and what you timelessly are—to awaken to the Spirit that is the actual author of this integral display.

And there, hidden in the secret cave of the Heart, where God and the Goddess finally unite, where Emptiness embraces all Form as the lost and found Beloved, where Eternity joyously sings the praises of noble Time, where Shiva uncontrollably swoons for luminescent Shakti, where Ascending and Descending erotically embrace in the sound of one hand clapping—there forever in the universe of One Taste, the Kosmos recognizes its own true nature, self-seen in a tacit recognition that leaves not even a single soul to tell the amazing tale.

And remember? There in the Heart, where the couple finally unite, the entire game is undone, this nightmare of evolution, and you are exactly where you were prior to the beginning of the whole show. With a sudden shock of the utterly obvious, you recognize your own Original Face, the face you had prior to the Big Bang, the face of utter Emptiness that smiles as all creation and sings as the entire Kosmos—and it is all undone in that primal glance, and all that is left is the smile, and the reflection of the moon on a quiet pond, late on a crystal clear night.

APPENDIX

The Twenty Tenets

The twenty tenets are simply some of the tendencies of evolutionary systems wherever we find them; they are "Kosmic patterns." There is nothing sacrosanct about the number "twenty." Some of these are simple definitions, others are real tendencies. Tenet 2 actually has four; tenet 12 has five (that's nineteen); there are three additions (twenty-two); but at least two tenets are simple definitions (e.g., seven, nine), which gives around twenty. But the interested reader can probably find more to add (or subtract). . . .

1. Reality as a whole is not composed of things or processes, but of *holons* (wholes that are parts of other wholes; e.g, whole atoms are parts of whole molecules, which are parts of whole cells, which are parts of whole organisms, and so on).
2. Holons display four fundamental capacities: (a) self-preservation (agency), (b) self-adaptation (communion), (c) self-transcendence (eros), and (d) self-dissolution (thanatos).
3. Holons emerge.
4. Holons emerge holarchically.
5. Each emergent holon transcends but includes its predecessor(s).
6. The lower sets the possibilities of the higher; the higher sets the probabilities of the lower.
7. The number of levels that a holarchy comprises determines whether it is "shallow" or "deep"; and the number of holons on any given level we shall call its "span."
8. Each successive level of evolution produces greater depth and less span.

Addition 1: The greater the depth of a holon, the greater its degree of consciousness.

9. Destroy any holon, and you will destroy all of the holons above it and none of the holons below it.
10. Holarchies co-evolve.
11. The micro is in relational exchange with the macro at all levels of its depth.
12. Evolution has directionality.
    a. increasing complexity
    b. increasing differentiation/integration
    c. increasing organization/structuration
    d. increasing relative autonomy
    e. increasing telos

Addition 2: Every holon issues an IOU to the Kosmos.

Addition 3: All IOUs are redeemed in Emptiness.

Index